THE WAY MICROSOFT® WINDOWS® 95 WORKS

Simon Collin

Microsoft Press

Conceived, edited, and designed by DK Direct Limited and Microsoft Press.

Published by Microsoft Press.

DK DIRECT

Project Editors: Brian Cooper, Edda Bohnsack, Susan Schlachter; **Senior Art Editor:** Nigel Coath
Designers: Steve Cummiskey, Trond Wilhelmsen; **Production Manager:** Ian Paton
Series Editor: Robert Dinwiddie; **Series Art Editor**: Virginia Walter

MICROSOFT PRESS

Acquisitions Editor: Lucinda Rowley
Project Editor: Katherine A. Krause; **Technical Reviewer:** Marc Young

PRINCIPAL AUTHOR

Simon Collin

ADDITIONAL AUTHORS

Brian Cooper, Robert Dinwiddie, Susan Schlachter, Edda Bohnsack

ADDITIONAL CONTRIBUTORS

Illustrators: Anthony Bellue, Nigel Coath, Trond Wilhelmsen, Steve Cummiskey
Airbrushing: Janos Marffy; **Photography:** Tony Buckley, Steve Gorton, Andy Crawford, Sarah Ashun
Computer Support: Alan Greenwood; **Editorial Assistance:** Joe Elliot, John Watson, Tim Worsley

Library of Congress Cataloging-in-Publication Data

Collin, Simon.
The way Windows 95 works / Simon Collin.
p. cm.
Includes index.
ISBN 1-55615-680-4 : $19.95 ($24.95 Can.)
1. Operating systems (Computers) 2. Microsoft Windows 95.
I. Title.
QA76.76.063C648 1995
005.4'469—dc20

95-18875
CIP

Color Reproduction by Triffik Technology, UK

Printed and Bound in the USA

23456789 QEQE 98765

Flexibook

CONTENTS

INTRODUCTION

CHAPTER ONE

Getting to Know Windows 95

Welcome to Windows 95! In this introductory chapter, you'll explore the basic features of the operating system, find out how to view what's on your computer, launch programs, and use the help system.

CHAPTER TWO

Work & Play with Windows 95

Have fun with the creative accessories that come with Windows 95, such as WordPad, Paint, and Sound Recorder, and learn how to organize the files and folders on your PC.

CHAPTER THREE

Making Connections with Windows 95

Get connected with Windows 95. Learn how to set up and use a small network, share files and printers with others, exchange electronic mail, connect to remote PCs, and access the Internet and The Microsoft Network. This chapter also introduces a number of useful accessories for laptop users.

CHAPTER FOUR

Working Smarter

Discover a multitude of ease-of-use and power features that can improve your working efficiency.

REFERENCE

Reference Section

Turn to this section for advice on installing additional software and Windows 95 components on your PC. Find out how to and use passwords to protect files or folders on your computer.

About This Book

Welcome to *The Way Microsoft Windows 95 Works*, an easy-to-follow guide to all the main features of Windows 95 — and much more!

Unlike previous versions of Windows, Windows 95 is a complete *operating system* for IBM-compatible PCs. For example, Windows 95 controls and allows you to configure all your PC's hardware. In addition, it provides a host of accessories to help you get the most fun and use out of your PC — everything from running CD-ROM titles or "surfing" the Internet to more mundane tasks such as maintaining your PC's hard disk.

Tools and Accessories
Turn to page 42 for a quick tour of all the tools and accessories that come with Windows 95.

FORMER WINDOWS USER?
Although primarily intended for PC novices, this book should be useful even if you've previously used Windows or Windows for Workgroups and the MS-DOS operating system. Throughout this book, you'll find references to the ways in which Windows 95 improves upon previous versions of Windows. Former MS-DOS users will find a short section on the new MS-DOS in Chapter Four.

Multimedia Magic
Find out about Windows 95's enhanced support for multimedia and the enjoyment of CD-ROM titles on pages 60 to 67.

EXPLORING THE INTERFACE
You can use the book in one of two ways — by reading through from the beginning and completing all the step-by-step exercises (this is advised for complete beginners), or by browsing and dipping into the areas that interest you most. If you're a browser, be warned that a few exercises are linked to previous tasks in the book. These links are clearly marked by cross references.

The book assumes a "typical" installation of Windows 95. If any of the accessory programs described seem to be missing on your system, see "Adding Windows 95 Components" on page 123.

THE WYSIWYG CONCEPT
By the way, my name's the WYSIWYG wizard, and you'll find me popping up quite often in the pages that follow, handing out a few tips on Windows 95.

One of the first questions you may be asking is: What does the term WYSIWYG have to do with it? Well, WYSIWYG stands for "What You See Is What You Get." It was coined some years ago to describe programs with a special feature — namely that *what*

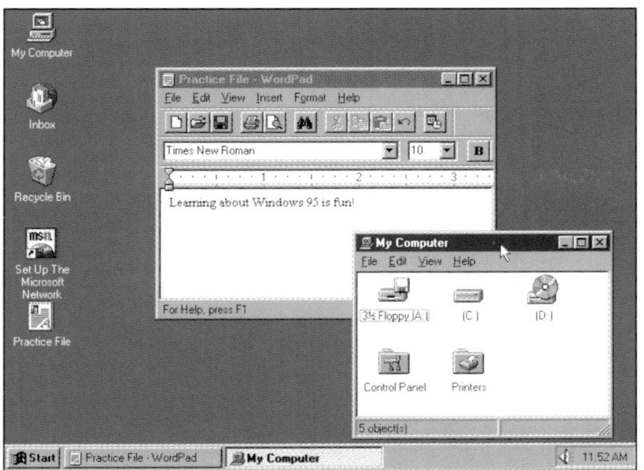

you see on the screen is the same as *what you get* when you print it out. In this book we'll be turning the WYSIWYG concept around a little bit. Throughout the book, the practical instructions for learning about Windows 95's features are accompanied by visual prompts showing exactly what is happening on your computer screen. In other words, *what you see* on the page is the same as *what you get* on the screen. Sometimes an instruction will be accompanied by a screen shot (like the one shown at left) showing how your screen will look at a particular stage in an operation. Or you may see a series of screen "fragments" (like those shown at right). These home in on where the action is as you follow a set of instructions.

Don't Close!
Avoid clicking on the Close button of any help window unless you want to close down the whole help system. When browsing the help system, you'll find that clicking on the *Help Topics* button will take you back to the *Help Topics* dialog box. Clicking on the *Back* button will take you back to the previous window.

TIPS AND SHORTCUTS

In addition to the insights I'll provide, you'll see various tips scattered throughout the book in colored boxes. The *pink* boxes contain warnings about some common pitfalls you may run into when using Windows 95 or offer advice on what to do when things go wrong. The *green* boxes provide some useful tips and shortcuts or answer some common queries.

REFERENCE SECTION

At the back of the book, you'll find a useful Reference Section. This includes information on how to install new software or components of Windows 95 and how to use passwords to protect your personal files and limit access to folders, files, and resources across a network.

Hide All?
You can minimize all open windows in one move by right-clicking a blank area of the Taskbar and then choosing *Minimize All Windows* from the pop-up menu.

MOUNTAINS INTO MOLEHILLS

Getting comfortable with software you're unfamiliar with can be a real uphill struggle. But with the right tutorial guide ready, the mountain quickly becomes a molehill. While this book doesn't explore every corner of Windows 95, you should be feeling confident of the basics by the end. We hope you enjoy reading and using *The Way Microsoft Windows 95 Works* — look for my handsome face in the pages that follow!

1

CHAPTER ONE

Getting to Know Windows 95

Using your computer should be fun and productive — and Windows 95 will help you achieve those goals. But before you get to work, you need to familiarize yourself with the Windows 95 interface — the various menus, tools, and icons that provide access to the programs and data on your PC. During the course of this chapter, you'll practice some basic skills, such as how to launch programs, manipulate windows, open and save documents, and browse what's on your computer.

WINDOWS 95 AND YOUR PC
WINDOWS 95 JUMPSTART • BROWSING YOUR COMPUTER
LAUNCHING PROGRAMS AND OPENING DOCUMENTS
THE CONTROL PANEL • GETTING HELP

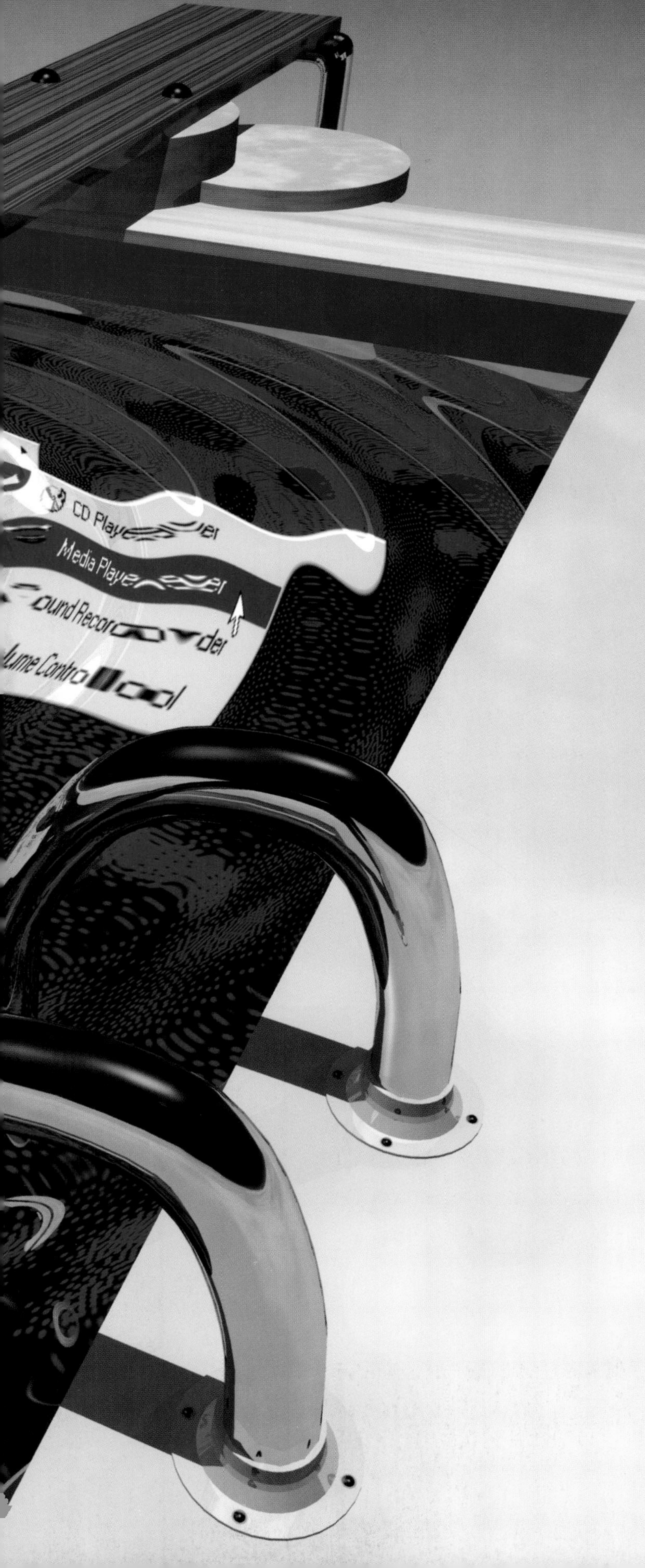

Windows 95 and Your PC

WHATEVER REASON YOU HAD FOR BUYING A PC — word processing, keeping accounts, writing a novel — you'll be pleasantly surprised at how many other activities suddenly become available to you. Computers these days can do much more than simply produce letters and spreadsheets. They can also educate, entertain, and even plug you into the "Information Superhighway." Windows 95, with its user-friendly appearance and extensive help system, provides the easiest way for you to get the most out of your PC.

How Is Windows 95 Different?
Windows 95 — the successor to Windows 3.1 and Windows for Workgroups 3.11 — has made the PC much easier to use. For example, filenames can now have a maximum of 255 characters (see page 25), and new Plug and Play facilities make the addition of new hardware an easy process (see page 60).

Graphical User Interface (GUI)
Symbols and icons make computing easy.

What Is Windows 95?

A PC consists of two parts: hardware (the mechanical pieces you can see and touch) and software (a set of instructions that tells the hardware what it should be doing). If it wasn't for software, the bits and pieces of hardware in your PC would have no way of responding to your actions and commands.

The main piece of software in a computer is the operating system. Windows 95 is an operating system — that is, it controls and manages the computer by translating your instructions into a language the hardware can understand. Windows 95 also lets you communicate with your computer in an intuitive way, through pictures and symbols on the screen (see left), rather than by typing in commands. This friendly face is known as a graphical user interface (GUI).

In addition to providing the link between you and your PC, Windows 95 also includes a set of tools to help keep your computer files in order. And with the new networking facilities in Windows 95, users can easily connect to each other — even across continents!

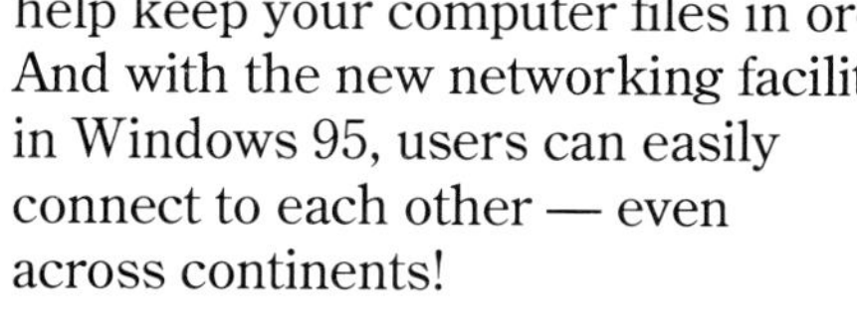

Plug and Play
Before Windows 95, installing a new piece of hardware in a PC was often a difficult process. Now, Windows 95 will automatically scan for new equipment and then help you set it up correctly.

What Equipment Do I Need?

To use Windows 95, your PC must be equipped with the following:

- A 386DX processor or higher and a hard disk with at least 35 to 40 megabytes (MB) of hard disk space.
- At least 4 MB (but preferably 8 MB) of random access memory (RAM).
- A VGA or higher resolution graphics card.
- A Microsoft mouse (or compatible).

For maximum enjoyment, we recommend a sound card and CD-ROM drive (see pages 60 to 61 for more information).

Communications

Windows 95 includes all the software you need to connect to other computers, whether they're in the same office or on the other side of the world. With the right hardware, you can send faxes, dial telephone numbers, and even connect to the Internet and The Microsoft Network.

Multitasking

The main use of a PC is to run applications, such as word processing and spreadsheet programs. With its built-in multitasking capabilities, Windows 95 lets users run several programs at once. Each program is displayed in its own window.

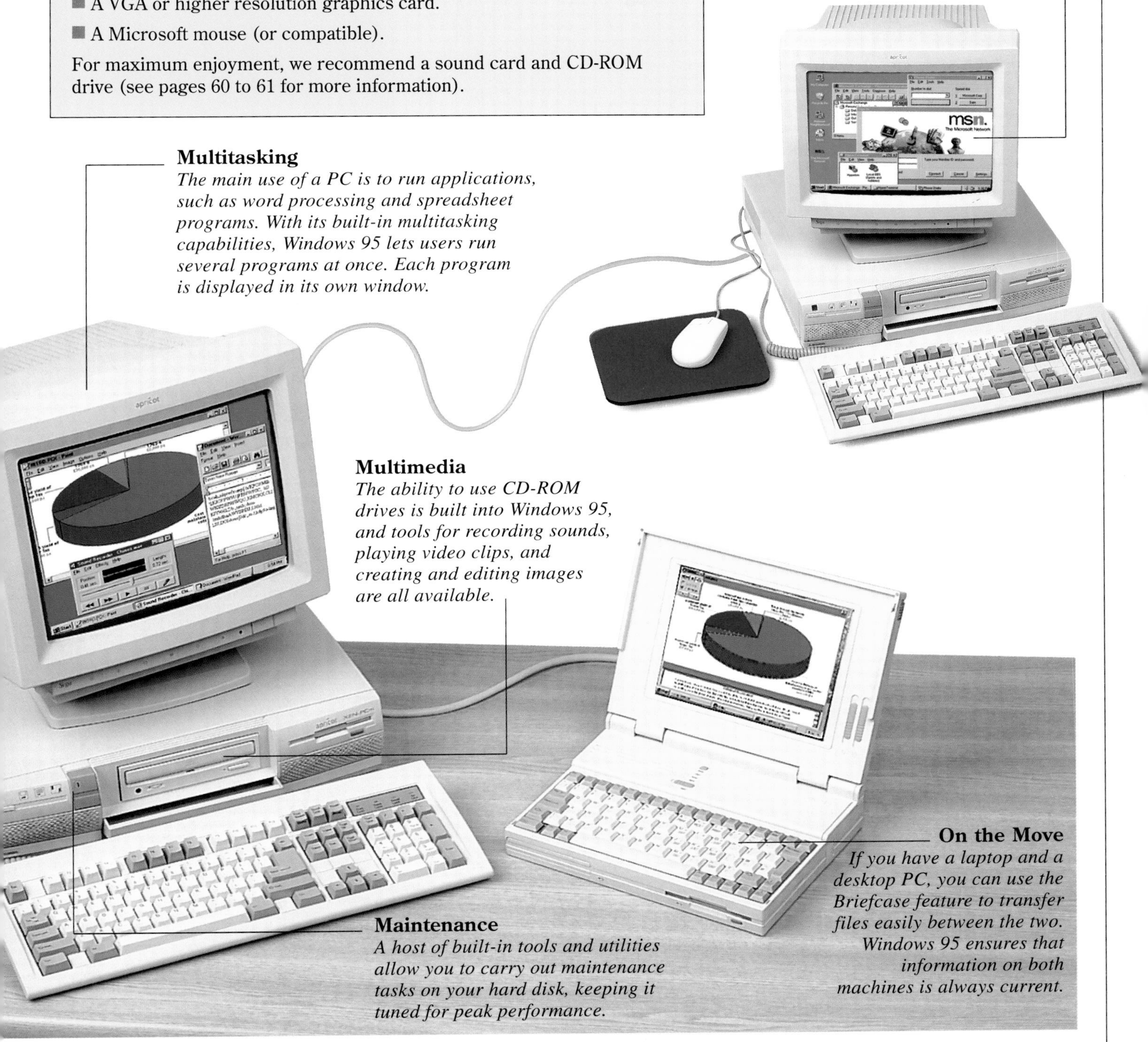

Multimedia

The ability to use CD-ROM drives is built into Windows 95, and tools for recording sounds, playing video clips, and creating and editing images are all available.

On the Move

If you have a laptop and a desktop PC, you can use the Briefcase feature to transfer files easily between the two. Windows 95 ensures that information on both machines is always current.

Maintenance

A host of built-in tools and utilities allow you to carry out maintenance tasks on your hard disk, keeping it tuned for peak performance.

Windows 95 Jumpstart

IN THIS SECTION, YOU'LL LOOK AT THE FEATURES of the Windows 95 Desktop and then embark on a practice session to get familiar with many of the most important features of Windows 95. For example, you'll find out how to use some major ease-of-use features such as the *Start* button and the Taskbar; you'll also open a Windows 95 accessory, create and save a document, and, last but not least, you'll practice shutting down Windows 95.

The Windows 95 Desktop

When you switch on your PC, you will soon see the message "Starting Windows 95 ..." appear on your screen (assuming Windows 95 is installed). Next, the words "Microsoft Windows 95" are displayed in large lettering. If your PC is connected to a network, a message may ask you to type a password to log on to the network server. After doing so, press Enter. If a *Welcome* box appears, press Esc. You will be left with the Windows 95 Desktop and other features, some of which are explained here, on your screen.

My Computer Icon
This icon allows you to browse the disk drives on your PC. The disk drives include the hard disk drive, one or more floppy disk drives, and possibly a CD-ROM drive. Hard disks, floppy disks, and CD-ROMs all store computer files.

Recycle Bin
This icon represents a temporary storage area on your hard disk for files you no longer need. If you want to retrieve a file that is in the Recycle Bin, you can do so, but once you've emptied a file from the Bin, it's irretrievable (see page 54).

Microsoft Exchange Inbox Icon
This icon provides access to Microsoft Exchange, a feature that allows you to send and receive electronic mail messages or fax messages and to view and organize all your messages in one place (see pages 80 to 85). Microsoft Exchange is an optional feature of Windows 95: If it hasn't been installed on your PC, you won't see this icon.

My Briefcase
This icon represents an optionally installed feature for transferring files between PCs (see pages 96 to 97). Files you put in the Briefcase can be carried to another machine. When you bring them back, you can automatically update the local copies.

Start Button
You'll use this button as the starting point for day-to-day activities such as running programs, opening and editing documents, and finding files. When the opening screen first appears, you'll see a message, "Click here to begin," that points at this button. When you do so, the Start *menu — a pop-up list of options — appears (see page 13).*

Start

Network Neighborhood Icon
This icon provides a gateway to any other computers connected to your PC as part of a network (see page 86).

Set Up The Microsoft Network
Use this icon to set up access to The Microsoft Network, which provides a variety of online services, technical support, and an Internet gateway (see page 94).

Desktop
The entire background area of your screen is known as the Desktop. The Desktop represents your working environment when you are operating your PC. Initially, your Desktop appears uncluttered — there are just a few icons placed on it, representing the items you have access to. Later in this book, you'll find out how to put extra icons onto the Desktop for programs or documents you use often, so that you can access these directly (see pages 100 to 101).

Taskbar
The Taskbar helps you monitor and switch between the various activities you'll perform. During a typical Windows 95 session, you'll open several different windows for activities such as running programs or browsing through the files on your hard disk. To switch between windows, you simply click on the appropriate Taskbar button (see page 17).

4:18 PM

Sound Volume Control
For multimedia computing, this icon provides a quick way of changing the sound volume (see page 66).

Time Box
You'll see the current time displayed at the right end of the Taskbar. You can easily reset the time if you notice that it's wrong (see page 114).

Learning to Use the Mouse

If you've never used a mouse before, now is the time to start! Although it's possible to operate Windows using the keyboard alone, for the majority of tasks it's much simpler to use the mouse. Most of the step-by-step instructions throughout this book assume use of the mouse.

You use a mouse to choose various commands and options and to manipulate objects on the screen. The four actions you can perform with a mouse are moving, clicking a mouse button, double-clicking, and dragging. You'll practice each of these in the step-by-step tutorial session that follows. Unless otherwise stated, all clicking, double-clicking, and dragging actions described in this book refer to the *left* mouse button. However, with Windows 95, many timesaving shortcuts are available using the *right* mouse button. When we refer to these shortcuts, the right mouse button is always specifically mentioned.

Use a Mouse Pad
You will find it much easier to move the mouse smoothly if it is on a flat, textured surface. Rolling it on a smooth surface may cause the ball to slip. Ready-made mouse pads provide the best surface.

Wrong!
Wrist and arm held too high, which makes muscles tense.

Wrong!
Wrist and arm held too low, fingers arched up.

Right!
Wrist and arm held horizontally, fingers relaxed.

How a Mouse Works
As you guide the mouse over a flat surface, a ball on the underside rolls in the direction of movement and turns two rollers. These rollers turn sensors that send signals, via a cable, to the PC, causing a pointer to move on screen in unison with the movement of the mouse. You can perform special tasks on the screen through actions such as clicking or holding down the buttons on top of the mouse.

How to Hold the Mouse
If you use your mouse a lot and do not hold it properly, you risk suffering from repetitive strain injury (RSI). To avoid problems, keep your arm and wrist as horizontal as possible and rest your wrist lightly on the table or desk as you move your mouse.

Switch Buttons?
If you are left-handed or simply prefer to use the mouse with your left hand, you can tell Windows to swap the orientation of the left and right buttons. You can then use the right mouse button as the main controller and the left button for the timesaving shortcuts. See the instructions under "Taming Your Mouse" on page 116.

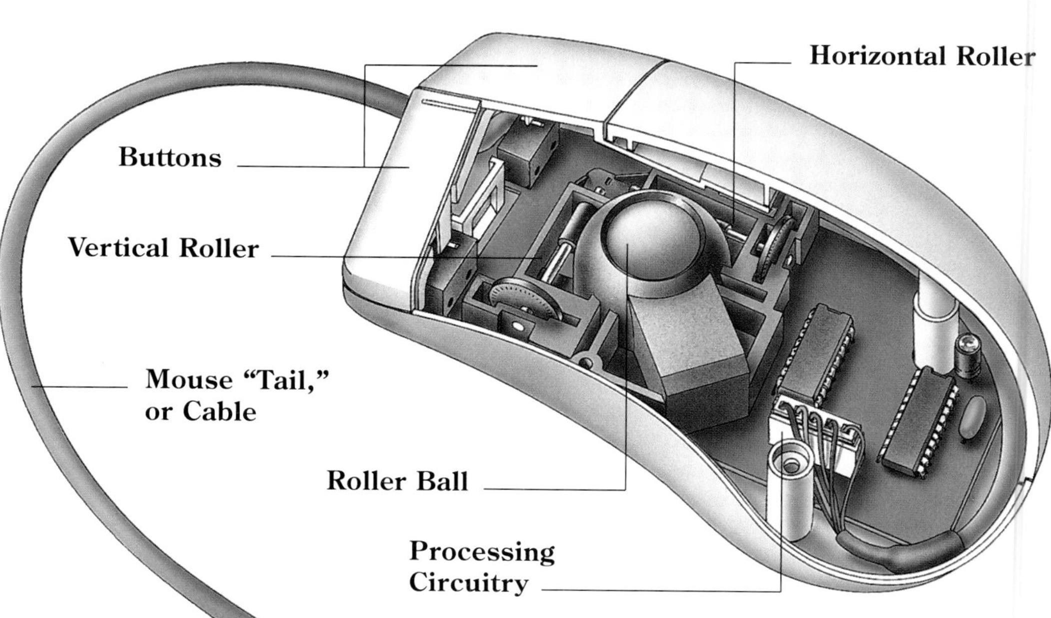

Let's Go!

Now let's get started actually using Windows 95. Over the next few pages, you'll find out how to launch a program from the *Start* menu, how to manipulate and switch between windows, how to save a document, and how to use the Taskbar. At the same time, you'll practice the full range of mouse skills. So place your mouse on a mouse pad, put your hand on the mouse, and follow the step-by-step instructions starting at the right.

1 First just practice moving the mouse on your mouse pad to "point" the arrow on-screen to various objects. Move it to point the arrow at the words *My Computer* or at the icon of a computer above those words.

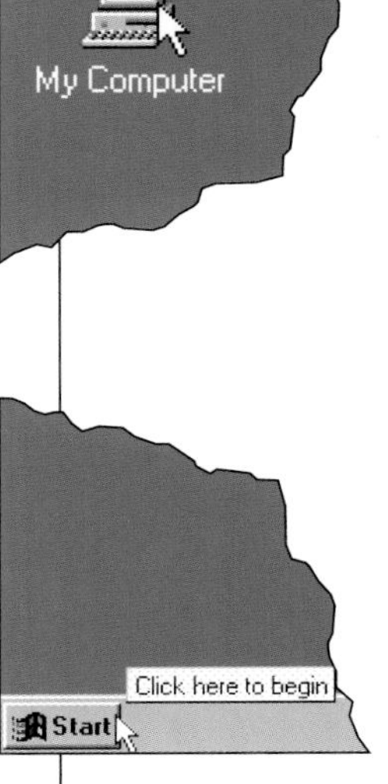

2 Now practice clicking. Press and then quickly release the left mouse button. If you have clicked correctly, you should see both the icon and the background to the words *My Computer* change color. An object that is highlighted in this way is said to be *selected*. For now, move the mouse pointer to a blank space away from the *My Computer* icon and click once. This deselects the icon.

3 Now point to and click on another object. Point to the *Start* button and you'll see a message appear — "Click here to begin." Do just that.

4 A pop-up list of options, called commands, appears.

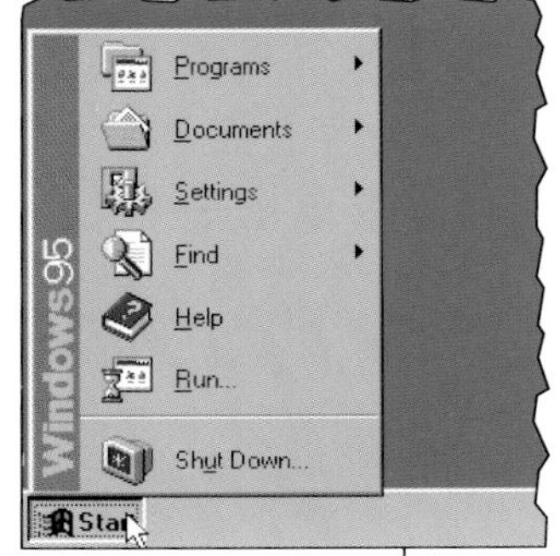

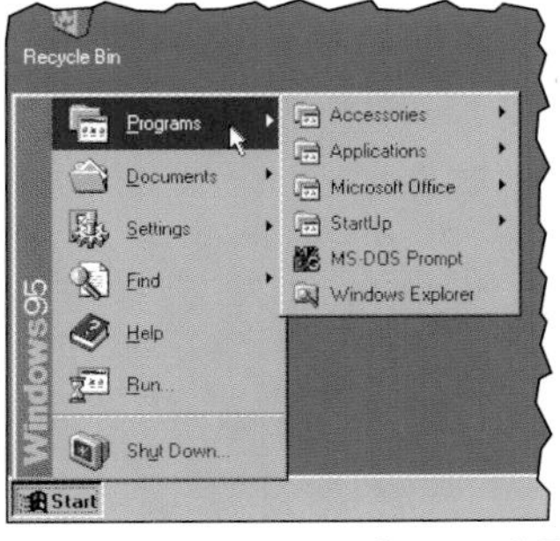

5 Move the mouse pointer to highlight the word *Programs*. To the right of this word you'll see a right-pointing arrowhead, which indicates that a submenu of options is available. As the mouse pointer moves over the word *Programs*, the submenu appears. The submenu contains several *program groups* — collections of related programs — as well as some special items, such as *Windows Explorer*, and *MS-DOS Prompt*.

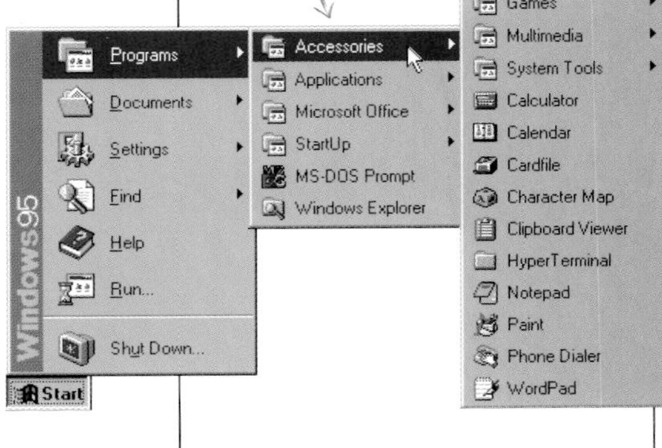

6 Move the mouse pointer immediately to the right over the word *Accessories*, and another submenu appears. The *Accessories* group of programs consists of various utilities that can help you get the most out of your PC. You'll be learning about most of these later in this book.

7 Move the mouse pointer to highlight *WordPad*. Now click the left mouse button to launch WordPad — a simple word-processing program. After a few moments, you'll see a window entitled *Document - WordPad* appear on your screen. At the same time you'll see that a button, also labeled *Document - WordPad*, appears on the Taskbar at the bottom of the screen.

A Typical Window

The *WordPad* window that you now see on your screen is a fairly typical window. The features of the window that are common to all windows are labeled below. Features that are specific to WordPad are not labeled but are described in the section on WordPad itself on page 44. For the moment we'll concentrate on the properties of windows in general and how to manipulate windows.

Menu Bar
Clicking on a name in this bar causes a drop-down menu to appear, containing commands relevant to the contents or selected items in the window. The names in this bar vary among windows.

Maximize/Restore Button
Clicking here toggles (switches) the window between its maximum size and the smaller size to which it was previously set.

Title Bar
This bar contains the window's name, in this case Document - WordPad.

Control Icon
Clicking here opens a menu of commands for moving, resizing, and closing the window.

Minimize Button
Clicking here shrinks the window so that it appears only as a button on the Taskbar.

Close Button
Clicking here closes the window.

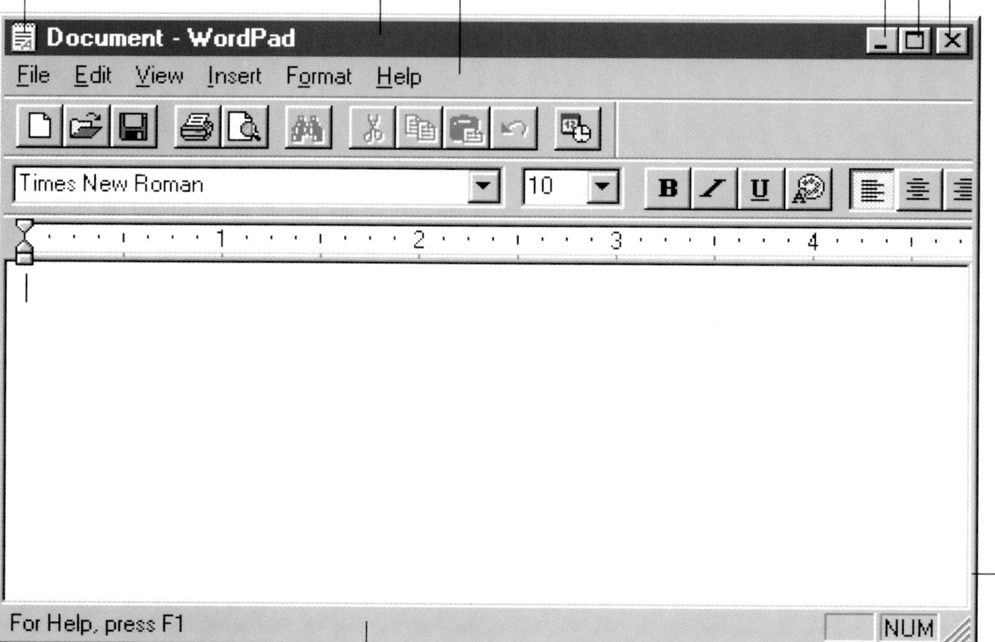

Status Bar
This bar contains information or messages relevant to the contents or activity in the window.

Window Borders
Dragging these resizes the window.

MAXIMIZING, RESTORING, AND RESIZING

You can alter the area that a window occupies on your screen in various ways. Practice the following techniques on the *WordPad* window.

Window Maximized — Click to Restore

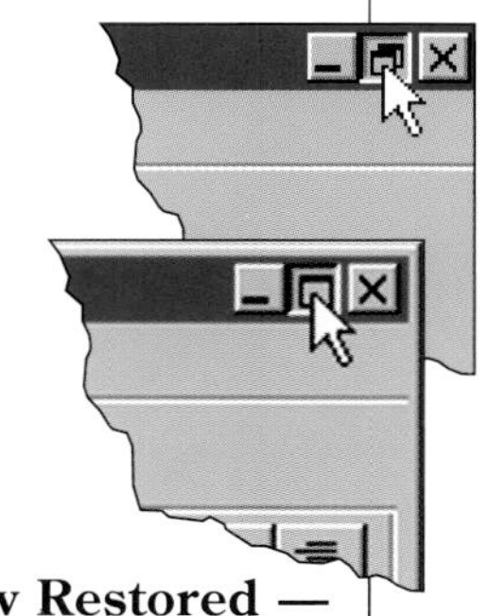

Window Restored — Click to Maximize

1 Click several times on the Maximize/Restore button. Doing so toggles (switches) the window between its maximum size and a smaller size. The appearance of the button varies according to whether the window is maximized or restored. Leave the window at its restored (smaller) size.

2 Now try resizing the window. This requires a new mouse skill called *dragging*. Move your mouse pointer over the right-hand border of the window, and you will see the pointer change into a double-headed arrow. This indicates that the border can be moved either to the left or right.

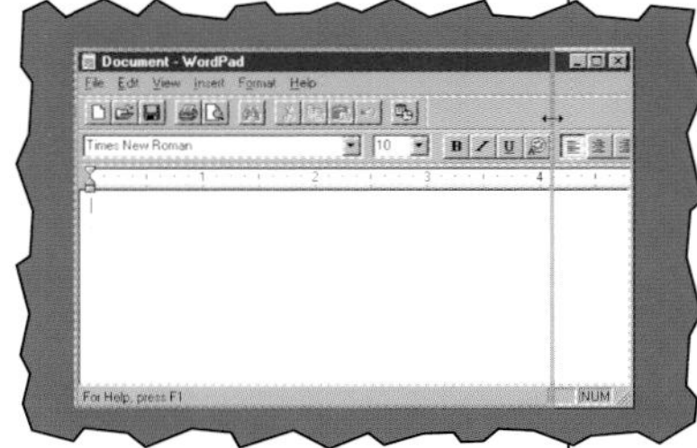

3 Hold down the mouse button and move the mouse to the left. As you do so, you will see that the window border is "dragged" to the left. Now release the mouse button, leaving the window at the reduced width.

4 You can also resize a window vertically by dragging its top or bottom border, or resize horizontally and vertically at the same time by dragging a corner. Place your mouse pointer over the bottom right corner of the *WordPad* window and drag the corner diagonally until the window occupies about one third of the total screen area. Then release the mouse button.

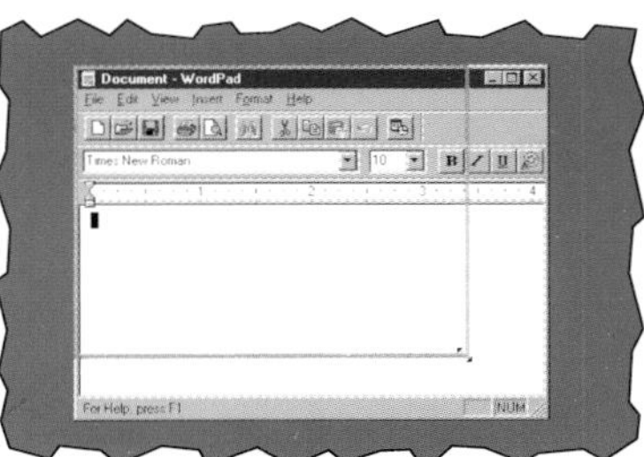

CHOOSING COMMANDS

Before you practice some more techniques for manipulating windows, try creating and saving a document using WordPad. This will show you how to choose a command from a drop-down menu and will also introduce you to your first Windows 95 dialog box.

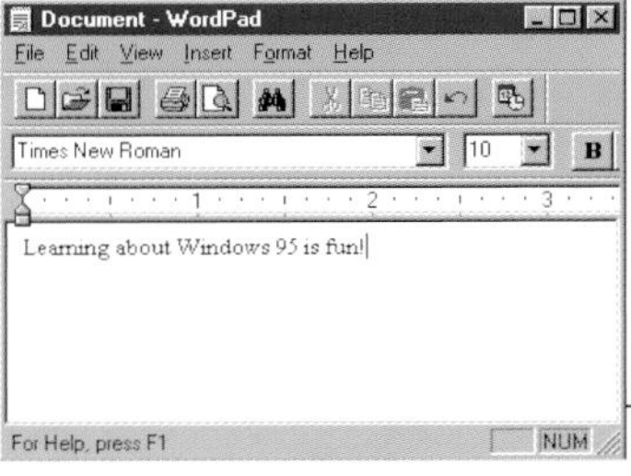

1 Type a sentence on your keyboard. Because WordPad is open and active, you will see the sentence appear in the *WordPad* window. As you type each character, you will see a flashing text insertion point move along to the right.

2 Click on the word *File* in the menu bar and a drop-down menu of commands appears.

3 Click on the *Save As* command in the drop-down menu. The *Save As* dialog box appears. A dialog box is a special window in which you give Windows more information about how you want a command performed.

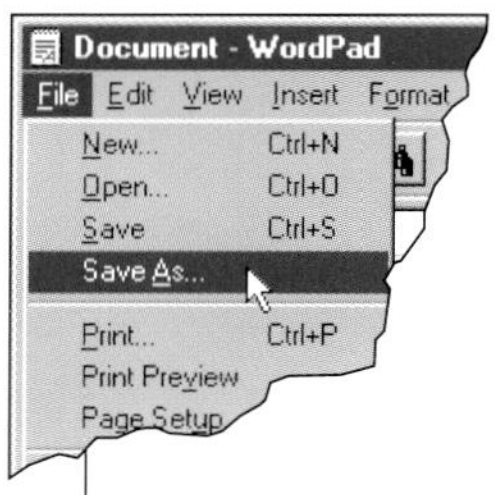

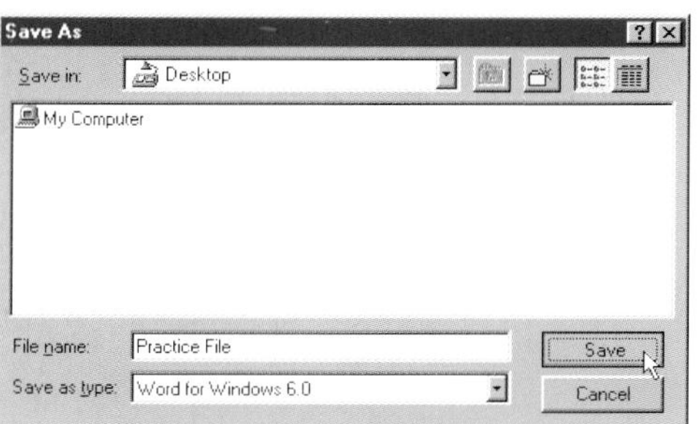

4 For now, just type **Practice File**. You will see these words appear in the box next to *File name*. Now click on the *Save* button in the dialog box.

5 The sentence you typed is now saved to your PC's hard disk as an electronic document named **Practice File**. You will see that the title bar of the *WordPad* window has changed to *Practice File - WordPad*.

You'll find out more about saving and naming files later on in this chapter (see page 32).

OPENING AND MOVING A SECOND WINDOW

When you're working with Windows 95, you'll often want to have more than one window open on the screen simultaneously and switch between windows. To see how that works, let's open a second window.

Double Trouble!
If you are not yet accustomed to using a mouse, you may need a little practice to perfect your double-clicking technique. If the second click does not follow fast enough after the first, Windows may interpret the mouse action as two single clicks. Make sure that you don't move the mouse between clicks. If you have chronic trouble with double-clicking, see "Taming Your Mouse" on page 116.

1 Move the mouse pointer to point at the *My Computer* icon. (If the icon is hidden, restore and/or resize the *WordPad* window to uncover it.) Now double-click the mouse button. To do so, quickly press and release the mouse button twice.

2 A second window, entitled *My Computer*, appears on the screen. (You'll find out more about the contents of this window on page 22.) A *My Computer* button appears on the Taskbar.

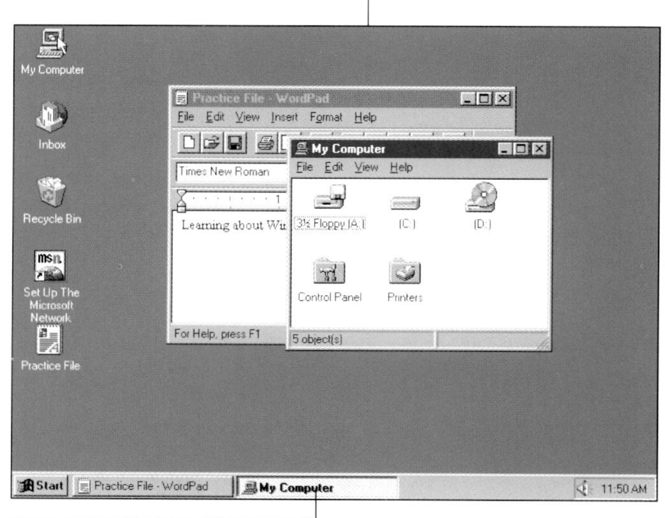

Taskbar Button

3 The *My Computer* window may partly or wholly obscure the *Practice File* window. To move it out of the way, first move your mouse pointer over the *My Computer* title bar.

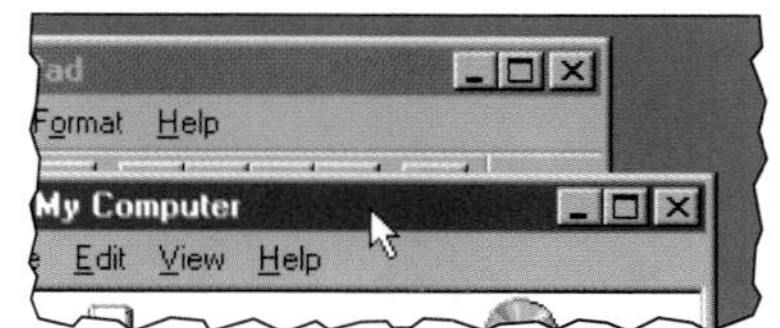

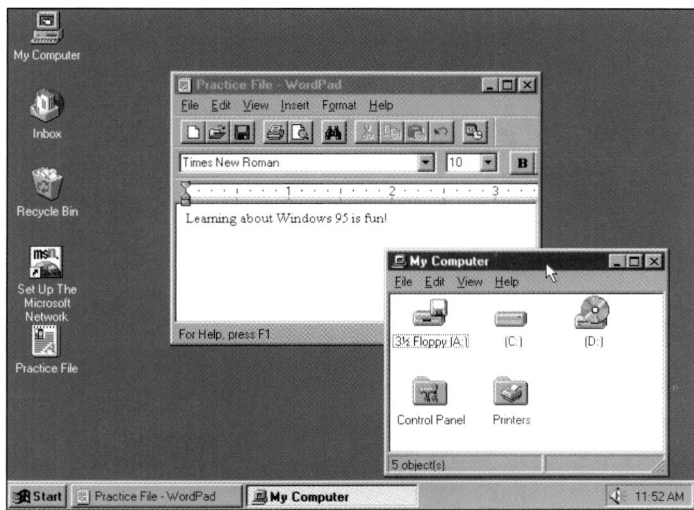

4 Hold down the mouse button and move the mouse. You'll find that by dragging the title bar, you can move the whole window to a new position.

Keyboard Cycle
If you press Alt and Esc repeatedly on your keyboard, Windows will cycle between each open window, making each one the active window in turn.

SWITCHING BETWEEN WINDOWS

If you look at the two windows on your screen, you'll see that the *My Computer* window has a highlighted (colored) title bar, whereas the *Practice File* window's title bar is gray. The *My Computer* window is said to be the *active* window. A window must be active before you can perform any operations on its contents. When two or more overlapping windows are open on the screen, the active window is always the one on top.

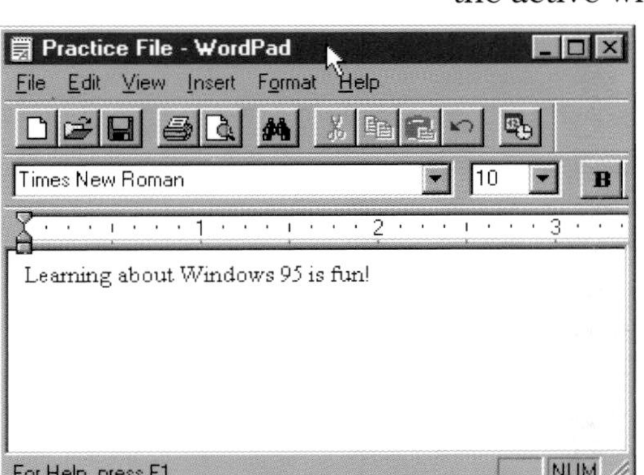

With Windows 95, it's particularly easy to switch between windows — i.e., change which window is active. There are two main methods — clicking on the window, or using the Taskbar. Follow these steps to practice each in turn.

1 Move your mouse pointer over the *Practice File* window's title bar or over any blank area of the window and click. You'll see the window's title bar is highlighted, indicating that the window is now active.

2 To revert to *My Computer* as the active window, use the second switching method. Just click on the *My Computer* button on the Taskbar. This is the most convenient method of activating any window that is obscured by other windows.

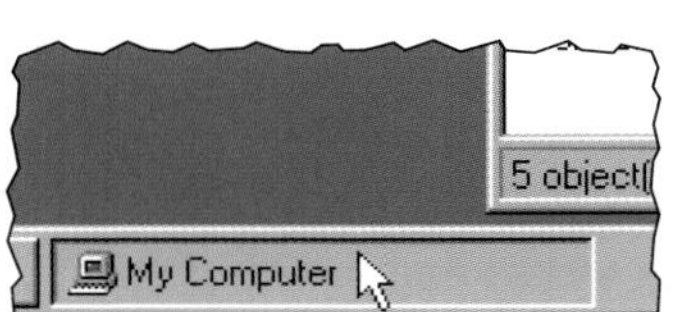

Lost Window?
Remember — if you ever "lose" a window that you know is open, you can always make it the active window simply by looking for and clicking on its Taskbar button.

A THIRD WINDOW

To make things a little more complicated, open a third window and continue practicing switching between windows.

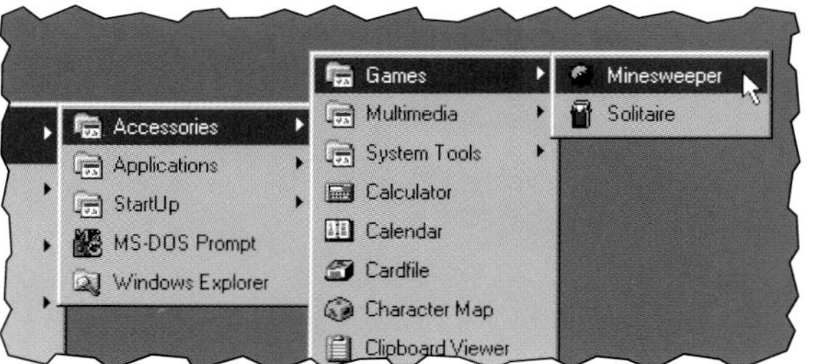

1 Click on the *Start* button, then point to *Programs*. Point to *Accessories*, then to *Games*, and finally click on *Minesweeper*.

Crowded Taskbar?
If you open so many windows that the Taskbar becomes congested, you can increase the Taskbar's depth by dragging its top border upward using the mouse.

2 The *Minesweeper* window opens. Minesweeper is a tricky little game you might like to play for a while. You'll find a brief explanation of the game in the box on the next page.

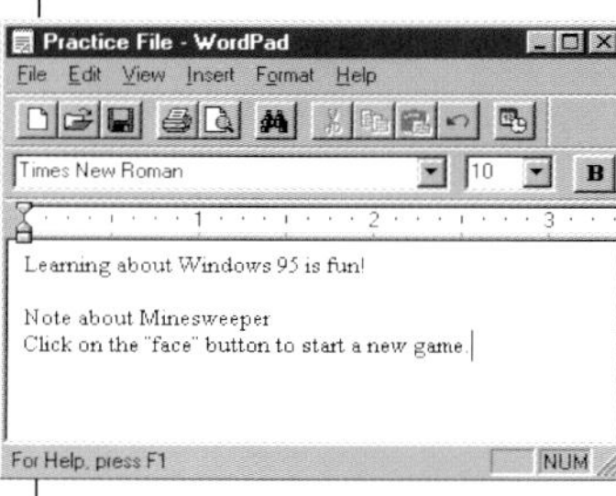

3 Switch back to the *Practice File* window by clicking its Taskbar button. You might like to add a comment about Minesweeper to the document. Press Enter to start a new line and type your comment. Then click on the Save button (the floppy disk symbol) at the top of the *Practice File* window to save the change.

4 Try one more method for switching between windows. Hold down Alt and then press Tab. Icons for your three open windows pop up. Continue to press Tab to cycle through the icons. When the Minesweeper icon is selected, release Alt and the *Minesweeper* window becomes active.

USING THE RIGHT MOUSE BUTTON

The quickest way to perform a variety of Windows 95 tasks and actions is to use the right mouse button. You can point to virtually any item on screen, click the right mouse button, and up pops a context-sensitive menu of commands that can be applied to that item. Let's practice with an example:

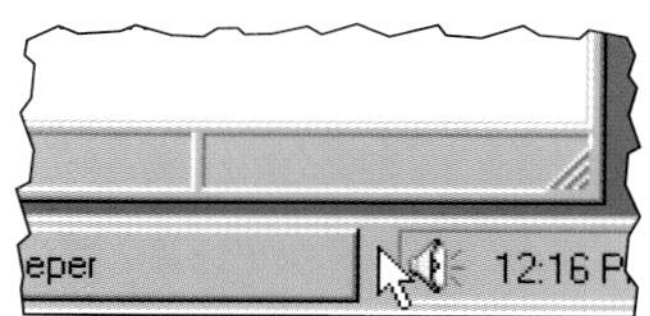

1 Point to a blank area of the Taskbar and click the right mouse button.

2 A menu of commands pops up that can be applied to your current "tasks"—i.e., the three windows on screen.

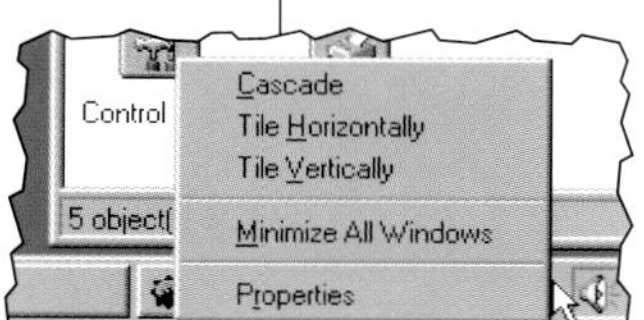

Minesweeper

In Minesweeper, the central grid of squares hides several explosive mines — 10 in the beginner version of the game. These are scattered randomly over the grid. To win the game, you must correctly "flag" the mine-containing squares and reveal the contents of all other squares.

To reveal the contents of a square, click on it using the left mouse button. To flag a square that you've identified as a mine, click on it using the right mouse button. Where a square contains a number, the number indicates how many of the surrounding squares contain mines. If you open a square that contains a mine, you lose the game. To start a new game, choose the *New* command from the *Game* menu or click on the smiley face button.

Exploded Mine

Flagged Mine-Containing Square

A Lost Game

3 Click on *Cascade* in the pop-up menu.

4 Your three windows now appear cascaded (neatly overlapped) on screen.

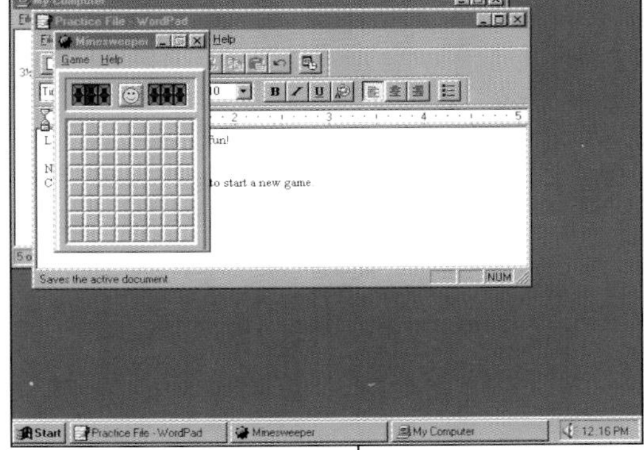

MINIMIZING A WINDOW

Sometimes you'll want to hide or shrink a window on your screen so that it's effectively invisible, without actually closing (shutting down) the window. This can help you keep your Desktop uncluttered, and it's easily achieved by means of the Minimize button.

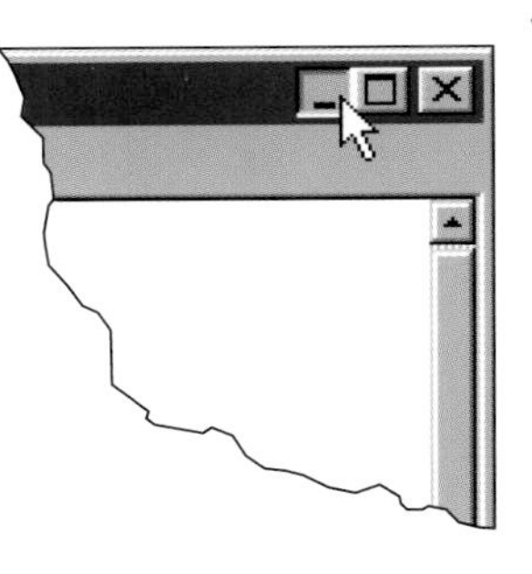

1 Activate the *My Computer* window and click on the Minimize button at the top right corner of the window. You'll see an animation as the *My Computer* window "shrinks" into its button on the Taskbar.

2 To reveal a minimized window, click on its Taskbar button. You'll see another animation as the window expands out of the button.

Hide All?

You can minimize all open windows in one move by right-clicking a blank area of the Taskbar and then choosing *Minimize All Windows* from the pop-up menu.

The Microsoft Natural Keyboard

If you do a lot of touch typing or have ever suffered symptoms of RSI (repetitive strain injury) you might like to try out the new ergonomically-designed keyboard called the Microsoft Natural Keyboard. The main keys are spread over two sections angled away from each other for typing comfort, and a section at the front has been molded to act as a palm rest. If your hands aren't horizontal when using the rest, as they should be, you can heighten the front by pulling down a flap on the underside. The keyboard has three extra keys that can sometimes be used for special functions, depending on the program you are using.

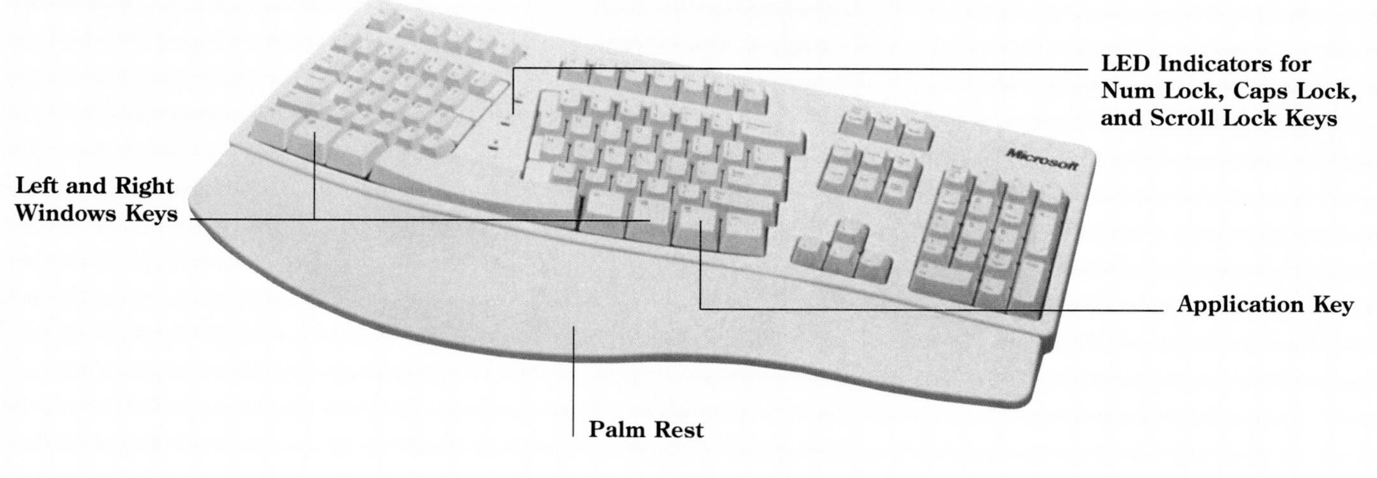

CLOSING WINDOWS

When you minimize a window, it is still open — that is, the window, and any program that might be running in the window, is still available and can be readily displayed by clicking on the appropriate Taskbar button.

If you want to shut down a window and remove it from the Taskbar, you must close the window. There are various ways of closing windows, so practice each of these in turn.

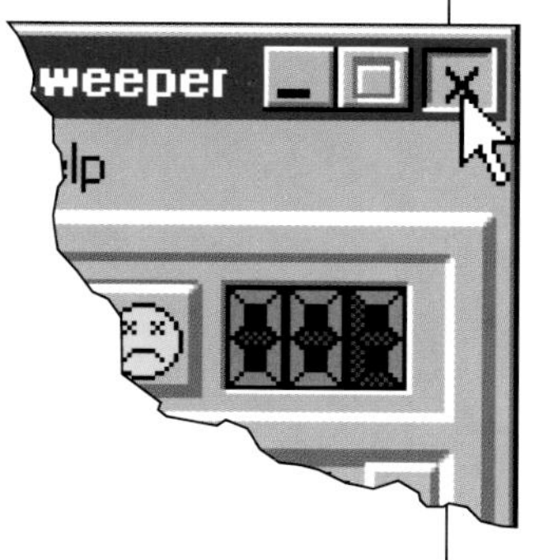

1 Activate the *Minesweeper* window and click on its close button (the button labeled with an x at the top right of the screen). The window closes.

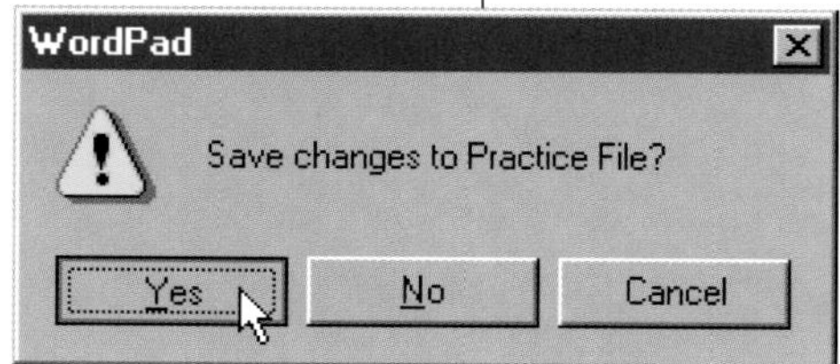

2 Activate the *Practice File - WordPad* window and then press Alt and F4 together. This keyboard combination closes the active window. If you have made changes to the **Practice File** document that you have not previously saved, the message shown above appears. Click on *Yes*.

3 On the Taskbar, click on the *My Computer* button using the right mouse button. Choose *Close* from the pop-up menu.

How to Shut Down Windows 95

When you've finished a Windows 95 session, you should shut down the program in a safe and proper way, otherwise you may corrupt some of the Windows program files, which could adversely affect the performance of your PC. The same applies if you wish to restart Windows 95 (see "Why Restart?" below).

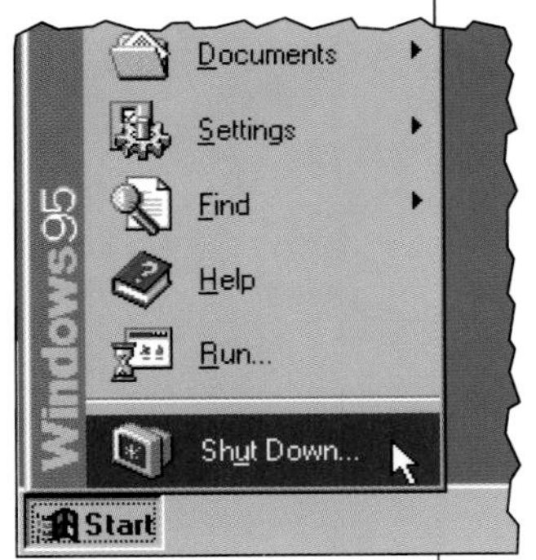

1 Click on the *Start* button and choose *Shut Down* from the *Start* menu.

2 A dialog box entitled *Shut Down Windows* appears. Click on one of the options listed and then click on *Yes* (or on *No* if you have changed your mind).

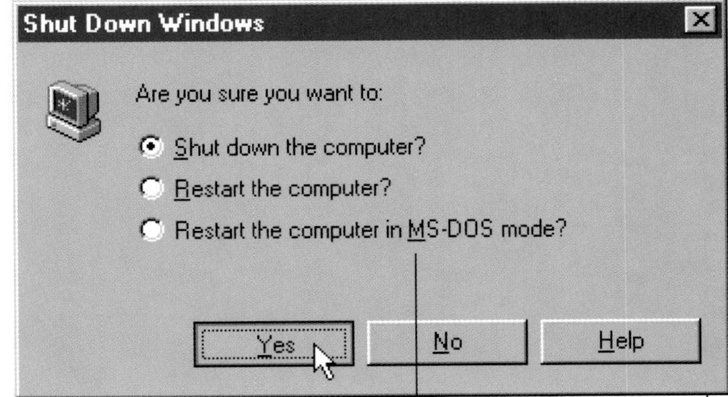

MS-DOS Mode?
If you're not sure what "MS-DOS mode" means, see pages 106 to 107.

You should wait until a message appears confirming that you can safely turn off your computer before you press the power off switch or use the keyboard combination Ctrl-Alt-Delete to restart Windows.

Why Restart?

You may sometimes need to restart Windows 95 after you have made changes to your computer's configuration — for example, after you have installed a new hardware device (see page 61) — so that the changes can take effect. Windows 95 will usually display a message telling you to restart and you should use the *Shut Down* command on the *Start* menu and then choose the *Restart the computer* option.

You may also need to restart if a program "hangs" or "freezes" and stops responding to your keyboard and mouse actions. In such circumstances, you will obviously not be able to use the *Shut Down* command. Instead, press the Ctrl, Alt, and Delete keys on your keyboard at the same time or press your PC's reset button.

Ctrl Key **Alt Key** **Delete Key**

Browsing Your Computer

EVERY LETTER, DATABASE, OR PICTURE YOU CREATE and every program you install on your computer is stored as a *file,* normally on the PC's hard disk or sometimes on a floppy disk. Imagine that your computer is like your desk: if you stored all your work in one big heap, what a mess your desk would be! Over the next few pages, you'll find out how most of the files stored on your computer are organized into *folders*. You'll practice a variety of techniques for browsing your computer's disks and the folders and files they contain.

What's on Your Computer?

Everything in your computing environment is arranged in a hierarchy. At the apex of this hierarchy is the Windows 95 Desktop, which provides access points both to your own computer and to other computers to which your PC is connected. Your computer provides access to a hard disk and floppy disks, these disks contain folders, and the folders contain subfolders and individual files.

To go one level below the Desktop in this hierarchy, start up your PC and double-click on the *My Computer* icon on the Desktop. This opens the *My Computer* window, which contains icons representing some of the main items associated with your PC.

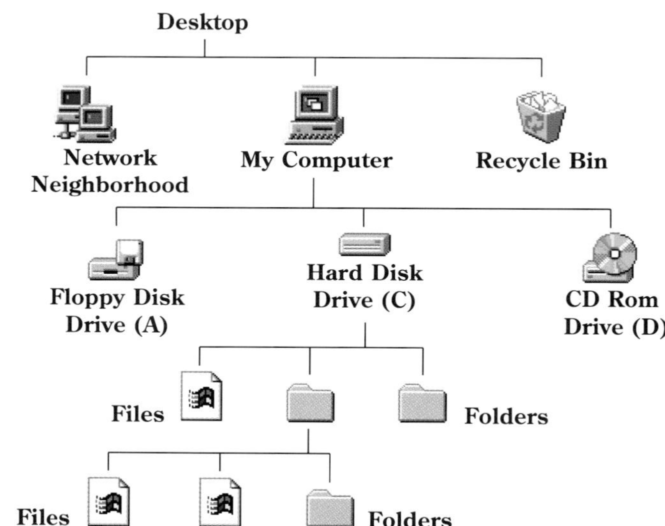

Hard Disk Drive Icon
Provides access to the contents of your PC's hard disk. The hard disk drive is normally called drive C.

Floppy Disk Drive Icon
Provides access to the contents of any disks placed in your PC's floppy disk drives. A single floppy disk drive is called drive A. If your PC has two floppy disk drives, they are called drives A and B.

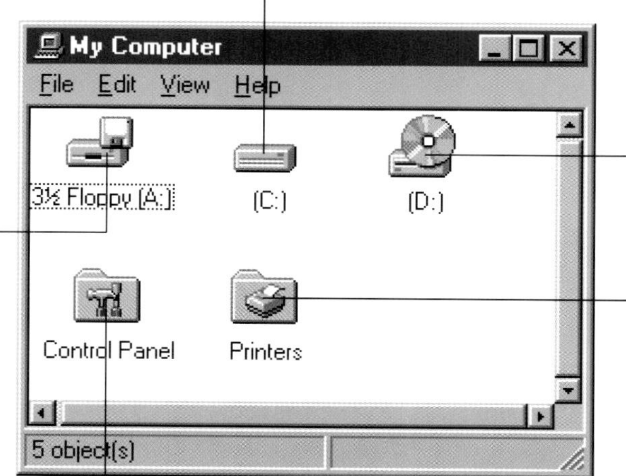

CD-ROM Drive Icon
Provides access to the contents of any CD-ROM placed in a CD-ROM drive on your PC. The CD-ROM drive is usually labeled drive D.

Control Panel Folder
Provides access to the Control Panel, a collection of tools for configuring or altering the settings of your PC's hardware and software (see page 34).

Printers Folder
Provides access to the printers attached to your PC, either directly or via a network (see pages 72 through 75).

Disk Storage and Memory

A crucial concept to understand about a PC is the difference between memory and storage on a disk. Your PC's disks (usually the hard disk) are used to store programs and data when they are not being worked on by the computer. When you run a program, the program and some data are loaded into RAM (random access memory) — special memory chips inside your PC. However, when the PC's power is switched off, anything in memory is lost — that's why your PC needs a hard disk for long-term storage.

Both disk storage and memory are measured in megabytes (millions of bytes), abbreviated as MB. One byte is enough space to store a single character. The storage capacities of different types of disks and memory chips typically used with PCs are shown below.

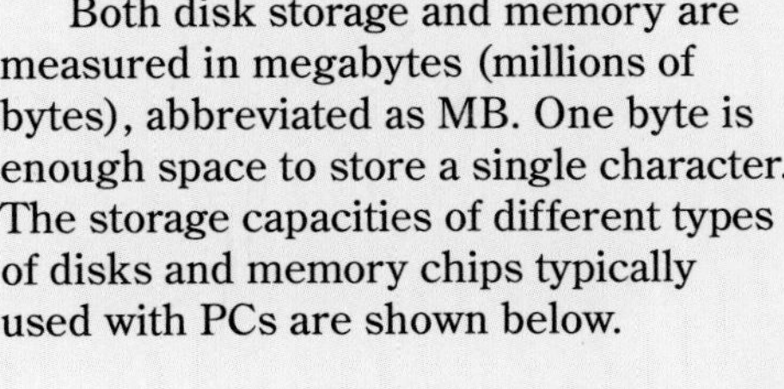

High-density 3½-Inch Floppy Disk
1.44 MB

Hard Disk
Usually holds between 100 and 500 MB

CD-ROM
650 MB

Memory Chip
Typically 4 MB or 8 MB of RAM

How Much Memory?
To find out how much memory you have installed in your PC, double-click on the *My Computer* icon and then double-click on the *Control Panel* icon to open the *Control Panel* window. Now double-click on the icon labeled *System*. The next window displays the amount of memory installed in your PC.

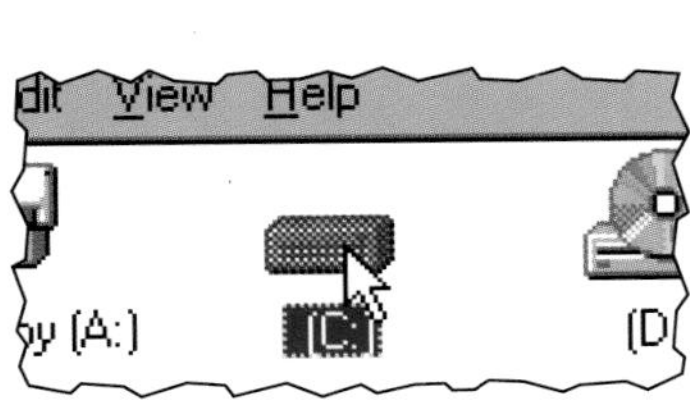

The Hard Disk Drive

Now let's move down a level and look at what's on your PC's hard disk. To do so, double-click on the hard disk icon, labeled *[C:]*, in the *My Computer* window. A new window titled *[C:]* appears on the screen.

C Drive Contents
The [C:] *window contains file and folder icons. Each file and folder has a name. The actual files and folders in your* [C:] *window may differ from those shown here, but you should see a* ***Windows*** *folder, a* ***Dos*** *folder, and a folder for any other major application that's been installed on your hard disk. You'll also see some files that are stored "loose" on your hard disk — for example, a file called* ***Autoexec****.*

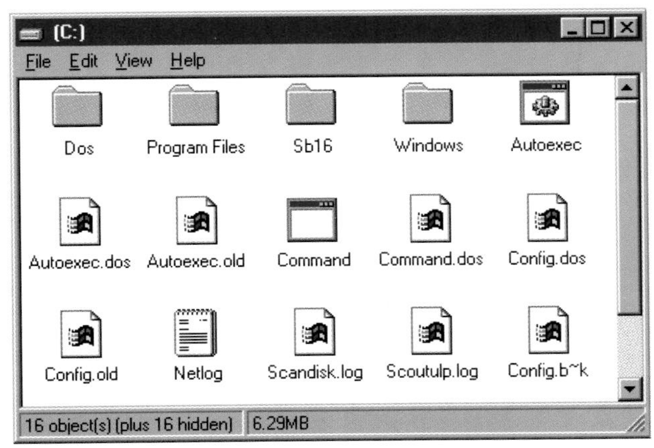

Folder Icon

File Icons

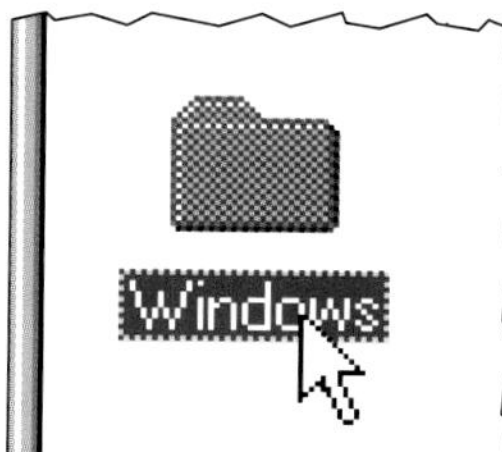

The Windows Window

Let's look at the contents of a folder in the *[C:]* window — the **Windows** folder. To do so, double-click on the *Windows* icon. A *Windows* window appears. If the window does not appear as shown below, choose *Large Icons* from the *View* menu.

Scroll Box
You can use your mouse to drag the box in this bar up or down. This action causes the contents of the folder to move in procession through the window — an action called scrolling.

Menu Bar
All folder windows (and also drive windows and the My Computer *window) have a menu bar containing the menu names* File, Edit, View, *and* Help. *You can use commands in these menus to perform a variety of operations on the files and folders in the window or to obtain help.*

Folder Icons

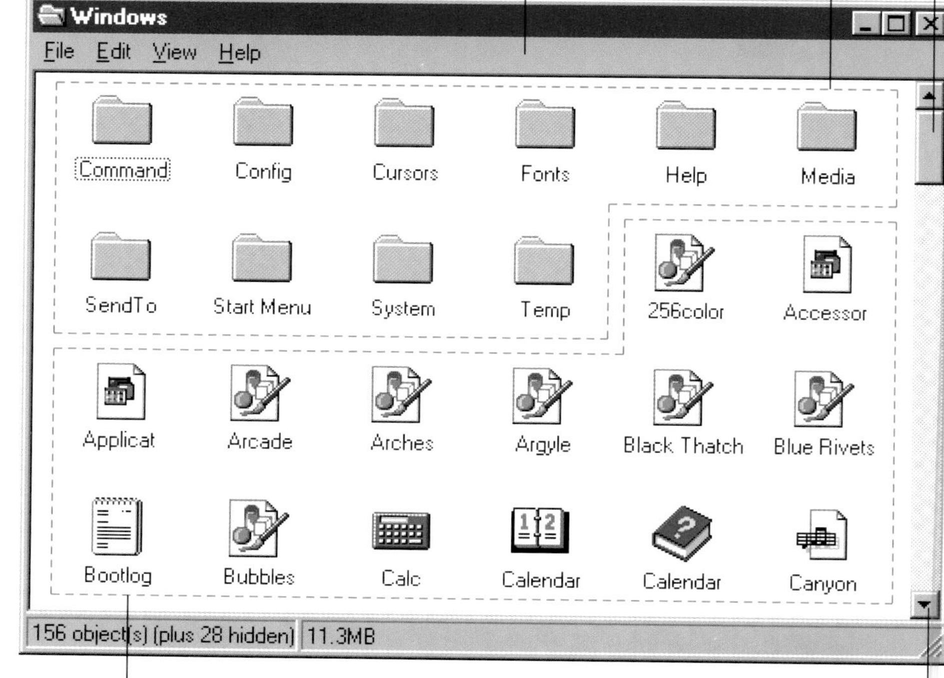

File Icons

Scroll Bar Arrow
Clicking on this arrow or the similar upward-pointing arrow at the top of the scroll bar scrolls the contents of a folder up or down one row of icons at a time. Pointing at an arrow and holding down the mouse button produces continuous scrolling.

Window Control
By default, whenever you open a new folder window, the window for its parent folder also remains open. If you want this to stop happening, choose *Options* from the *View* menu. This opens the *Options* dialog box. In the *Folder* flipcard, click on the option button labeled *Browse folders by using a single window....* and then click on *OK*.

You can see that the **Windows** folder contains several folders within it. These are subfolders of the **Windows** folder. Remember that folders are used to store related files in one place, where they can easily be found. For example, there's a **Media** folder for storing the sound and video files supplied with Windows 95, a **Help** folder for storing help files, a **System** folder that's used to store various program support files, and so on. The **Windows** folder also contains a large number of loose files, each with a name and represented by an icon.

Files and Icons

Program Files
These always have a unique icon. You can start a program by double-clicking on its icon (see more on page 29).

Calculator
A program that mimics a hand-held calculator

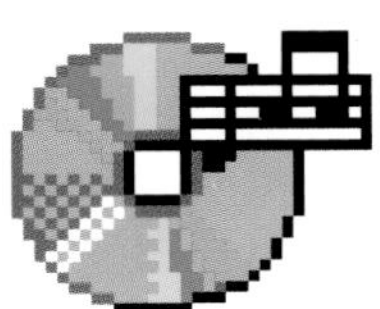

CD Player
A program for playing audio CDs in a CD-ROM drive

Solitaire
A card game

Defrag
A program for optimizing file storage on your hard disk

Most computer files fall into one of two categories — program files and data files. A program file contains instructions to the computer that describe how a particular program looks and works. Programs range from small accessories supplied with Windows 95, like Calculator, to huge applications, like Microsoft Excel. Data files, which are sometimes called "documents," include text files, graphics files, sound files, and spreadsheet files.

In drive and folder windows, each file is represented by an icon. A small selection of file icons that you might come across when browsing through your hard disk are shown at left and right.

Shortcut Icons
Some icons have a small arrow in the bottom left-hand corner. These icons are called shortcut icons. The icon actually points the way to a file that's stored in a different folder. To find out more about shortcuts and their uses, see page 100.

Filenames

Windows 95 files can have names up to 255 characters long. However, you'll sometimes come across files with short, odd-looking names, like Win386.swp.

These files are holdovers from an old filenaming system that worked with previous versions of Windows and with the MS-DOS operating system (see page 106). Under this system, filenames could have a maximum of eight characters, followed by a period and a three-character extension. The extension described the type of file. For example, EXE meant an executable (or program) file. Windows 95 looks at existing files on a disk, works out from each file's extension what sort of file it is, and assigns an icon to the file. If Windows 95 doesn't recognize the file's extension, it displays the original name derived from the old filenaming system.

Data Files
You'll notice that within the same folder there are sometimes several files with the same icon but different labels. These are usually data files that have all been created with the same program. For example, in the ***Windows*** *folder the files labeled* ***Cars***, ***Castle***, ***Walls***, *and* ***Argyle*** *are all picture files created with a program called Paint.*

Sound File

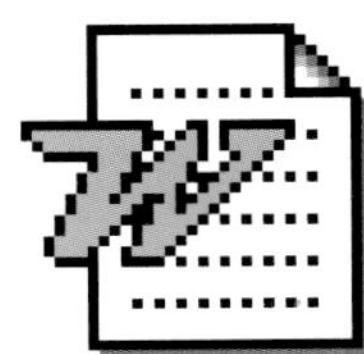

Microsoft Word Document

Paint Picture

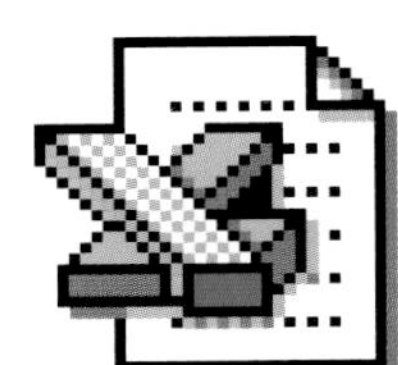

Microsoft Excel Spreadsheet

Browsing Aids

The contents of your **Windows** folder are currently displayed in large icon view. This option provides the clearest view of individual icons. When a folder contains a large number of files and folders, however, you may only see a fraction of a folder's contents within that folder's window. You can use the scroll bar to help you browse, but that can be time-consuming.

Fortunately, Windows 95 offers a number of options that can assist you in your browsing sessions. Activate the *Windows* window, maximize it if you have not already done so, and then do the following:

Small Icons?
If you choose *Small Icons* instead of *List* from the *View* menu, you'll see a similar view to the list view, except that the icons run in order across rows instead of down columns.

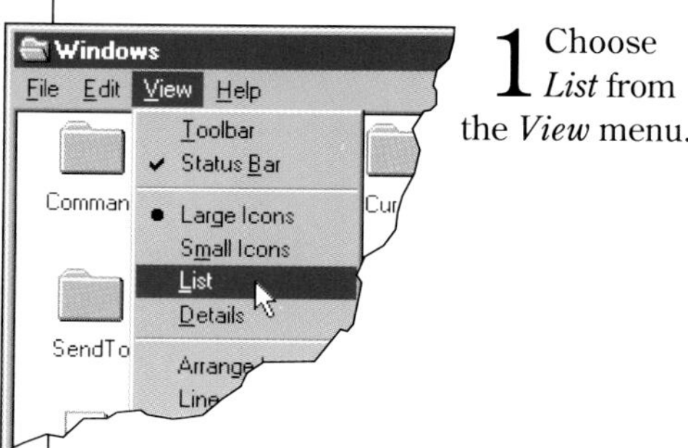

1 Choose *List* from the *View* menu.

2 All the icons are now small, so you can see more of the folder's contents at the same time. The files are ordered in columns across the window and the vertical scroll bar is replaced with a horizontal scroll bar.

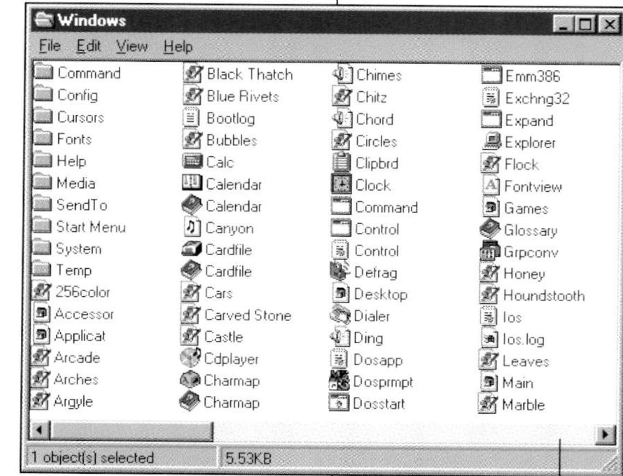

Horizontal Scroll Bar

OTHER VIEWING OPTIONS

You can also view files sorted according to their types, sizes, or ages, instead of by name (alphabetically); and you can view details about your files, such as their sizes, types, and when they were last modified. With your *Windows* window still active, do the following:

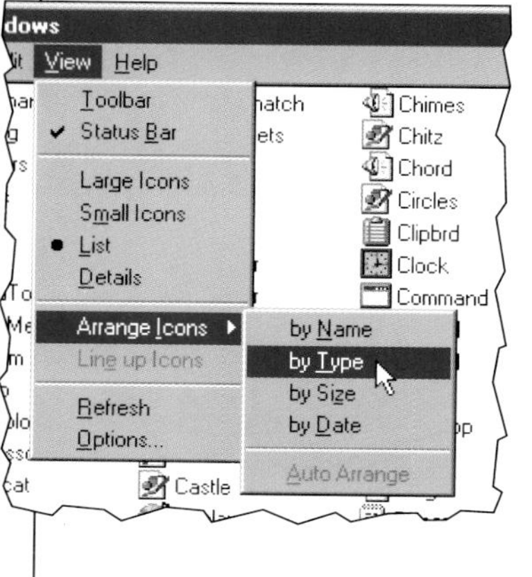

1 Choose *Arrange Icons* from the *View* menu and *by Type* from the submenu.

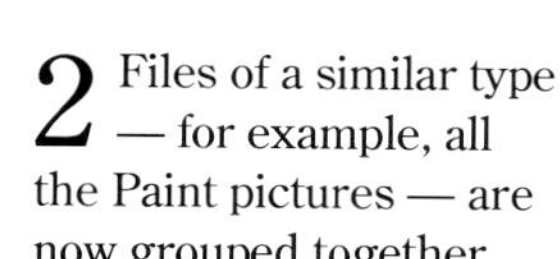

2 Files of a similar type — for example, all the Paint pictures — are now grouped together.

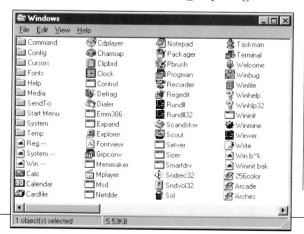

Any Old Files?
If you are looking for any old or very big files that you might be able to delete to save space on your hard disk, try arranging the file icons in a window sorted by age or by size.

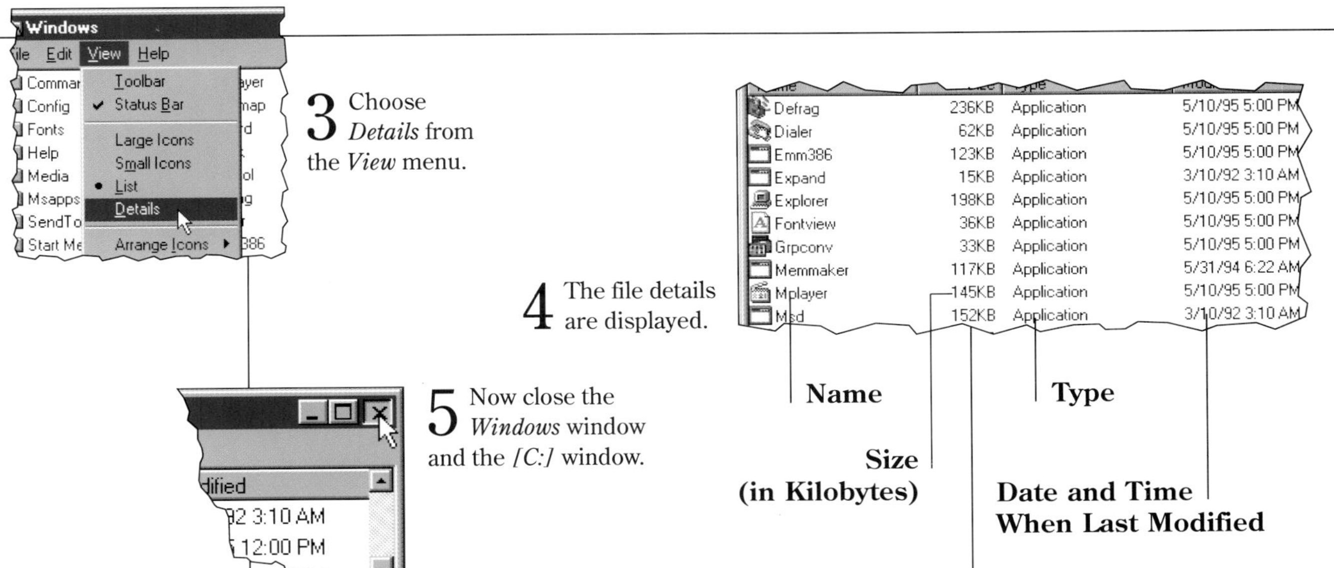

3 Choose *Details* from the *View* menu.

4 The file details are displayed.

5 Now close the *Windows* window and the *[C:]* window.

Browsing Other Drives

So far you have explored only what's stored on the hard disk drive inside your PC. You can use all the techniques already described to explore what's on floppy disks or CD-ROMs.

Browsing a Floppy Disk

1 Put a floppy disk in its appropriate disk drive. Activate the *My Computer* window from the Taskbar, and then double-click on the icon for that disk drive.

2 A window showing the floppy disk contents opens. You can perform the same operations on the contents of the floppy disk as you have already performed with the hard disk — for example, browse individual folders, find out details about the files, change the view of a folder's contents, and so on.

Now close all the open windows on your Desktop. In Chapter Two, in the section on "Organizing Files and Folders," you'll find out about some operations you can perform on the contents of drive and folder windows — such as moving or copying files to a new folder.

My Icons Look Messy!
In large icon and small icon views, you can move icons around within a window by dragging them with the mouse. But if you move icons around a lot, the window may start to look messy. Choose *Line up Icons* from the *View* menu to reorganize the icons neatly.

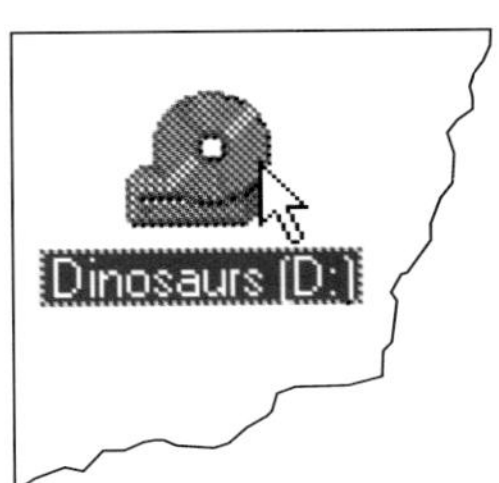

Browsing a CD-ROM
If you have a CD-ROM drive installed in your PC and would like to see what files and folders are on a CD-ROM, just insert the disc in the drive. In the My Computer *window, the name of the CD-ROM will appear below the [D:] drive icon. To see the contents of the CD-ROM, simply double-click on this icon.*

Launching Programs and Opening Documents

During most Windows 95 sessions, you'll want to launch at least one program in addition to Windows itself. The program might be an accessory or a tool provided with Windows 95, or it might be an application, such as a word processing, graphics, or spreadsheet program that's been installed on your PC. In this section, you'll take a closer look at launching programs, opening documents, and saving documents to disk.

Launching Programs

When you launch a program, you are instructing Windows 95 to open the program so that you can work with it. There are several different ways to launch a program.

USING THE PROGRAMS MENU

This is the standard method, which you have already used in "Windows 95 Jumpstart" to launch both WordPad (see page 13) and Minesweeper (see page 18). Let's look at this method a little more closely.

1 Click on the *Start* button to open the *Start* menu.

2 Point to *Programs,* and the *Programs* menu appears. Most or all of the programs on your computer should be available via this menu. The items with identical folder and window icons are called program groups, and each represents a collection of programs. The groups you'll see on your own *Programs* menu will probably differ from those shown at right.

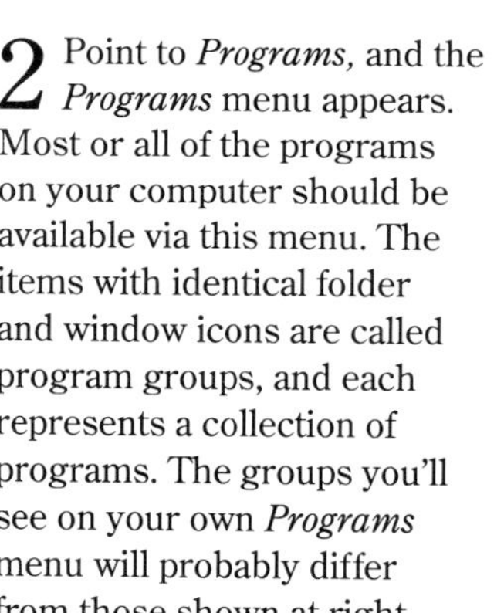

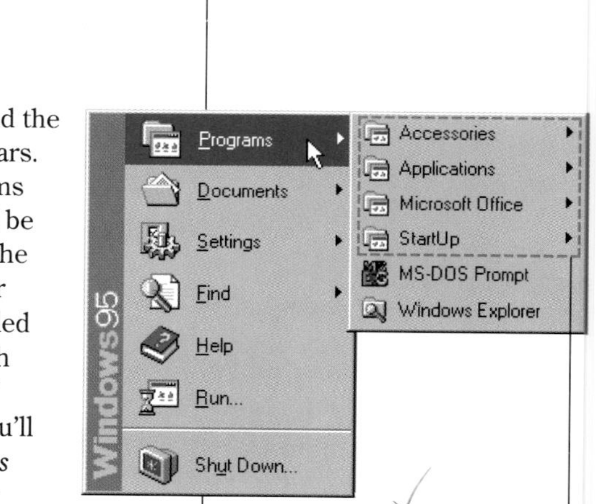

3 Point to each program group in turn and look at the programs it contains, which appear in submenus. You can launch any program by clicking on its name. In the example at right, Microsoft Excel is being launched from the *Microsoft Office* program group. Try launching a few of the programs on your own computer — you may find there are more than you imagined! Once you've done this, close all the programs — you can close any Windows-based program by clicking on its Close button.

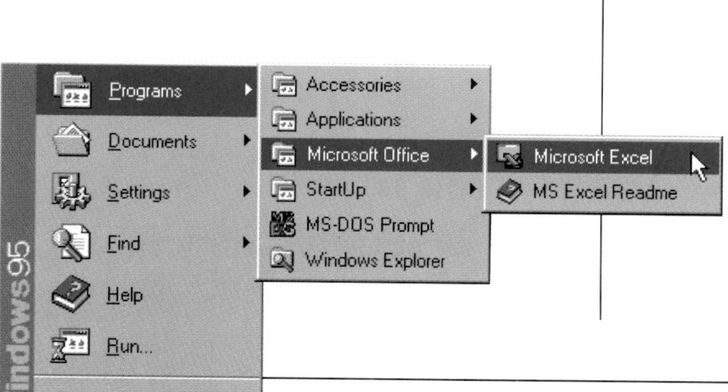

Program Groups

The program groups you'll see on your own *Programs* menu depend on what software has been installed on your computer.

■ When Windows 95 is installed on a PC as an upgrade to Windows 3.1 or 3.11, all existing program groups (which in the previous Windows versions appeared within a window called Program Manager) are put on the *Programs* menu.

■ Whether or not you upgraded from a previous Windows version, Windows 95 puts an *Accessories* program group on the *Programs* menu. The *Accessories* group contains a collection of utilities supplied with Windows, like WordPad and Paint. Nested within the *Accessories* group you'll see at least three more program groups — a *Games* group, a *Multimedia* group, and a *System Tools* group (see page 42).

■ When you install programs on your PC, Windows 95 may create a new group to hold that program or may place it into an existing group. For example, when you install Microsoft Excel or Word, Windows 95 puts these programs into a group called *Microsoft Office*.

■ Turn to page 103 to find out how to create new program groups and add programs to those groups.

LAUNCHING FROM A FOLDER WINDOW

There's a second method of launching a program — by finding a program's icon in the folder where it's located, and then double-clicking on the icon. You might use this method if you can't find the program via the *Programs* menu but know where to look for the program in your PC's drive and folder hierarchy. Try the following to launch a program called Calculator that comes with Windows 95:

1 Double-click on the *My Computer* icon.

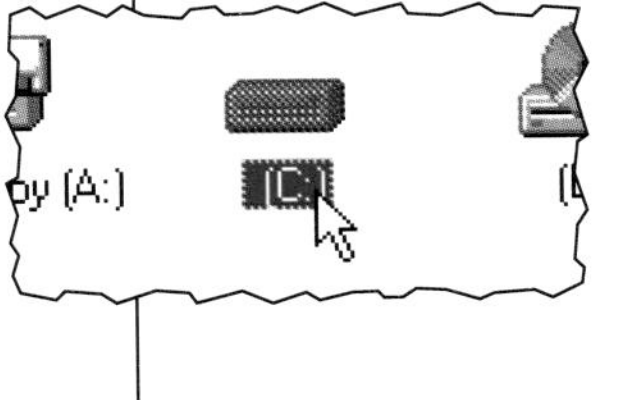

2 Double-click on the *[C:]* drive icon to display the contents of your hard disk.

3 Double-click on the icon for the **Windows** folder to display its contents.

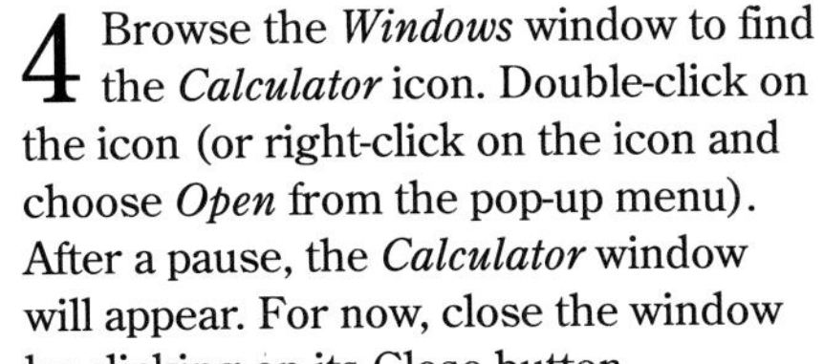

4 Browse the *Windows* window to find the *Calculator* icon. Double-click on the icon (or right-click on the icon and choose *Open* from the pop-up menu). After a pause, the *Calculator* window will appear. For now, close the window by clicking on its Close button.

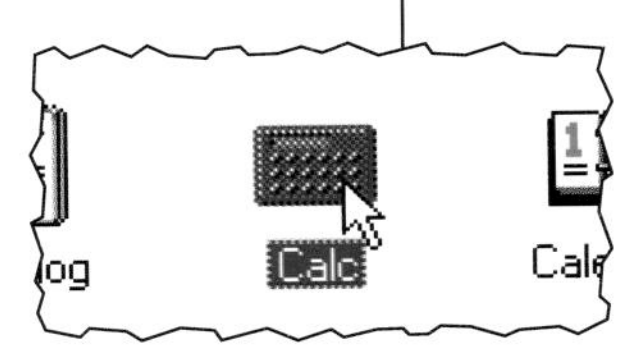

What Is Windows Explorer?

In addition to program groups, you'll see some individual programs on your *Programs* menu, such as Windows Explorer. Windows Explorer is a special utility that replaces the File Manager found in previous versions of Windows. You'll find out how to use it on page 56 in Chapter Two.

USING THE RUN COMMAND

If you don't know where to look for a program in your folder structure, there's one more method you could try — the *Run* command.

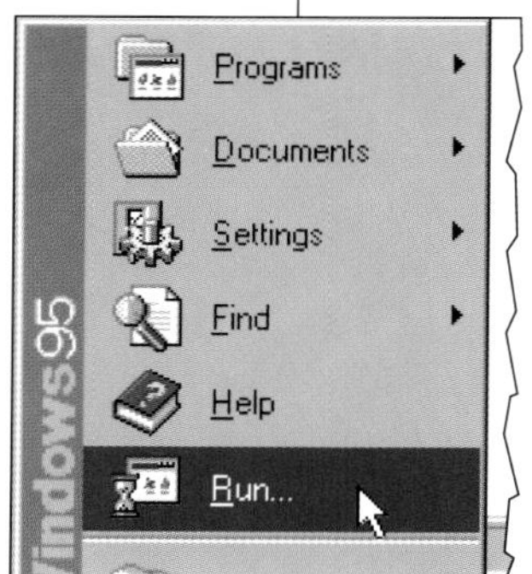

1 Choose *Run* from the *Start* menu. The *Run* dialog box appears.

2 Type the name of the program you want to launch into the *Open* box. For example, type **Wordpad**. Now click on *OK*. Windows 95 will search the hard disk for a program with this name and then launch it. When WordPad (a mini word processor) opens, close it down again by clicking on the Close button.

What's a Parent Folder?
In your PC's drive and folder hierarchy, a folder's *parent* is the folder or drive one level above that folder. For example, within the **Windows** folder, there is a **System** folder, so the **Windows** folder is the parent of the **System** folder.

Opening Documents

Once you've launched a program like WordPad, Paint, or Microsoft Excel, you'll usually want to do one of two things — create a new document (data file) or open an existing file in order to edit or print it.

Creating a new document is easy. When you launch a program like WordPad or Paint, the program automatically opens an empty, untitled document file. You can immediately start adding content to the file and at any time you can save and name the file using the *Save As* command, as explained on page 16.

To open an existing file, you use the *Open* command and dialog box. For example, launch WordPad from the *Accessories* program group, and then do the following:

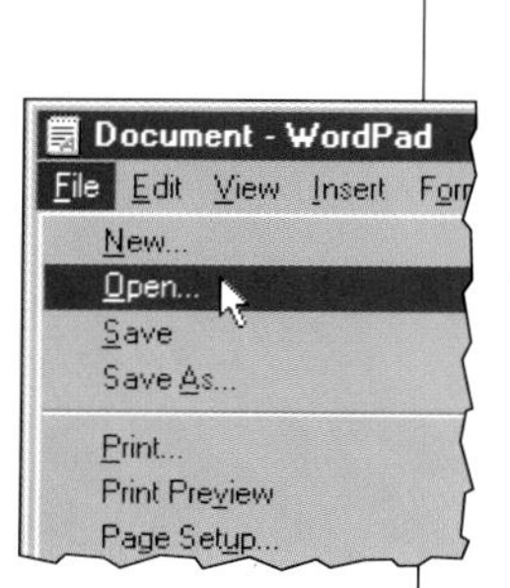

1 Choose *Open* from the *File* menu in the WordPad window.

2 The *Open* dialog box will appear.

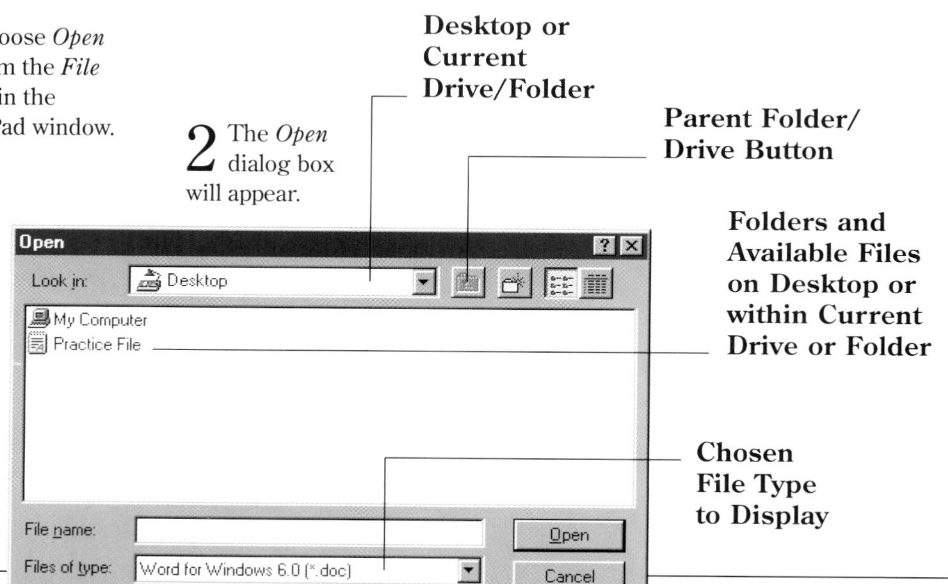

Desktop or Current Drive/Folder

Parent Folder/ Drive Button

Folders and Available Files on Desktop or within Current Drive or Folder

Chosen File Type to Display

USING THE OPEN DIALOG BOX

The *Open* dialog box looks similar and works in the same way no matter what Windows 95 application you find it in. Once you've mastered how to use this dialog box to load a file in one Windows program, you'll know how to use it in any other program.

In the *Look in* box, either *Desktop* or the name of the current drive or folder appears. The central area of the dialog box displays all the folders on the Desktop, or the folders within the current drive or folder, together with all files that belong to the file type displayed in the *Files of type* box.

If you can see the file you want to open in the dialog box, you just double-click on the file to open it, or click on it once and then click on the *Open* button.

If you don't see the file you want to open, you need to "navigate" through your computer's drive and folder hierarchy until the file appears in the window, and then double-click on its icon. Try navigating to and opening a text file called **Country** in the **Dos** folder. (If you can't find **Country**, open the file called **Readme**.)

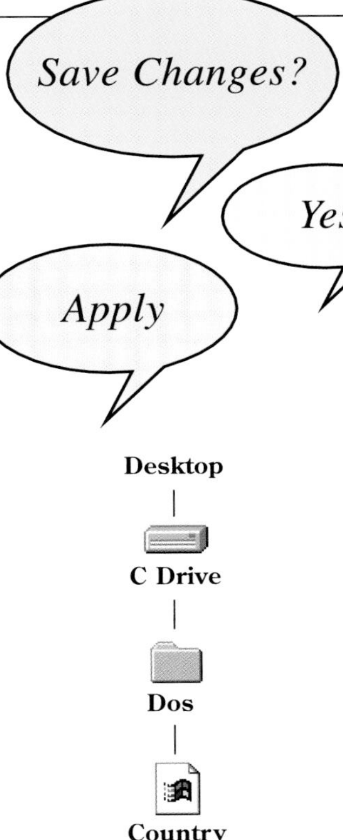

Going Down Country
To get to the **Country** *file, you must first access the folders on your C drive and then go down one level to access the contents of the* **Dos** *folder.*

Setting up Shortcuts
If you use a particular file or program every day, you might wish that there was a really quick way of launching it. There is! You can create a special shortcut icon on your Desktop that points directly to the file or program. See page 98 for details.

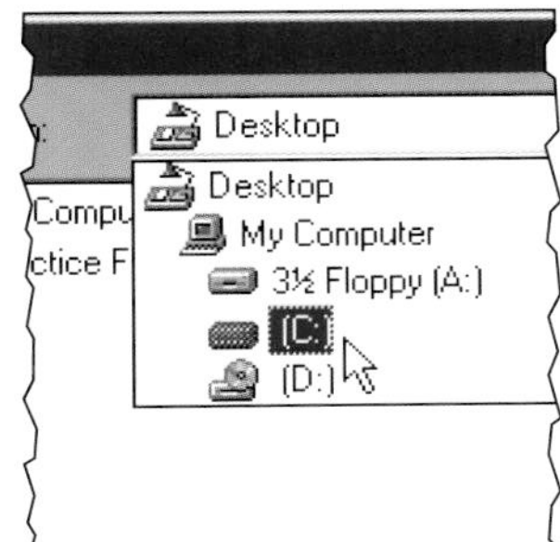

1 First click on the down arrow next to the *Look in* box and choose *[C:]* from the drop-down menu. You are now addressing the C drive.

2 Now you need to move one level down the hierarchy — to the **Dos** folder. Because the **Dos** folder is one of the main folders on the C drive, you should see it in the main area of the dialog box. Double-click on the icon for the **Dos** folder.

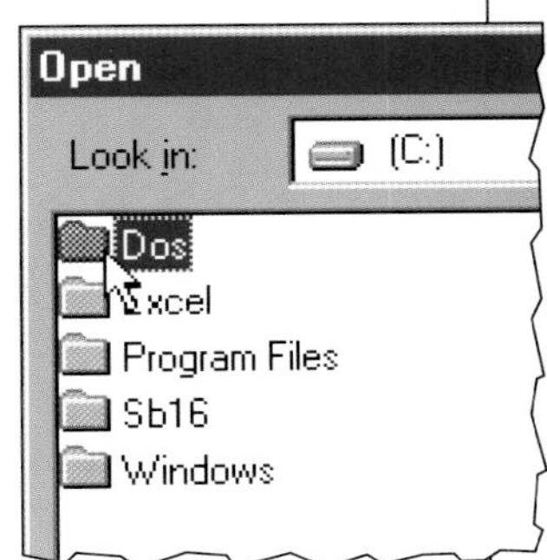

3 The **Dos** folder is now your current folder. Now you need to find the **Country** file in the **Dos** folder. Click on the down arrow at the right of the *Files of type* box. Choose *Text Documents (*.txt)* from the drop-down list that appears. If you are not sure about the type of file you're looking for, choose *All Files* to see them all.

Quick Open?
A quick shortcut to the *Open* dialog box is to use the Ctrl-O key combination.

4 You should now see some text-only files, including **Country**, in the main area of the dialog box. Double-click on the **Country** file and it should open in WordPad. For now, minimize the WordPad window.

OPENING A DOCUMENT FROM ITS FOLDER WINDOW

You can also open a document by double-clicking on the file's icon in its folder window. When you do so, Windows will automatically launch the application that was used to create the document and will then load the document.

For example, if you want to launch the Paint program automatically and load the picture file called **Leaves**, which is in the **Windows** folder, first open the **Windows** folder by double-clicking on its icon in the *[C:]* window, and then do the following:

1 Find the Paint picture icon labeled *Leaves* and double-click on it (or right-click it once and choose *Open* from the pop-up menu).

2 Windows will launch the Paint application, which created this file, and load the **Leaves** picture file. You can now close the window.

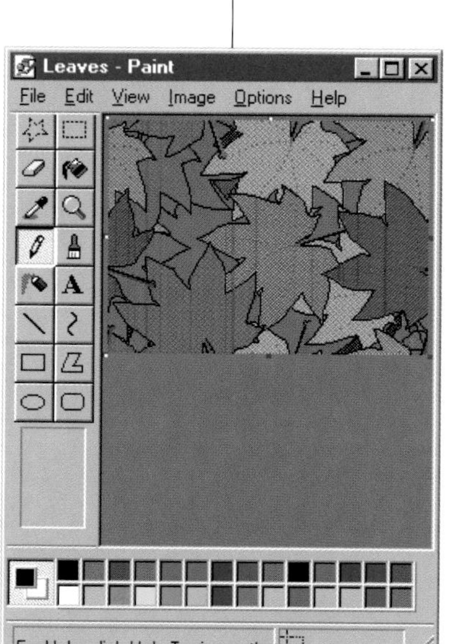

Last Fifteen
Windows 95 keeps a record of the last 15 documents (data files) that you have opened and stores these in the *Documents* menu, available via the *Start* button. To open a document that you have worked on recently, click on the *Start* button, point to *Documents*, and then choose the file you want.

Saving a Document

Once you've made any changes to a named document, you can save the file with its original name and to its original folder by choosing *Save* from the program's *File* menu. If you want to close the document and save it, you can close the program window and confirm that you want to save changes when a question box pops up. Many programs offer a *Close* command on the *File* menu that allows you to close and save a document without exiting the program.

SAVING OPTIONS

To save a copy of a document to a new location or as a new file type, or to save a version of the document with a new name, you use the *Save As* command and dialog box. As an example, follow the steps starting on the opposite page.

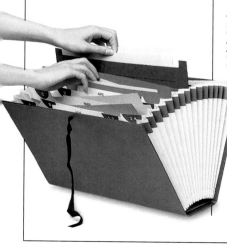

Save Your Work!
Remember that you should save your work often to guard against power failures and software crashes. Anything that you've created on your computer screen but have forgotten to save will be irretrievably lost if the program or the computer unexpectedly shuts down.

Different File Types? Some types of data files can be saved to a disk in a number of different formats or types — for example, a text document can be saved as text-only or with information about the formatting (styling) of the text included. The choice of type in which a data file is saved is controlled by means of the *Save as type* box in the *Save As* dialog box.

1 Activate the WordPad window containing the **Country** file by clicking on its Taskbar button.

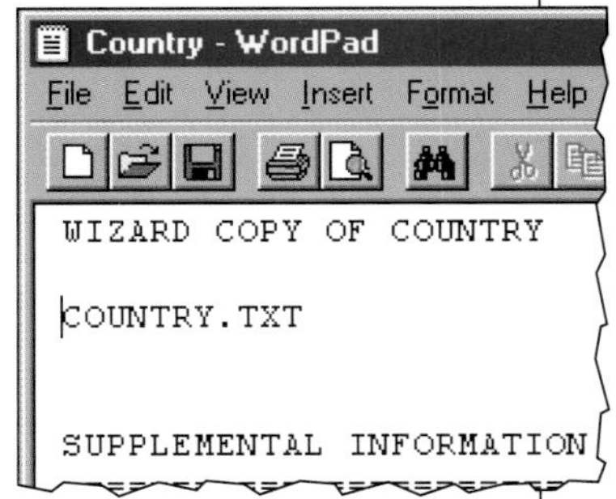

2 Type **WIZARD COPY OF COUNTRY** at the top of the document (make sure you don't omit the word "**Wizard**") and press Enter a couple of times. Now choose *Save As* from the *File* menu.

3 The *Save As* dialog box opens. In the *Save in* box, the **Dos** folder is shown as the current folder. Click on the Parent Folder/Drive button.

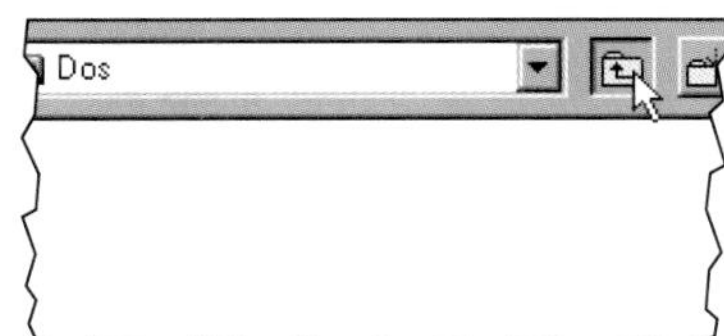

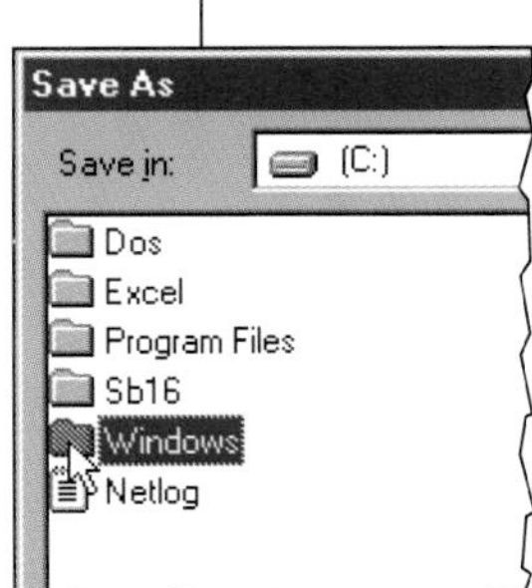

4 Now double-click on the **Windows** folder in the central area of the dialog box to choose this as the folder in which you would like to save the slightly altered copy of the **Country** file.

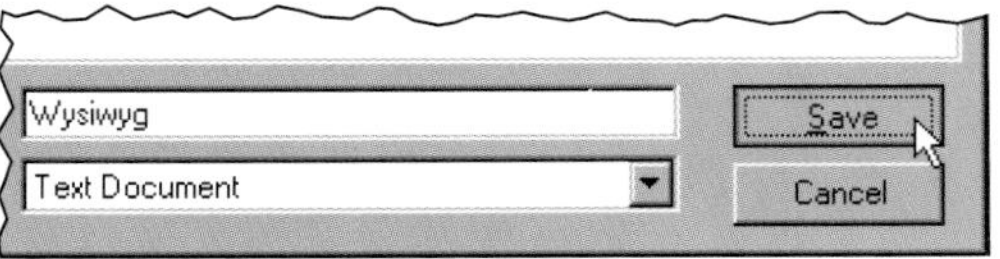

5 In the *File name* box, place the mouse pointer over the file's current name, double-click to highlight it, and then type **Wysiwyg**. Finally, click on the *Save* button, and then close WordPad. The **Wysiwyg** file is now stored in the **Windows** folder, while the original **Country** file remains in the **Dos** folder.

Quick Viewing

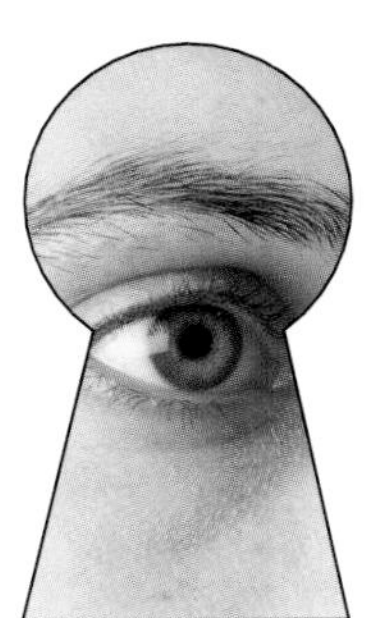

The Quick View feature lets you look at what's inside a text or picture file without allowing you to change or print the file. Quick View can be useful when you just want to see what's in a file, perhaps to check that you've found the right file before opening it. If Quick View does not appear on the pop-up menu, see "Adding Windows 95 Components" on page 123. To preview a file follow these steps:

1 Find any Paint picture file in the **Windows** folder on your hard disk. Right-click on the file's icon and choose *Quick View* from the pop-up menu. The Paint picture appears in a *Quick View* window.

2 If you decide you would like to open the file to edit or print it, choose *Open File for Editing* from the *File* menu. In this case, click on the Close button.

The Control Panel

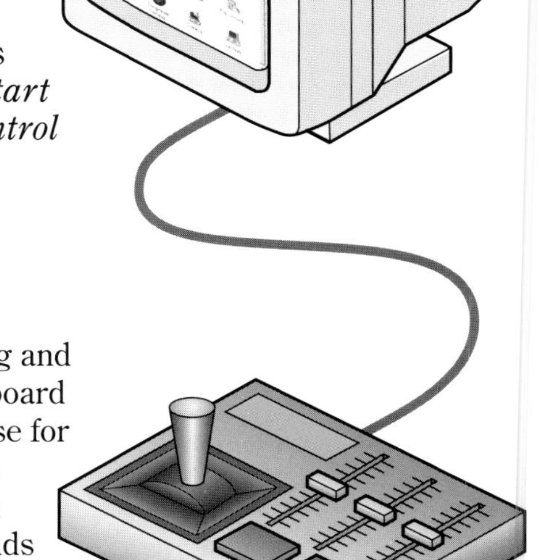

In the Control Panel folder, you will find a number of utilities that allow you to set up Windows 95 and your computer hardware in a way that suits you best. You will learn to use many of these utilities in later sections of this book. To open the Control Panel, click on the *Start* button and then choose *Control Panel* from the *Settings* menu. The *Control Panel* window will appear.

Control Panel
You may find some additional icons such as Microsoft Mail Postoffice in your Control Panel. These are optionally installed items (see page 123).

Customization Tools

The Control Panel contains tools for customizing and altering items such as the behavior of your keyboard and mouse (you can, for instance, set your mouse for a right-handed or left-handed person). From the Control Panel, you can set or alter features such as the appearance of your Desktop and the sounds that are linked to different Windows events.

The Control Panel is also the place where you set up and configure hardware devices such as modems, CD-ROM drives, and printers. Installing a new piece of equipment is easy with the Hardware Installation Wizard, which you access by double-clicking on the *Add New Hardware* icon; but always remember that, as the keeper of configuration settings, the Control Panel should be treated with care!

The Control Panel Tools

Most of the individual tools in the Control Panel will be discussed in more detail later on in the book. For now, let's just take a quick glance inside the folder to see what kinds of functions are available.

Add New Hardware

Add New Hardware
Accesses the Hardware Installation Wizard, which you use to add new hardware, such as a sound card (see page 61).

Date/Time

Date/Time
Changes the current time or date settings. The Time Zone option also allows you to check the time in different parts of the world (see page 114 for more details).

Fonts

Fonts
*Opens the **Fonts** folder. In the* Fonts *window you can view the fonts that Windows 95 provides for you. You must also access this window to install new fonts.*

Add/Remove Programs

Add/Remove Programs
Lets you install new programs from a floppy disk or CD-ROM drive, remove programs, and modify your Windows 95 setup (see page 64 for more details).

Display

Display
Lets you change your Windows 95 color scheme, screen resolution, or Desktop's appearance (see the examples above opposite and on page 115).

Keyboard

Keyboard
Adjusts keyboard settings, such as specifying layouts for different languages.

A CUSTOMIZATION EXAMPLE

You can use the *Display* tool in the Control Panel to customize the way Windows 95 looks by altering items such as the color of menu bars. You can also brighten up your Desktop by changing the background color or pattern or by choosing a picture to put in the background as *wallpaper*. If you're bored with the background color, it's easy to choose a new one; it's more fun, however, to replace it with a picture.

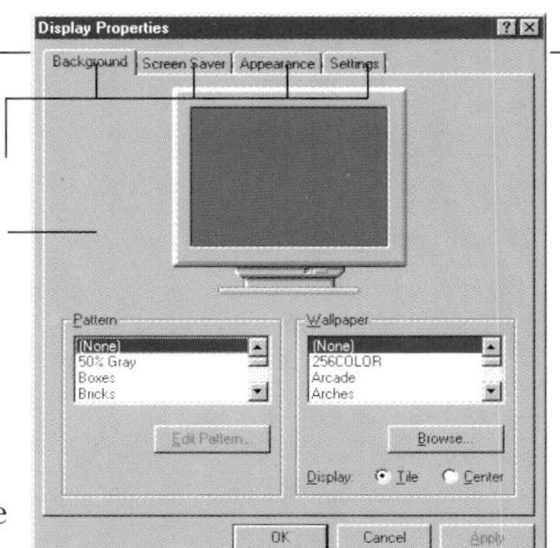

Tabs

Flipcard

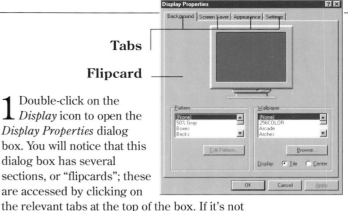

1 Double-click on the *Display* icon to open the *Display Properties* dialog box. You will notice that this dialog box has several sections, or "flipcards"; these are accessed by clicking on the relevant tabs at the top of the box. If it's not at the front, click on the *Background* flipcard.

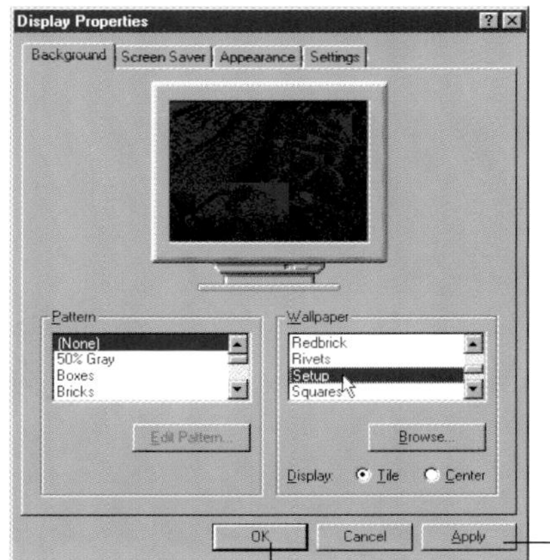

2 Below the preview screen are two lists called *Pattern* and *Wallpaper*. Scroll through the *Wallpaper* list until you see *Setup*. Click on this option and a representation of the picture will appear on the preview screen.

OK Button
Click here to apply your changes, close the dialog box, and return to the Desktop.

Apply Button
Click to apply and view your changes without closing the dialog box.

3 Click on *OK* and your Desktop's appearance will change (close the Control Panel to see the whole picture).

Modems
You can install a new modem or change modem settings with this tool (see page 88 for more details).

Network
This option lets you browse or change the network settings for your PC and install additional network components.

Regional Settings
Defines the symbols used for currencies and the standards used for the display of times, dates, numbers, and measurements (see page 114).

Mouse
Specifies settings such as the mouse pointer speed (see page 116 for more details).

Passwords
This option lets you set up a password for yourself and anyone else who uses your PC (see page 124).

Sounds
Use this to specify sounds to accompany Windows 95 events, such as opening a program (see page 62 for more details).

Multimedia
You can change settings for multimedia devices here (see page 67 for more details).

Printers
*Opens the **Printers** folder, where you can add a printer or define the printer to be used (see page 72 for more details).*

System
Provides access to various system settings.

Getting Help

IF YOU EVER NEED HELP WHEN USING WINDOWS 95, you just need to ask for it! The main Windows 95 help system consists of step by step instructions on hundreds of Windows tasks. There are specific Help systems for each Windows 95 accessory (such as WordPad). You'll also find pop-up help windows in dialog boxes that explain specific dialog box elements.

The Main Windows 95 Help System

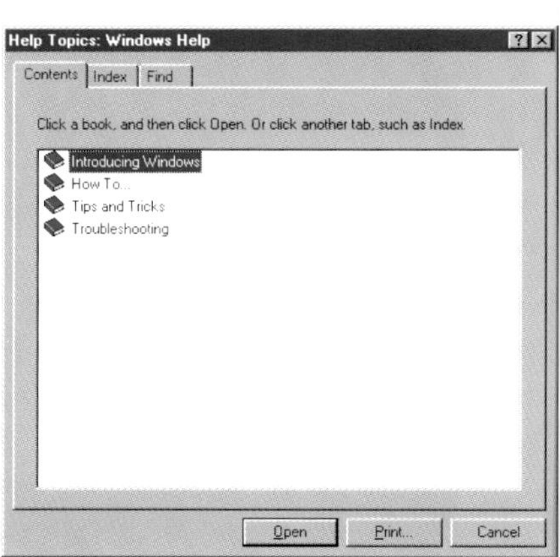

Help Topics: Windows Help **Dialog Box**

To access the main Windows 95 Help system, open the *Start* menu and click on *Help*. Alternatively, just press the F1 key (first switch out of any Windows accessory or application you are using by clicking on the Desktop). In either case, a dialog box entitled *Help Topics: Windows Help* appears. This contains three flipcards — a *Contents* flipcard, an *Index* flipcard, and a *Find* flipcard — that can be accessed by clicking on the *Contents*, *Index*, and *Find* tabs at the top. The flipcards provide access to hundreds of help topics, but the method of access is different in each case. Let's look at how to use each of these flipcards in turn.

CONTENTS FLIPCARD

The *Contents* flipcard organizes information like a table of contents in a book. When you first open the flipcard, you will see four main books of topics (*Introducing Windows 95*, *How To...*, and so on). Each book contains further books nested within it, and these nested books contain individual help topics. Try accessing help on how to copy a file or folder.

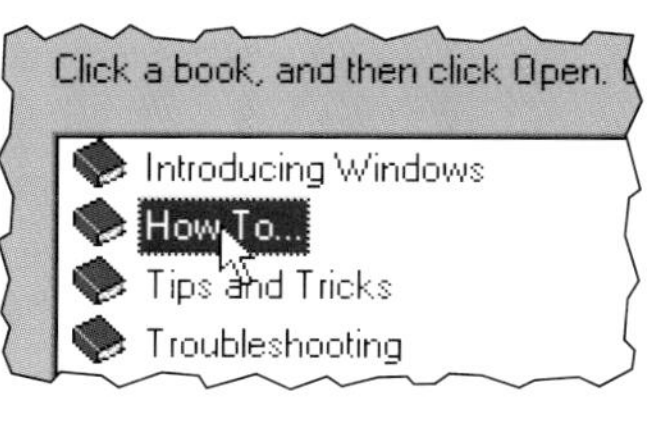

1 Double-click on the words *How To...* or on the accompanying book icon.

2 The closed book icon changes into an open book and a list of the books nested within it appears. Double-click on the book labeled *Work with Files and Folders*.

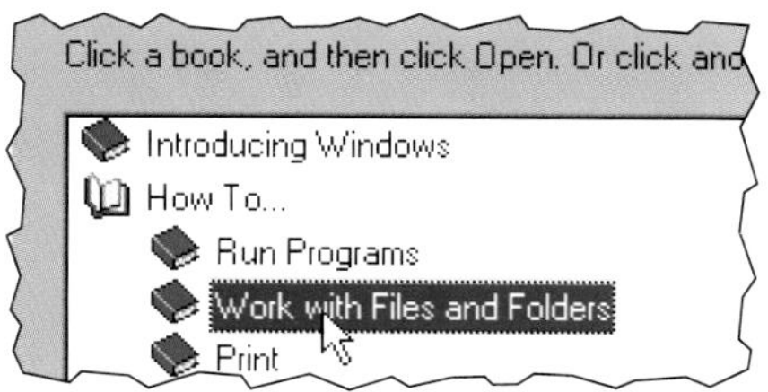

Help When Browsing?
If you want to access the main help system when browsing the *My Computer* or *Network Neighborhood* windows or any drive or folder window, you can do so by choosing *Help Topics* from the *Help* menu.

Printing Help Topics
From the *Contents* flipcard of the *Help Topics* dialog box, you can print all the topics in a book, including any nested books, by selecting the book and clicking the *Print* button. To print an individual help topic, open the topic and then click on the *Menu* button and choose *Print Topic...* from the pop-up menu.

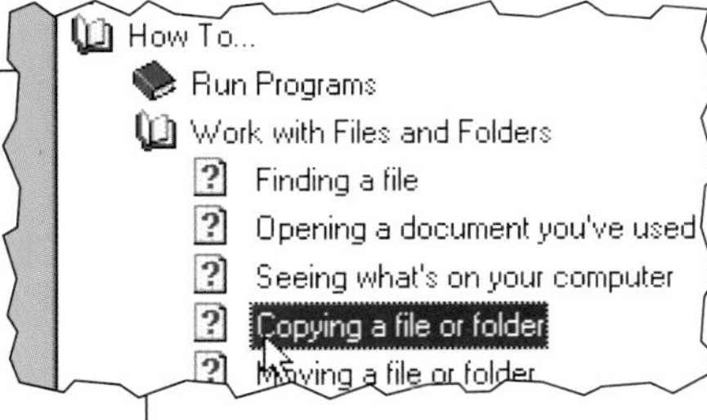

3 A list of help topics opens. Double-click on *Copying a file or folder*, or click once on the topic and then click on the *Display* button.

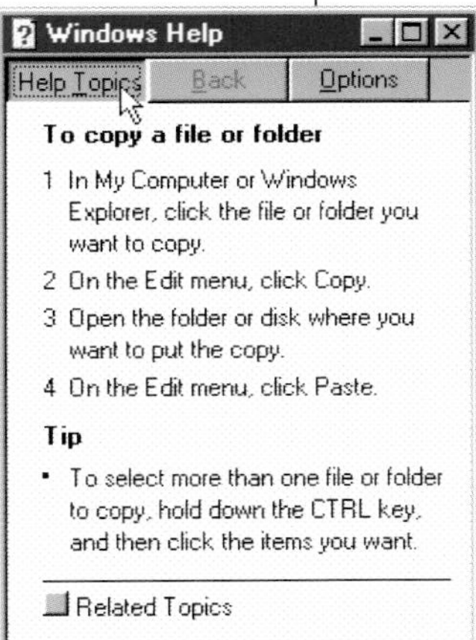

4 A help topic window opens, containing step by step instructions for copying a file or folder. After reading through the topic, you can click on the *Related Topics* button for a list of related help topics, click on the *Help Topics* button to return to the *Contents* flipcard of the *Help Topics* dialog box, or click on the Close button to close the help system. For now, click on the *Help Topics* button.

Don't Close!
Avoid clicking on the Close button of any help window unless you want to close down the whole help system. When browsing the help system, you'll find that clicking on the *Help Topics* button will take you back to the *Help Topics* dialog box. Clicking on the *Back* button will take you back to the previous window.

When browsing the books in the *Contents* flipcard, note that by double-clicking you can close open books (thus hiding their contents) in the same way that you can open closed books (revealing their contents).

Seeing Green?
In some help topic windows, you will see some terms that are colored and underlined. Click on any of these and a box containing an explanation of the term pops up. Click again to close the box.

INDEX FLIPCARD

Now take a look at the *Index* flipcard of the *Help Topics* dialog box. Click on the *Index* tab to view this flipcard. The *Index* flipcard contains a conventional, alphabetically arranged list of help topics and subtopics. To browse through these, you can use the scroll bar and scroll arrows, but if you want help on a specific topic, it's usually quicker to type in the first word or even a few letters of the topic into the box at the top. As an example, try accessing help on formatting floppy disks.

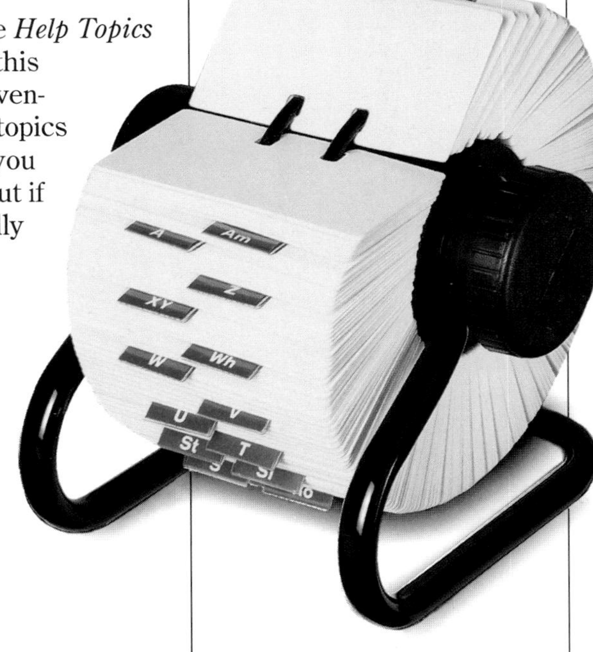

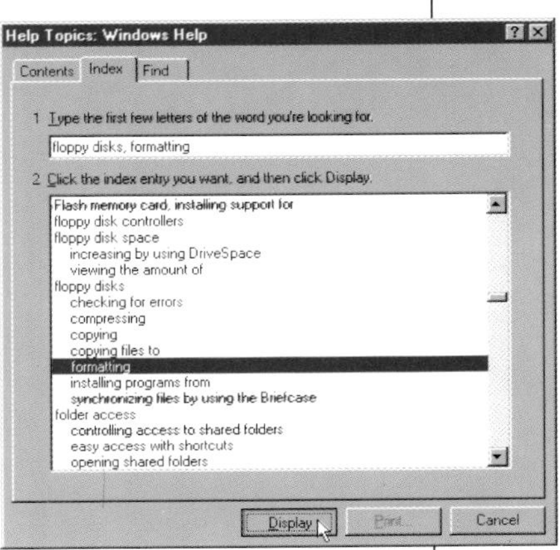

1 Type **floppy** into the box at the top. A list of topics related to floppy disks appears in the scrolling list box below. Click on *formatting* under *floppy disks*, and then click on the *Display* button.

2 A help topic window appears with instructions for formatting a disk. (You could also have arrived at this window by typing **formatting** or **disks** in the *Index* flipcard and then choosing *formatting, floppy disks* or *disks, formatting,* respectively.) After reading the help topic, click on the *Help Topics* button to return to the *Index* flipcard.

Windows Help
Help Topics
Back
Options
To format a disk
1 If the disk you want to format is a floppy disk, insert it into its drive. Otherwise, go to step 2.
2 Double-click the My Computer icon, and then click the icon for the disk you want to format.
Be sure not to double-click the disk icon, because you can't format a disk if it is open in My Computer or Windows Explorer.
3 On the File menu, click Format.
Notes
• Formatting a disk removes all information from the disk.
• You cannot format a disk if

SHORTCUTS IN HELP TOPICS

The information in help topic windows is generally short and task-oriented. Many of the help windows include shortcut buttons that will take you to appropriate dialog boxes or applications to help you complete a task. Try the following to find out how to adjust the cursor blink rate in Windows 95 programs such as WordPad.

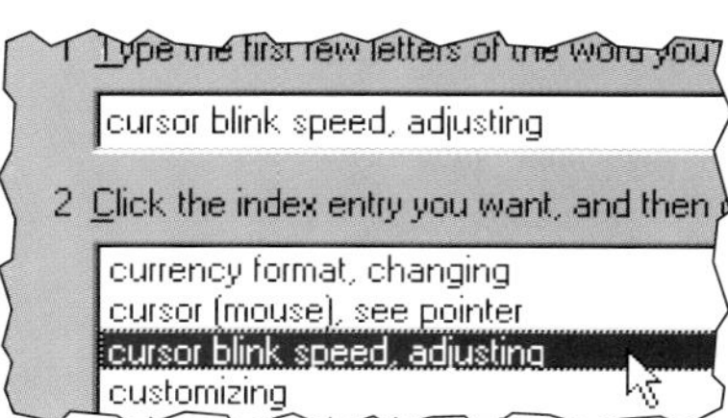

1 In the *Index* flipcard of the *Help Topics* dialog box, type **cursor** into the box at the top. Double-click on *cursor blink speed, adjusting* in the scrolling list box.

Find Flipcard?
The *Find* flipcard enables you to search for help topic entries that contain specific words. It works in a similar way to the *Index* flipcard. When you first access the *Find* flipcard, you are told that Windows 95 must first create a database of all words in your help files. Click on *Next* and then on *Finish*.

2 The help topic window that appears contains a shortcut button to access the *Keyboard Properties* dialog box. Click on this button.

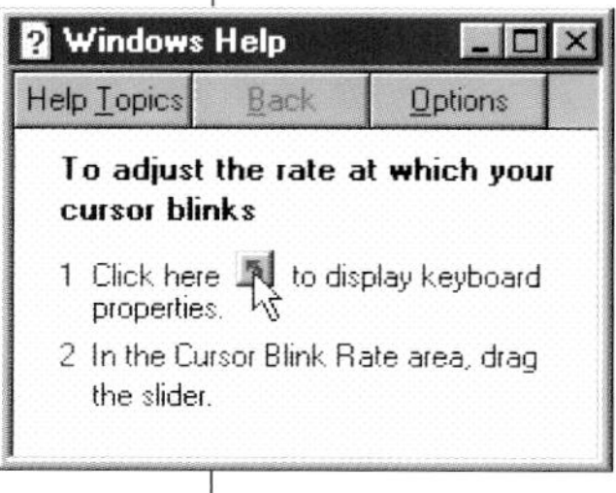

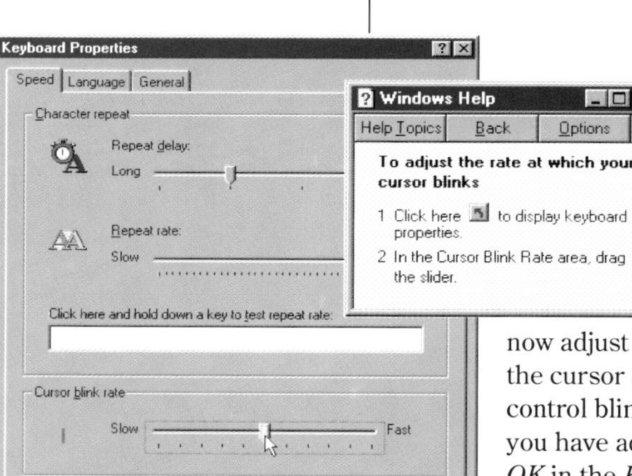

3 The *Keyboard Properties* dialog box appears. Using this dialog box and the information in the help topic window, you can now adjust your cursor blink rate until the cursor at the left of the sliding control blinks at the desired rate. Once you have adjusted the setting, click on *OK* in the *Keyboard Properties* dialog box, and then click on the *Help Topics* button of the help topic window.

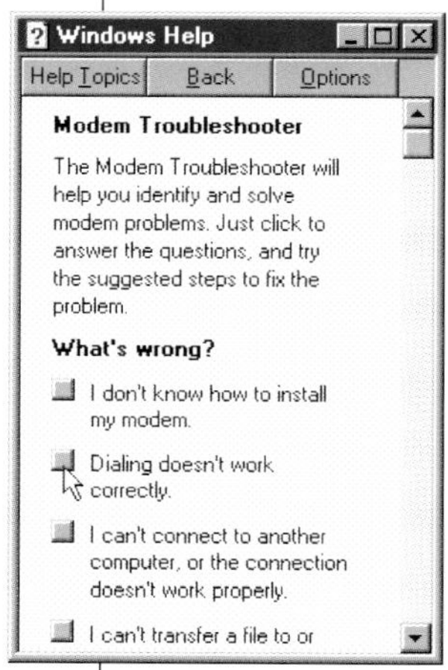

TROUBLESHOOTING TOPICS

Sometimes a help topic window is the starting point for an extensive interactive troubleshooting system. For example, suppose you have a problem with a modem. Use the *Index* flipcard of the *Help Topics* dialog box to choose the topic *modems, troubleshooting*. The help topic window shown above right appears. Start by choosing your response to the question *"What's wrong?"* Then answer the questions that appear in the series of dialog boxes that follow to trace the solution to your problem.

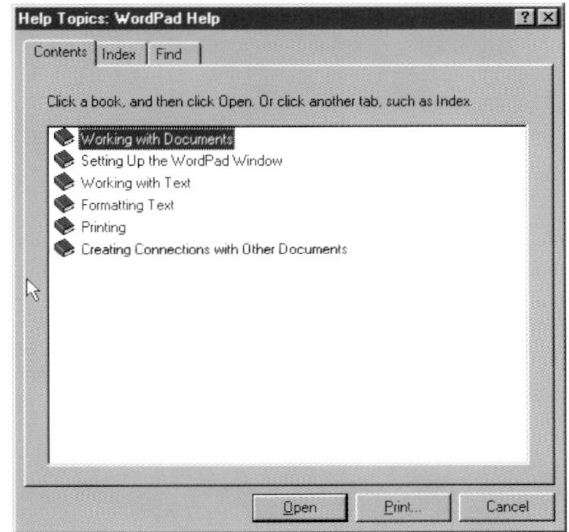

***Help Topics: WordPad Help* Dialog Box**

Help with Windows 95 Accessories

When using a Windows 95 accessory such as WordPad, Sound Recorder, CD Player, Paint, or Calculator, choosing *Help Topics* from the *Help* menu or pressing the F1 key brings up a special *Help Topics* dialog box that is specific to that accessory. The dialog box works in the same way as the main Windows *Help Topics* dialog box, but only help topics relevant to that accessory are included.

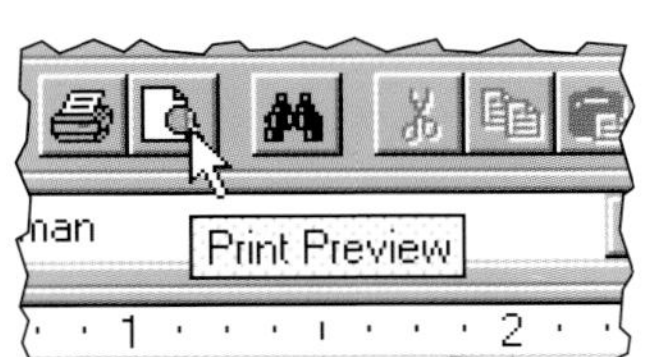

ToolTips

Many Windows accessories include toolbars — arrays of buttons that if clicked on carry out actions such as saving or printing. If you place the mouse pointer over any button on a toolbar, after a short pause a "ToolTip" — a box briefly explaining the function of the button — appears. The example at left shows the ToolTip for the Print Preview button in WordPad.

Shortcut to What's This?
Instead of using the What's This? button and mouse pointer, you can obtain pop-up help in dialog boxes by clicking with the right mouse button on the object you want to know more about and then choosing *What's This?* from the pop-up menu that appears.

What's This?

All Windows 95 dialog boxes offer a type of help called "What's This?." It can help you find out more about particular options or controls featured in the dialog box. As an example, follow the steps starting below:

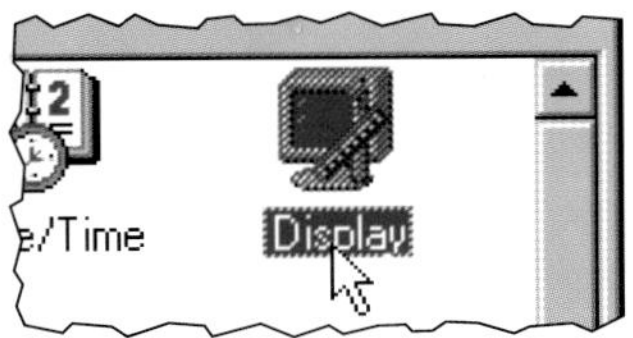

1 Open the Control Panel (see page 34) and double-click on the *Display* icon.

2 In the *Display Properties* dialog box, click on the *Settings* tab to open the *Settings* flipcard.

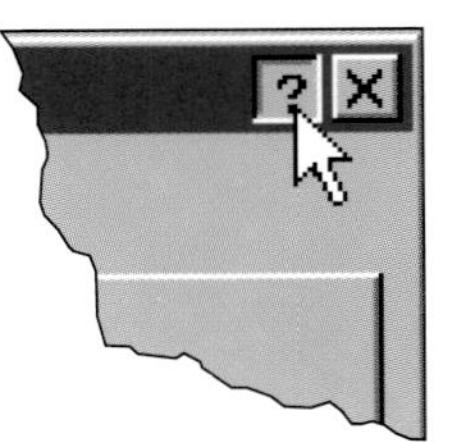

3 Click on the What's This? button at the top right of the dialog box. A question mark appears next to the mouse pointer arrow.

4 You can now click on any item in the flipcard to pop up a short description of that item. Try clicking on the box labeled *Desktop area*.

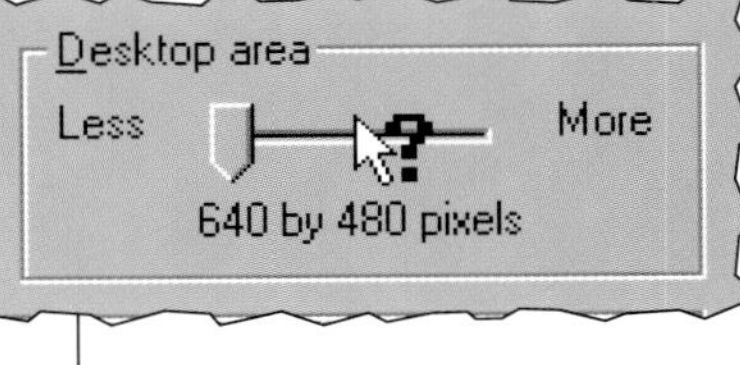

5 The explanation of the *Desktop area* settings pops up. You can click anywhere to close it. If you want to print the information in a pop-up help box, right-click inside it, and then choose *Print Topic*.

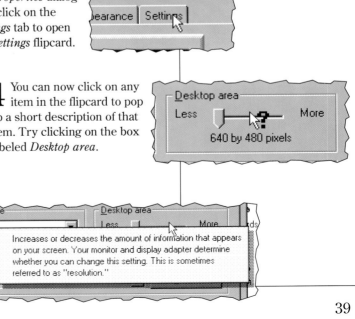

Increases or decreases the amount of information that appears on your screen. Your monitor and display adapter determine whether you can change this setting. This is sometimes referred to as "resolution."

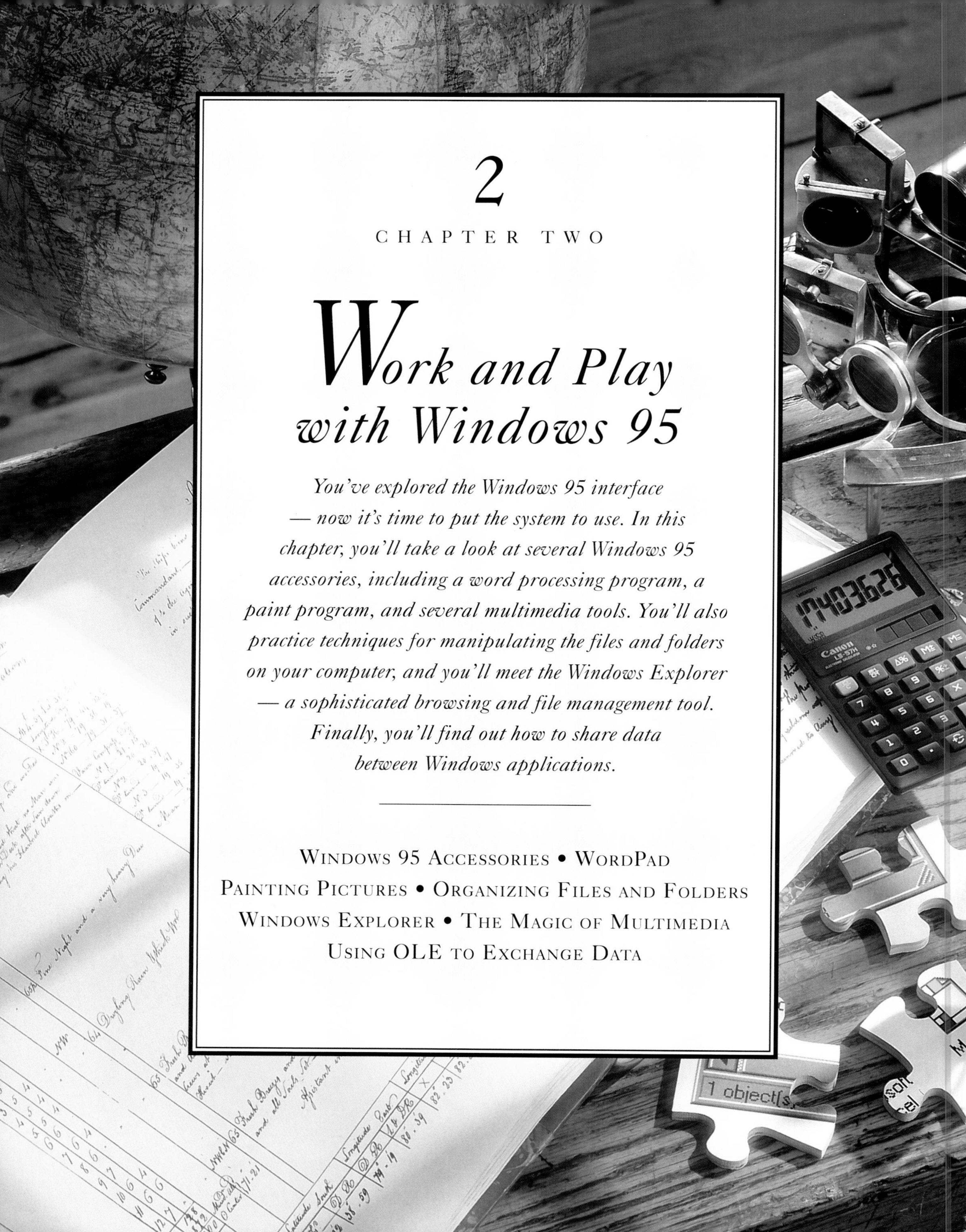

2

CHAPTER TWO

Work and Play with Windows 95

You've explored the Windows 95 interface — now it's time to put the system to use. In this chapter, you'll take a look at several Windows 95 accessories, including a word processing program, a paint program, and several multimedia tools. You'll also practice techniques for manipulating the files and folders on your computer, and you'll meet the Windows Explorer — a sophisticated browsing and file management tool. Finally, you'll find out how to share data between Windows applications.

WINDOWS 95 ACCESSORIES • WORDPAD
PAINTING PICTURES • ORGANIZING FILES AND FOLDERS
WINDOWS EXPLORER • THE MAGIC OF MULTIMEDIA
USING OLE TO EXCHANGE DATA

Access
File
Edit
Winpad
Packager

Windows 95 Accessories

WINDOWS 95 COMES WITH A SET OF ACCESSORY PROGRAMS that are easy to use, surprisingly powerful, and, best of all, free! Among other features, Windows 95 includes a mini word processor, facilities for recording sound and creating images, tools for maintaining your hard disk, and (if you have any free time left!) a number of games. To see a list of the available accessories, click on the *Start* button, point to *Programs*, and then point to *Accessories*.

A Bagful of Accessories

Most of these accessories are described in more detail later on in the book; for now, we'll take a quick look at their functions. If you want to use an accessory that is shown here but does not seem to be installed on your PC, see "Adding Extra Windows 95 Components" on page 123.

System Tools
This program group contains tools for managing and maintaining your hard and floppy disks (see pages 108 to 113). Optional tools include backing up files (see page 118).

Scandisk
Use this to check your disk's surface, files, and folders for errors, and to repair damaged areas.

Disk Defragmenter
This rearranges files and folders on your hard disk so that programs can run faster.

Paint
Lets you create images (see page 46).

WordPad
A mini word processing program (see page 44).

Multimedia
To use the accessories in this program group (see pages 65 to 68) you need to have a sound card installed.

CD Player
Use CD Player to play audio compact discs in your CD ROM drive.

Media Player
Use this to play audio, video, or animation files and to control settings for multimedia hardware devices.

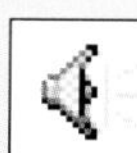

Sound Recorder
Use Sound Recorder to record, play, and edit sound files. You will need a microphone to record live sound.

Calculator
Helps you perform calculations (see opposite page).

Games
Inside this program group are some games. You've already played Minesweeper. FreeCell and Hearts are optionally installed card games.

Minesweeper

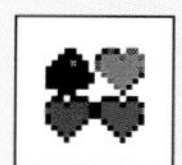

Hearts

FreeCell

HyperTerminal Connections
Lets you exchange files with a remote computer via a modem or connect to computer bulletin boards (see pages 92 and 93).

Phone Dialer
Allows you to automatically dial a telephone number from any PC with a modem attached.

Character Map
Allows you to insert special characters into documents (see opposite page).

Notepad
A very basic word processing program.

What a Character!
If you are going to use a certain symbol or character regularly, make a note of the keystroke information for that character, which appears in the bottom right corner of the Character Map. You can then generate the character whenever you need to by holding down the Alt key and typing the relevant numbers on the numeric keypad.

USING THE CHARACTER MAP

Character Map displays all the characters that are stored in a particular font file. For example, Times New Roman contains letters of the alphabet, numbers, and some special symbols; Wingdings, on the other hand, contains only special symbols, such as arrows and bullets. Any of the characters shown in Character Map can be copied and then inserted into documents.

Let's take a look at Character Map. To launch the program, display the contents of the *Accessories* program group and then click on *Character Map*.

1 When you open Character Map, it displays the characters of the most recently used font — in this case, the Symbol font.

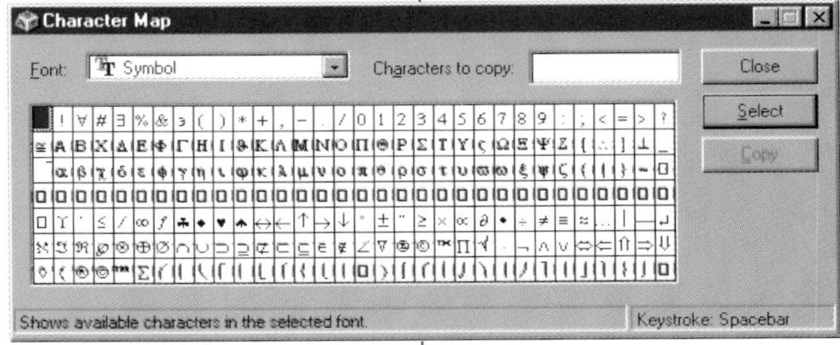

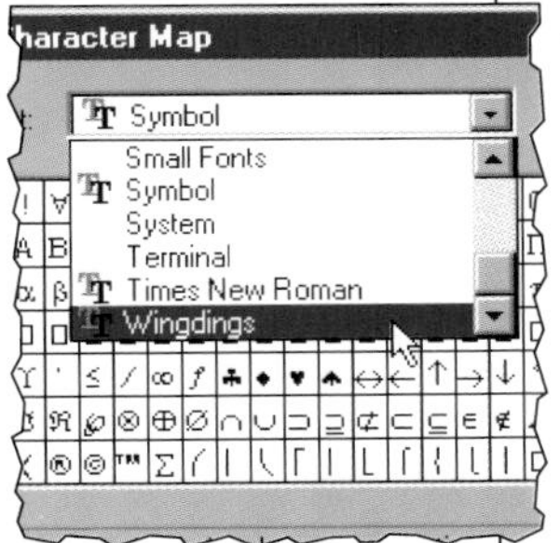

2 The list of available fonts is displayed in a drop-down scroll box in the top left-hand corner of the window. To change the font displayed, click once on the down arrow beside the entry. Scroll through the list and then click on *Wingdings*.

3 To magnify an individual character, place the mouse pointer over the character and click and hold down the mouse button. Try doing this with the bottom right-hand character of the Wingdings font. Note the keystroke information on the right of the status bar.

To insert a character into a document (such as a WordPad file), first double-click on the character and then click on the *Copy* button. This copies the character to the Windows Clipboard (a temporary storage area). Then open the document into which you wish to insert the character and choose *Paste* from the *Edit* menu.

USING THE CALCULATOR

Need to add up invoices or check your credit card bill? If so, you'll find the Calculator accessory a great help. Mathematicians needn't feel left out either; in addition to the usual functions, Calculator also offers a range of sophisticated scientific functions.

Click on *Calculator* in the *Accessories* program group to open this accessory. To calculate, click the relevant numbers, operators, and functions as you would with a real calculator. To view the Scientific layout, choose *Scientific* from the *View* menu.

Calculator Accessory

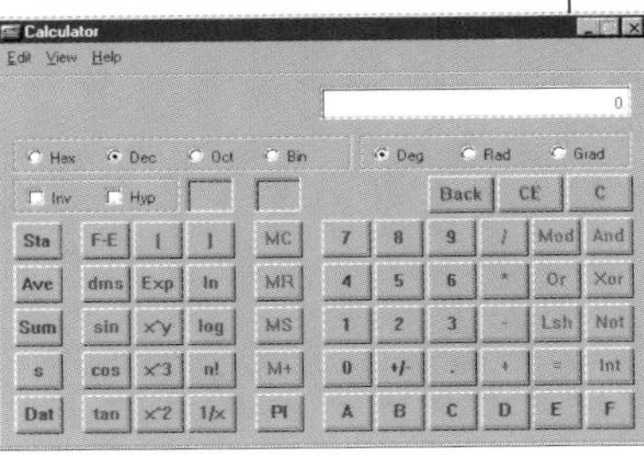

Calculated Moves!
If you need to enter a lot of numbers in Calculator, you might find it quicker to use the numeric keypad rather than clicking on the calculator's buttons. To do this, press the NumLock button on your keyboard (the NumLock light will illuminate). You can now use the numbers and functions on the numeric keypad.

WordPad

YOU MET WORDPAD EARLIER IN THE BOOK, when you created and saved the **Practice File** document (see pages 13 to 16). This mini word processor offers numerous editing and formatting options and can be used to write letters and memos. To see how it works, open WordPad. (Follow steps 3 through 7 on page 13 if you've forgotten how to do this.)

Creating a Document

To create a new document from the WordPad window, select *New* from the *File* menu. A message will appear asking what type of document you wish to create. For Word 6 and Rich Text documents, WordPad provides a Formatting toolbar for formatting documents. With Text Only documents, you're offered no formatting options. In this case, highlight *Word 6 Document* and click on *OK*. Then click on the Maximize button so that the window fills your screen.

Document Choice
When you open a new file in WordPad, a dialog box offers a number of options for the creation of documents.

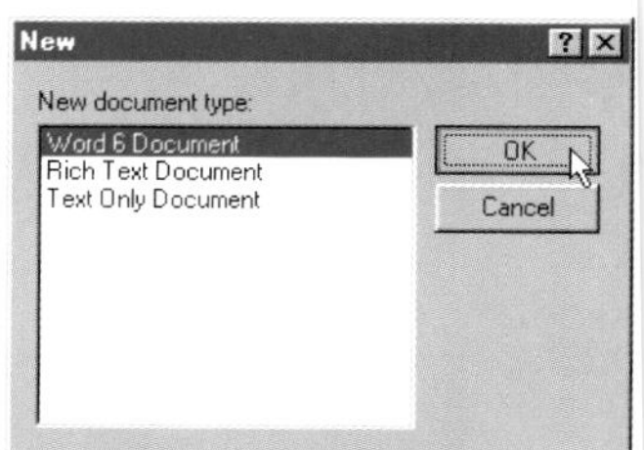

Formatting Toolbar
The buttons on this bar are used to change the appearance of text (for instance, the type style and color and paragraph alignment.)

Main Toolbar
This series of buttons provides a quick route to most WordPad operations.

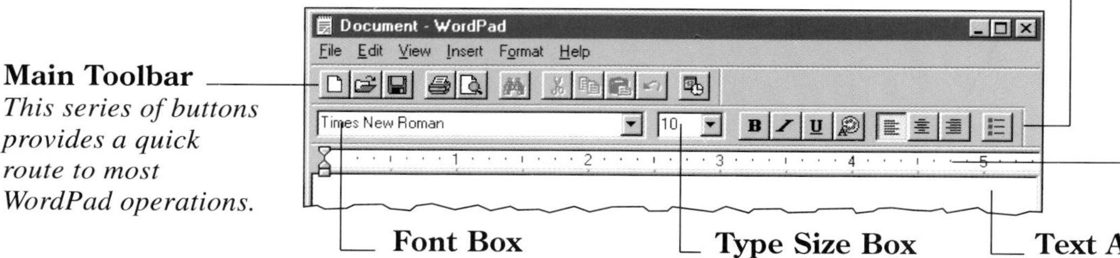

Ruler
The Ruler allows you to set tab stops and paragraph indents.

Font Box **Type Size Box** **Text Area**

The Toolbars

Here is a guide to the buttons on the WordPad toolbars. With a click of a button you can apply formatting styles to text or perform a number of file-related activities.

 **Creates a New Document**

 **Opens an Existing Document**

 **Saves Active Document**

 **Prints Active Document**

 **Displays a Document in Print Preview**

 **Finds Text**

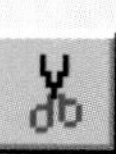 **Cuts Selected Text**

 **Copies Selected Text**

 **Pastes Text**

 **Undoes Last Action**

 **Inserts Date and Time**

 **Makes Selected Text Boldface**

 **Italicizes Selected Text**

 **Underlines Selected Text**

 **Applies Selected Color to Selected Text**

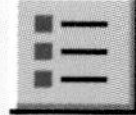 **Adds Bullets**

Aligns Paragraph to Left

 **Centers Paragraph**

 **Aligns Paragraph to Right**

TYPING AND FORMATTING A LETTER

To create any document with a word processor, you first type the text. As a practice exercise, type the letter shown at right, pressing Enter to start a new line only where you see <Enter>. Next, read and correct the text. To correct an error, click the I-beam pointer to the left or right of the mistyped character, press Backspace to erase the character to the left of the flashing insertion point, or Delete to erase the character to the right, and then type the correction.

Next you select any text to which you wish to apply special formatting, and then apply the formatting.

1287 Franklin Avenue<Enter>
Seaton Oregon 83754–5437<Enter><Enter>

October 26, 1995 <Enter><Enter>

Dear Jenny,<Enter>
Finally, here is our new address. After all those months we've spent traipsing between real estate agents, a classified advertisement in last month's local paper caught my eye. So here we are, safely ensconsed in a two bedroom cottage with fireplaces, wooden floors, and a huge back yard, all only five minutes walk from the beach. <Enter><Enter>

Still, that isn't the biggest event of the month, is it? The big event is your birthday, so Happy Birthday! You'll get a parcel in the mail soon; if the contents don't fit, bring them with you on your visit so they can be exchanged. <Enter><Enter>

Fond regards,<Enter>
Kate

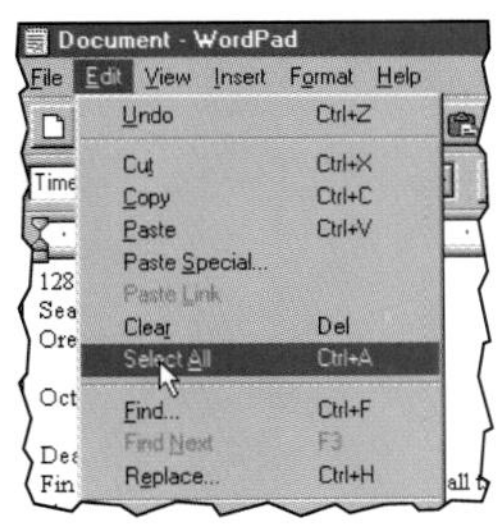

1 Select all the text by choosing *Select All* from the *Edit* menu (when selected, the text will appear white against a black background).

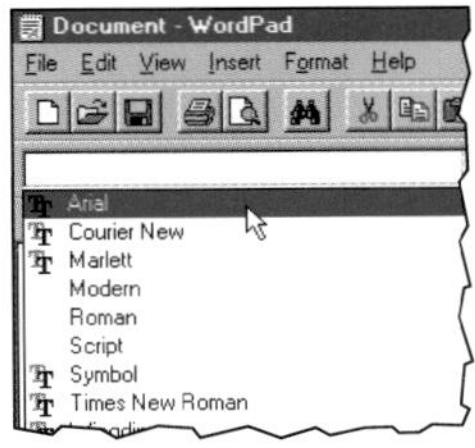

2 Click on the down arrow next to the Font box and a drop-down menu will appear. Use your mouse to scroll up and down the font list; when you see *Arial*, click on this to select it for use.

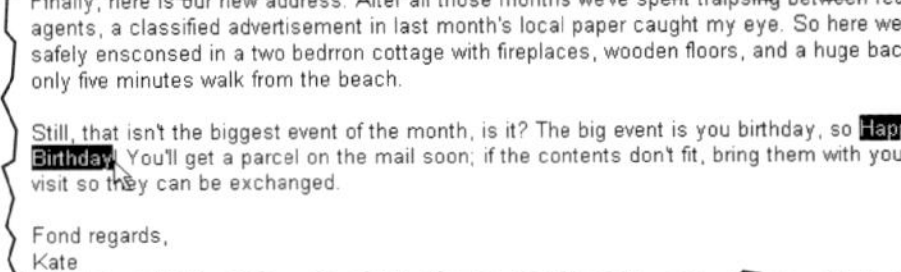

3 Click in the text area to deselect the text. Now highlight the words **Happy Birthday** by placing the I-beam pointer just to the left of the **H**, holding down the mouse button, and then dragging the pointer over the words you wish to highlight.

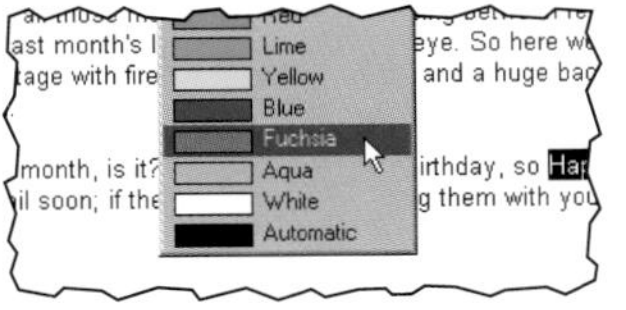

4 Click on the Bold button to make the text bold. Finally, give the words a festive feel by clicking on the Color button and choosing *Fuchsia* from the drop-down menu. Click in the text area to deselect the text.

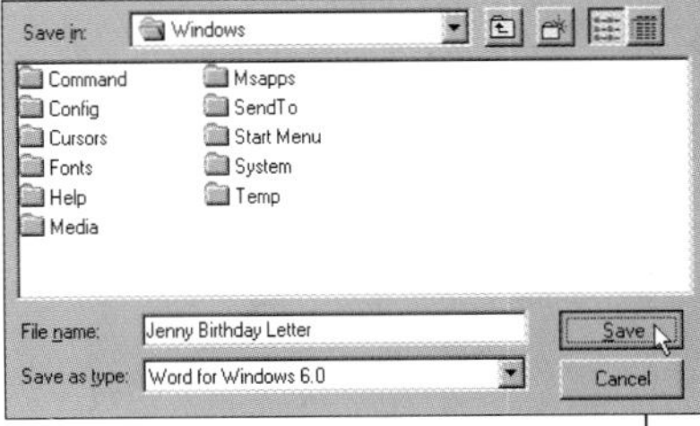

5 Click on the Save button and the *Save As* dialog box will open. Type **Jenny Birthday Letter** in the *File name* box, choose the **Windows** folder in the *Save in* box, and click on *Save*.

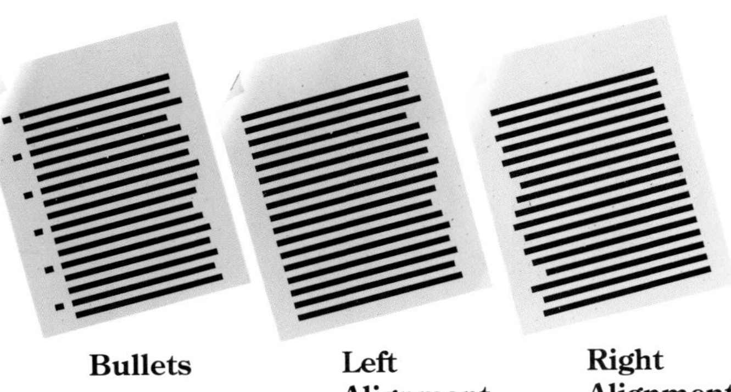

Bullets **Left Alignment** **Right Alignment**

OTHER FORMATTING OPTIONS

Once your letter is saved, practice using some of the other options in WordPad. Remember that each action can be undone with a click on the Undo button.

Try inserting bullets before each paragraph by clicking in the paragraph and then clicking on the Bullet button. You can also try the different paragraph alignments by clicking in a paragraph and then clicking on each of the alignment buttons.

When you close WordPad, you'll be asked if you want to save the changes to the document; click on *No*.

Painting Pictures

YOU DON'T HAVE TO BE AN ARTIST TO APPRECIATE PAINT — with its extensive range of drawing tools and large color palette, this program makes illustration easy for everyone. Paint can be used to create company logos, liven up personal letters with colorful sketches, make greeting cards and party invitations, or even illustrate newsletters and reports.

What Are Pixels?
Pixels are tiny dots that make up a picture on screen. The pixels form a grid of columns and rows; wherever you draw, the affected pixels are filled with your chosen color. When you enlarge an image, you can often see the pixels as a jagged edge.

The Paint Tools

In the *Start* menu, point to *Programs* and open the Paint program from the *Accessories* group. Maximize the window by clicking on the Maximize button. Most of the screen is filled with the drawing area; below this is the color palette, with the Toolbox on the left.

Experiment by clicking on various tools in the Toolbox. You'll see that when you click on a tool, an explanation of its use appears in the information bar below the palette. You'll also see that when you select certain tools, extra choices appear below the Toolbox.

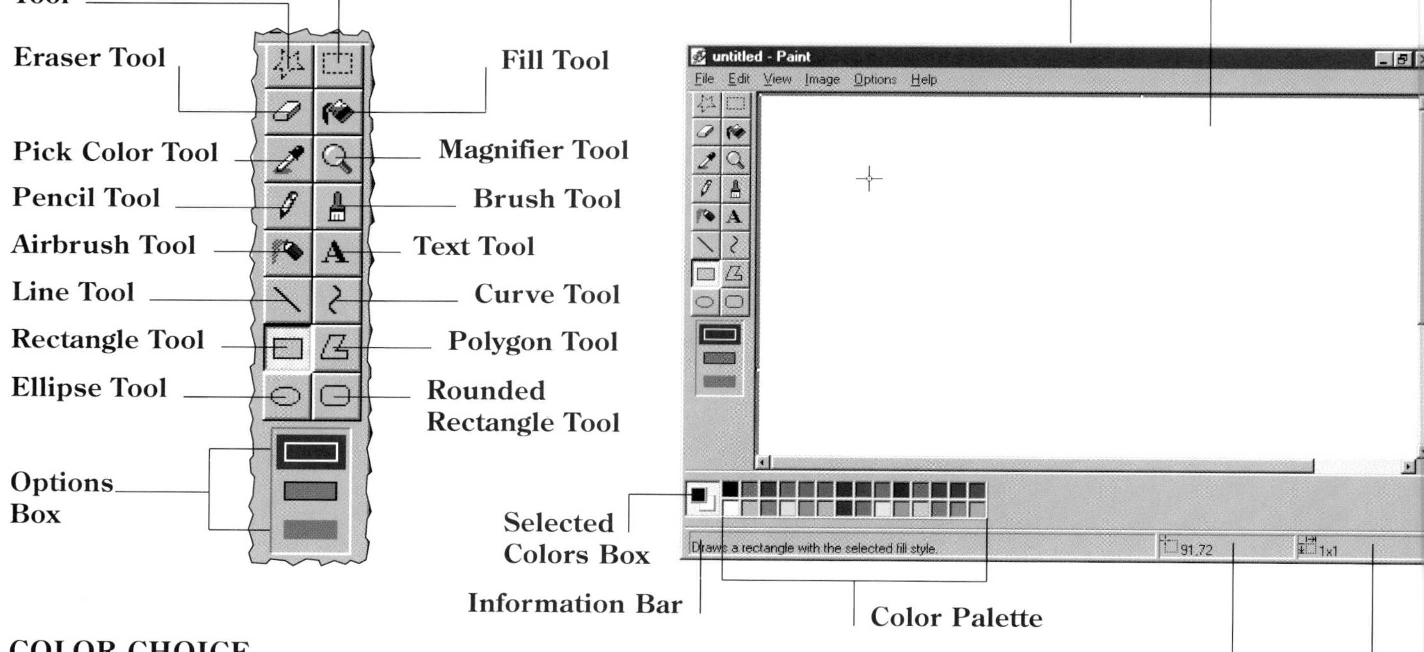

COLOR CHOICE
Before starting a drawing, you must select the background and foreground colors. Your choice will be reflected in the Selected Colors box; at the moment, the foreground is black and the background is white. To change the foreground color, simply click on your selection in the color palette; to change the background color, use the right mouse button to make your choice.

Cursor Placement
Move the mouse pointer around the drawing area and you'll see the numbers here change to reflect the mouse pointer's position on the grid of pixels.

Measuring Size
As you draw a shape or use a selection tool, this box shows its length and width (in pixels).

USING THE SHAPE TOOLS

Most tools use only the foreground color; the eraser and shape tools, however, also use the background color. To see how this works, follow these steps.

1 Click on the dark brown option of the color palette for the foreground, and then click on the lighter brown color with the right mouse button to make this the background color.

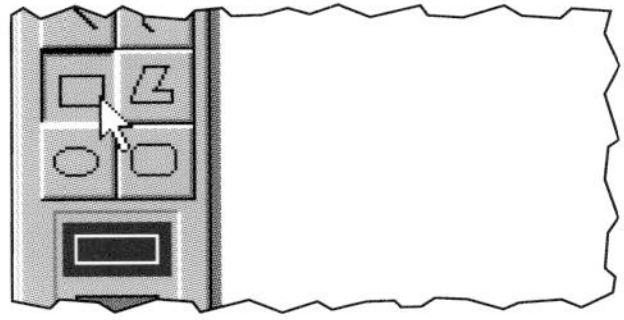

2 Click on the Rectangle tool. In the options box below the Toolbox, select the top option to draw an outline rectangle.

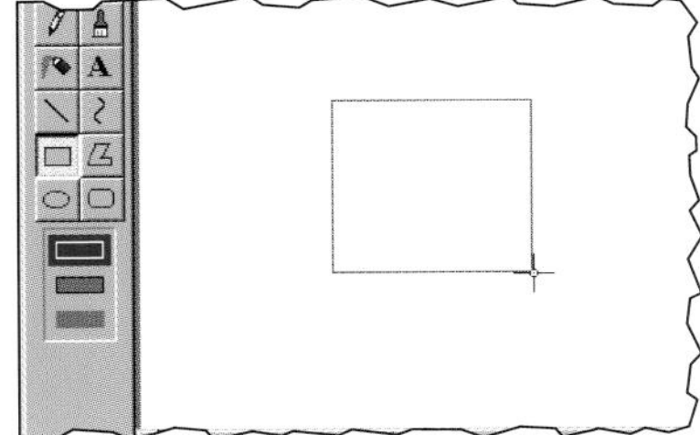

3 Place the cursor in the center of the drawing area and draw a small rectangle by holding down the left mouse button and dragging diagonally across the screen. Release the mouse button.

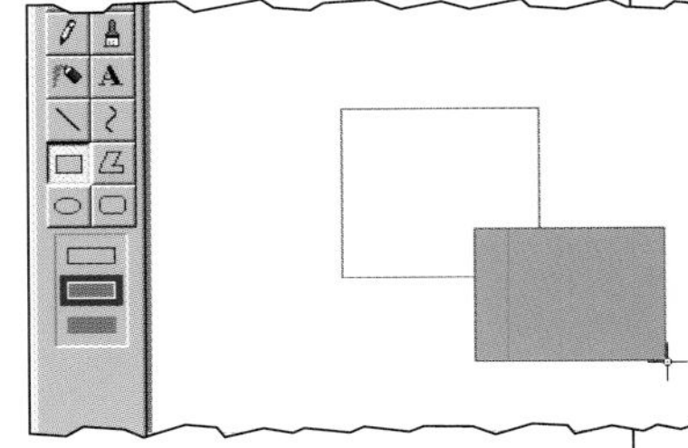

4 Now click on the middle rectangle in the options box and draw another rectangle. Note that this rectangle is filled with the background color, while its borders are the darker brown of the foreground color.

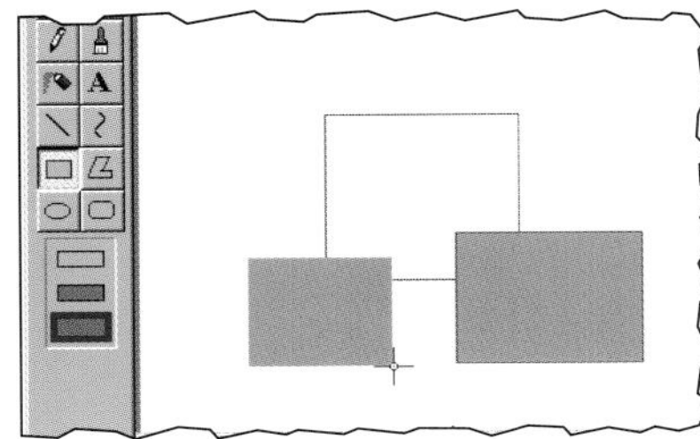

5 The bottom rectangle in the options box creates a filled shape using only the background color. Click on this option and draw a third rectangle to see how it works.

THE ERASER

When you erase any part of a drawing, the eraser tool leaves the selected background color in its wake. So, to delete anything you have drawn so far, you must first change the selected background color to white.

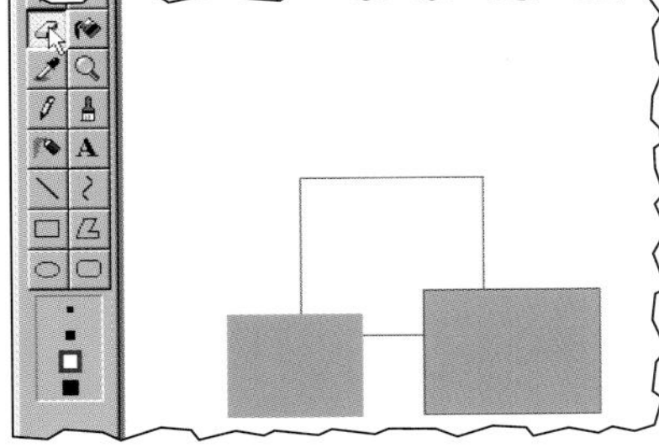

1 Using the right mouse button, click on white in the color palette. Now select the Eraser tool. Note that a selection of sizes appears below the Toolbox.

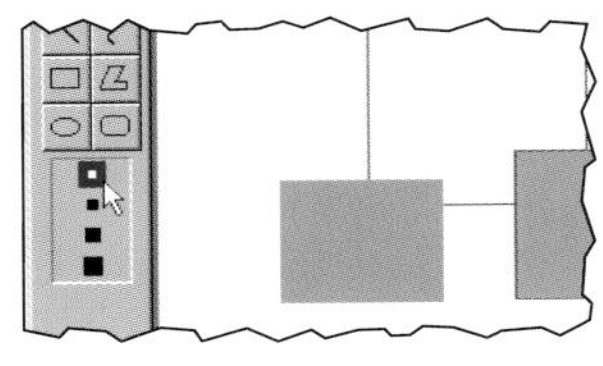

2 Let's erase the outline rectangle. The area where its border is overlapped by the other two shapes will need delicate erasing, so choose the smallest size for the eraser.

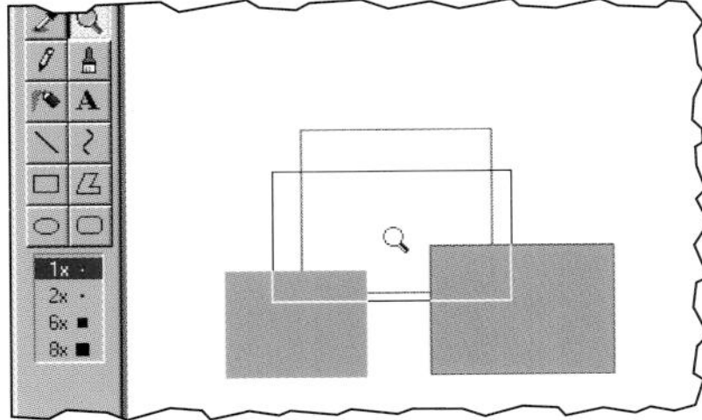

3 Now enlarge the area you wish to erase. Click on the Magnifier tool, choose the *1x* option below the Toolbox, and click on the area you wish to enlarge.

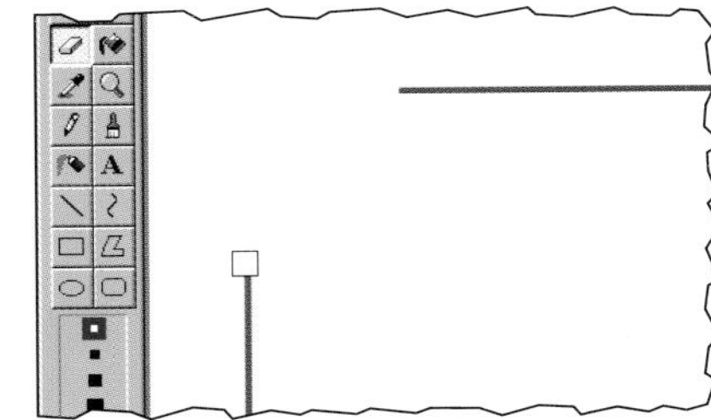

4 Erase the outline rectangle by dragging the eraser over its border (the small *Paint View* window on screen makes working at this magnification easier). When you've finished, choose *Zoom* from the *View* menu and *Normal Size* from the submenu.

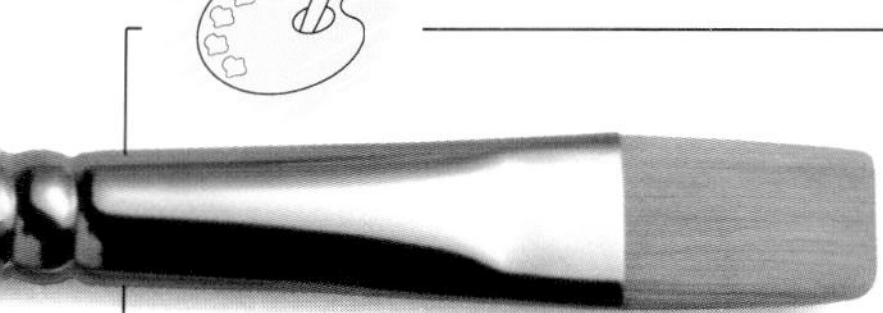

PAINTING A PICTURE

Let's draw a birthday card to go with the letter you've just written in WordPad — a picture of a cake seems apt. Choose *New* from the *File* menu to open a new file (don't save the changes made to the previous file).

1 Choose a foreground and background color for the cake. Select the Rounded Rectangle tool, choose the middle option from the three choices below the Toolbox, and draw a cake shape.

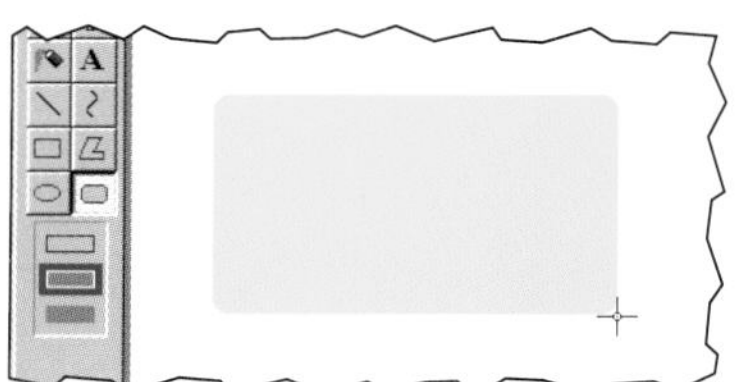

2 Now for some decoration. Choose a foreground color for the trim, click on the Airbrush tool, and choose the option highlighted at right from the options box. Now move the airbrush cursor around the bottom and top rims of the cake and click in bursts to apply a sprinkling of color.

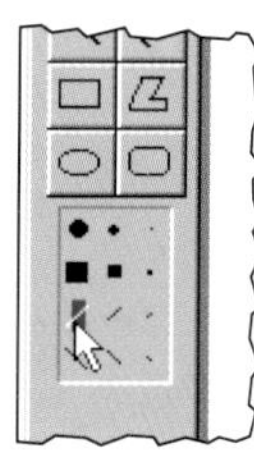

3 To add a ribbon to the middle of the cake, choose a color, click on the Brush tool, and then select the first angled line from the options box, as shown.

4 Place the cross-hair pointer on the left-hand side of the cake, hold down the mouse button, and draw a continuous wavy ribbon around the middle.

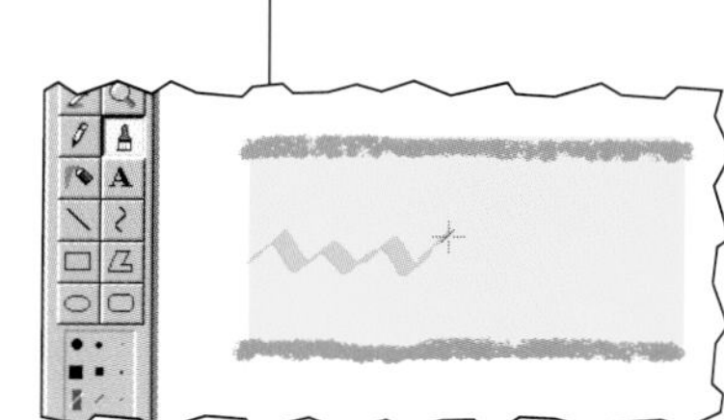

COPY AND PASTE

Before going any further, use the *Save As* command and dialog box (see pages 16 and 32 to 33) to save and name this file in case a sudden power failure undoes all your artistic effort. Call the picture **Birthday Cake** and save it to the **Windows** folder.

The next step — adding candles to the cake — involves using the *Copy* and *Paste* commands from the *Edit* menu. When a drawing includes a number of similar elements, it's usually easiest to draw one element and then copy it the required number of times.

Get in Shape!
To create a square, select the Rectangle tool and hold down the Shift key as you draw. You can also draw a perfect circle by holding down Shift as you draw with the Ellipse tool.

1 To draw the first candle, select the Line tool and then select the fourth thickness down in the options box.

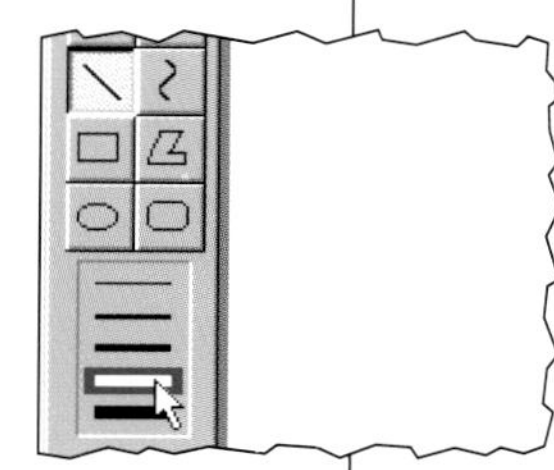

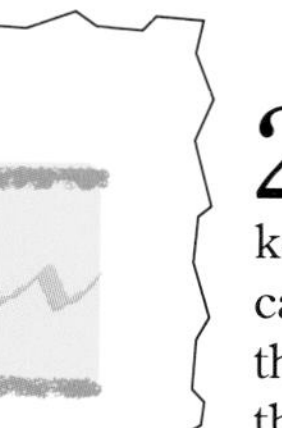

2 Choose a color from the palette. Now hold down the Alt key (this keeps the lines straight) and draw a candle on the cake by holding down the mouse button and dragging for the required length.

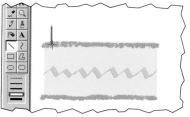

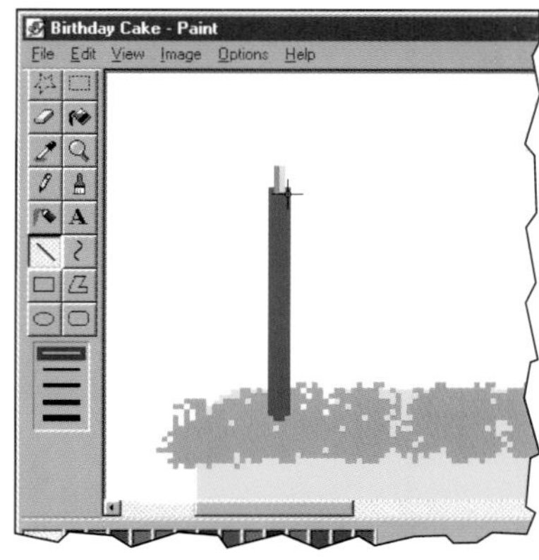

3 To add a flame to the candle, first zoom in closer. Select the Magnifier tool, make sure that the *1x* option is highlighted under the Toolbox, place the magnifying cursor on the candle, and then click once. Select the Line tool, choose the thinnest line, and draw a flame over the candle. You might want to use two strokes of color (orange and red).

4 To select the area to be copied, choose the Rectangle Selection tool at the top right corner of the Toolbox, and then drag the cursor so that the candle fits between the dotted lines of the selected area.

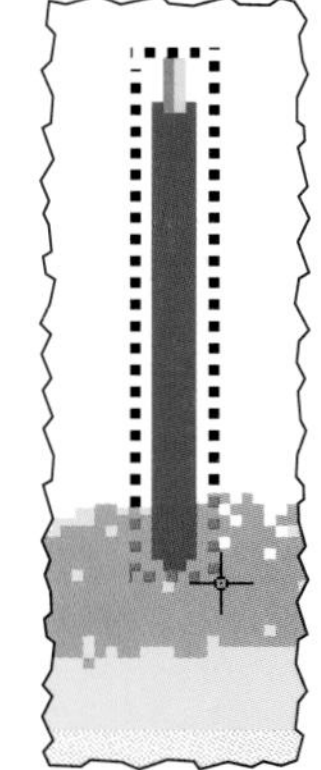

5 Choose *Copy* from the *Edit* menu and the selected area will be copied to the Windows Clipboard (a temporary storage area).

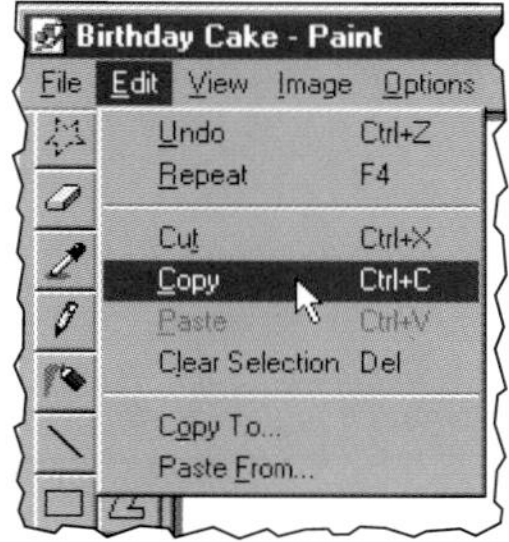

6 Go back to normal view by choosing *Zoom* from the *View* menu and *Normal View* from the submenu. Now choose *Paste* from the *Edit* menu. A copy of the candle appears in the left-hand corner of the drawing area. When you place the mouse pointer over the copy of the candle, it changes to a moving tool (a four-headed arrow); you can then drag the candle to the cake and position it next to the original.

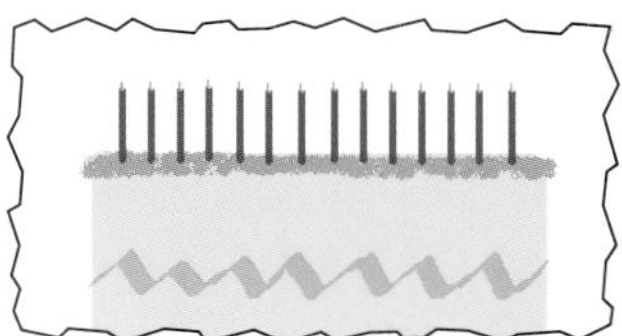

7 A copy of the candle will remain in the Clipboard until you use the *Copy* command again, so you can simply repeat step 6 until the cake is filled with candles.

ADDING TEXT TO ILLUSTRATIONS

Now that you've completed your drawing, you might like to use the Text tool to add a birthday greeting. Follow the steps below.

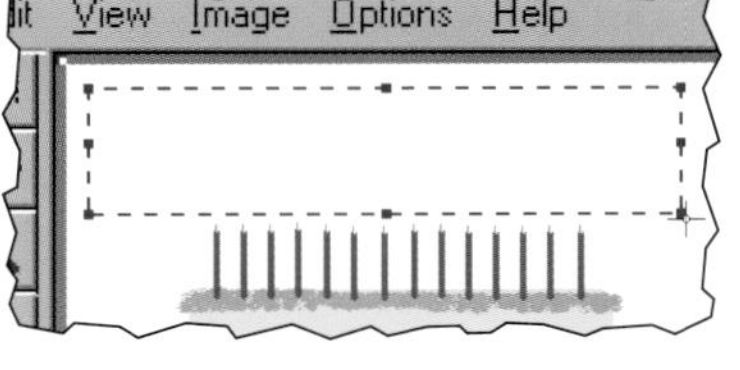

1 Select the Text tool and then create a text frame by dragging the cursor diagonally across the area where you want to place the message.

2 Choose a color for your text and then type your greeting into the text frame.

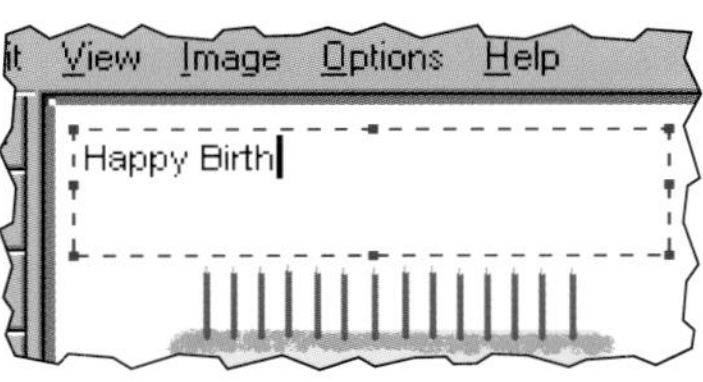

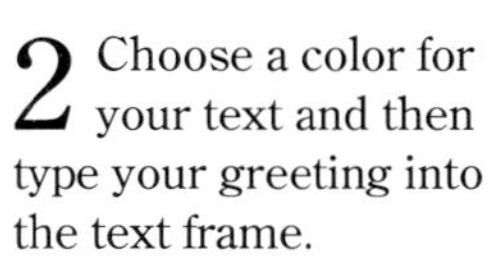

3 To change the style of the text, choose *Text Toolbar* from the *View* menu (if the toolbar entitled *Fonts* is not already visible.) Format the text using the font, font size, and style options on the toolbar; when you've finished, close the toolbar. Click outside of the text frame to insert the words into the picture.

4 To move text around on the screen, make sure the background color is set to white, and then select the relevant words using the Rectangle Selection tool; you can then drag the selection box to a new location.

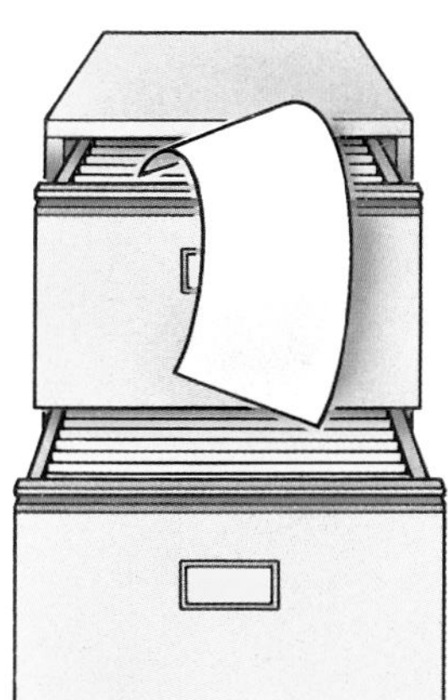

Organizing Files and Folders

AS THE NUMBER OF FILES YOU STORE on your hard disk increases, you may find that the overall organization of folders and files on your computer doesn't best suit your purposes. You may want to create some new folders, move existing files into those folders, and perhaps rename or delete some files. Windows 95 makes all of this simple and straightforward.

Creating and Naming a New Folder

You can create a new folder virtually anywhere in Windows 95 — on the Desktop or in any drive or folder window — with a few clicks of the mouse buttons. You can then name the folder as you like. Practice creating and naming a new folder within the **Windows** folder. Open the *Windows* window via the *My Computer* and *[C:]* drive windows and then do the following:

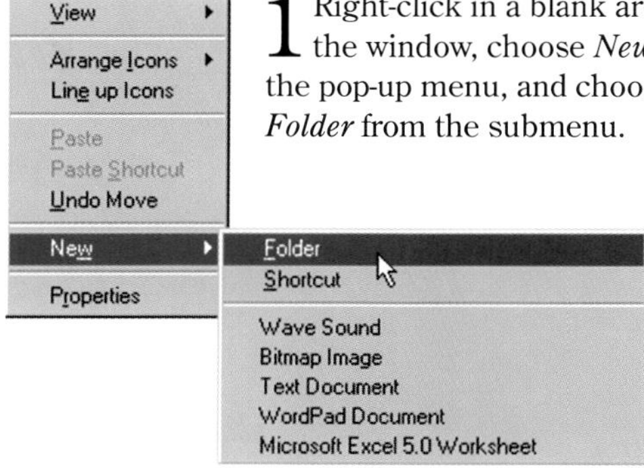

1 Right-click in a blank area of the window, choose *New* from the pop-up menu, and choose *Folder* from the submenu.

2 A new folder appears in the window. The folder name is highlighted and surrounded by a rectangular box. This indicates that you can give the folder a name of your choice simply by typing.

3 Type **Magic** to name the new folder you've created.

4 Press Enter to confirm that you want to call the folder **Magic**, and then click outside the folder to deselect it.

Renaming Files and Folders
If you want to rename a file, right-click on it, choose *Rename* from the pop-up menu, type the new name and press Enter. Windows 95 allows you to use up to 255 characters for file names, so you can give a description that accurately reflects the file or folder's contents. Follow the same procedure to rename folders.

Select All?
To select all the items in a folder or drive window, choose *Select All* from the *Edit* menu or press Ctrl and A together. You may sometimes see a *Select All* warning box, telling you that the folder contains hidden files, and advising you how to include these files in your selection.

Selecting Files and Folders

Windows allows you to perform a variety of operations on your files and folders. These operations include copying or moving files to new folders, renaming files or folders, or deleting them. Before you can perform any of these operations, you must first select the items by highlighting their icons.

Selecting a single item is easy — just click on the file or folder icon. To select multiple items, you hold down Ctrl and then click on each icon you want to select in turn. However, if the items are grouped together, there are shortcuts that use the Shift key or that "lasso" the items. Try each of these methods in the *Windows* window. First ensure all items appear in list view by choosing *List* from the *View* menu.

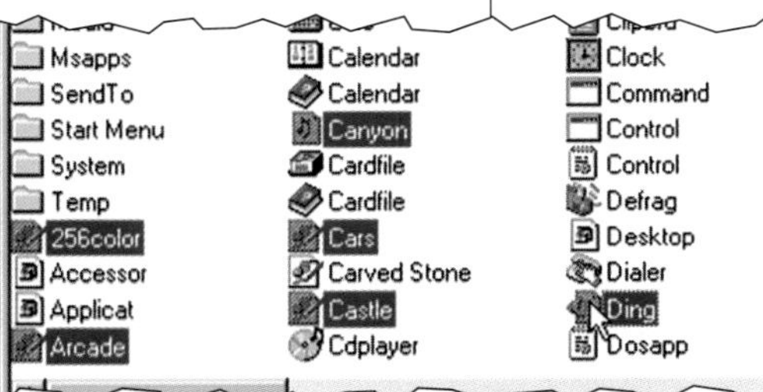

1 Hold down Ctrl and click on several nonadjacent file or folder icons to highlight each in turn. If you wanted, you could now perform an operation such as copying or deleting all these items simultaneously. For now, deselect the icons by clicking in a blank area.

2 Now select a group of adjacent items in a list. First click on the item at the top, and then hold down Shift and click on the item at the bottom. Again, deselect the icons by clicking in a blank area.

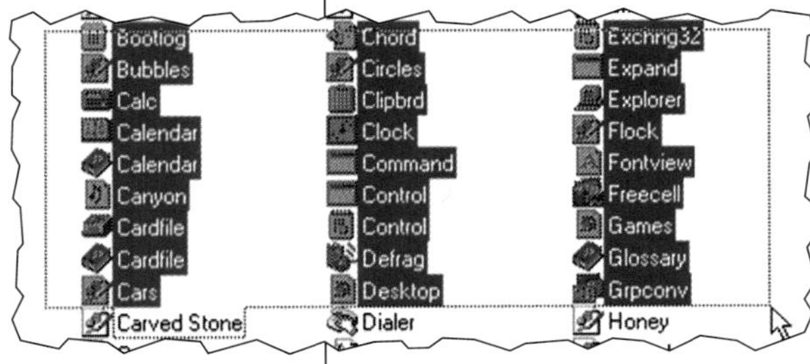

3 Now "lasso" a rectangular group of files or folders. Click to the left of the icon at the top left of the group, hold down the mouse button, and drag the mouse down and to the right. A rectangular selection frame appears. Release the mouse button when the whole block to be selected is highlighted. Then deselect the icons by clicking in a blank area.

Copying and Moving Files and Folders

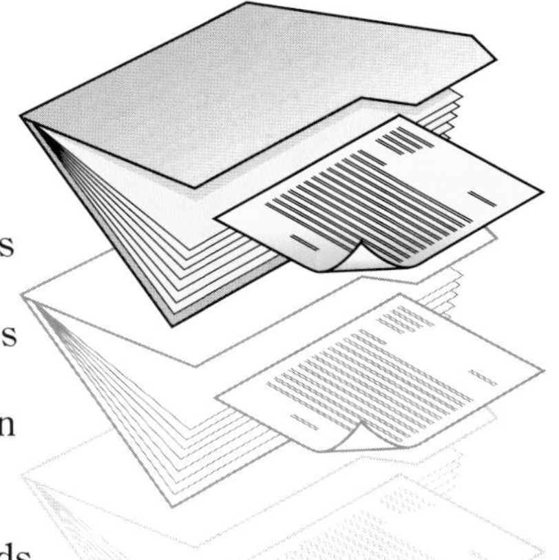

You can copy or move a file or a folder and its contents from one folder to another, or you can make a copy within the same folder. You can also copy or move files or folders from one disk drive to another — for example, from your hard disk to a floppy disk. You can copy or move by using a mouse technique called "drag and drop" or by means of menu commands. On the next page, you'll practice both of these methods.

MOVING A FILE TO A NEW FOLDER

First move a single file to a new folder using the drag and drop method. You can do this by dragging a file icon and dropping it directly onto the destination folder's icon. However, it's often more reassuring to open the destination folder window first because you can then see the files that you've moved appear instantly in the destination folder. As an example, move the **Wysiwyg** file that you previously saved to your **Windows** folder (see page 33) into the **Magic** folder that you've just created within the **Windows** folder.

1 Find and double-click on the icon for the **Magic** folder within the *Windows* window. The *Magic* window opens. If necessary, move the *Magic* window so it doesn't obscure the *Windows* window.

2 Find the **Wysiwyg** text file within the *Windows* window. Point to its icon and hold down the mouse button.

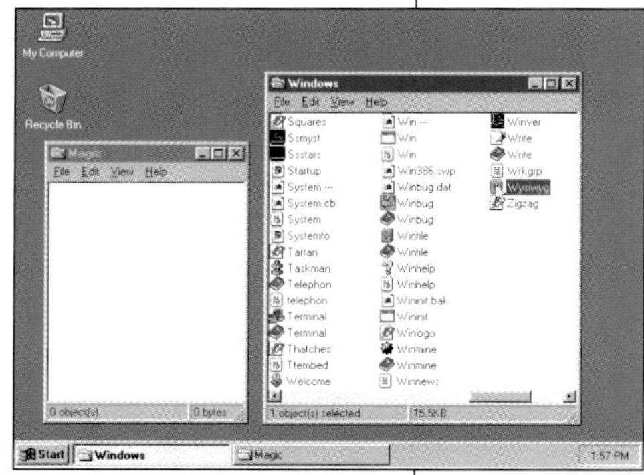

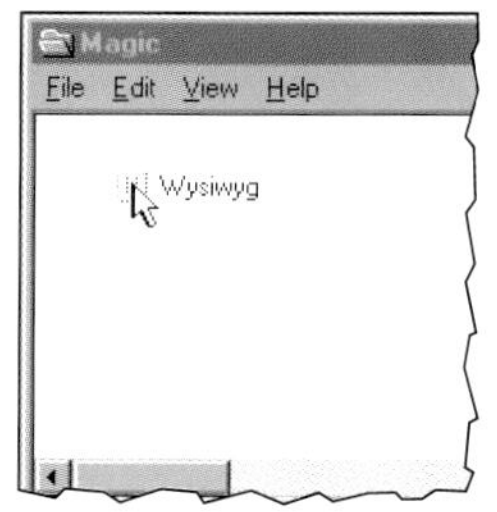

3 Move the mouse to drag the **Wysiwyg** file out of the *Windows* window into the blank area of the *Magic* window. Release the mouse button and you will see that the *Magic* window becomes active and the **Wysiwyg** file is now contained within it.

To copy instead of move a file, follow the same procedure, but hold down Ctrl while you drag the file. When a copy rather than a move is taking place, a tiny + sign accompanies the item being dragged.

COPYING MULTIPLE FILES TO A NEW FOLDER

Now try copying several files from the **Windows** to the **Magic** folder, using the *Copy* and *Paste* commands.

1 Select four files in the *Windows* window — any files will do (they don't need to be in a block).

2 Right-click on any one of the selected files and choose *Copy* from the pop-up menu.

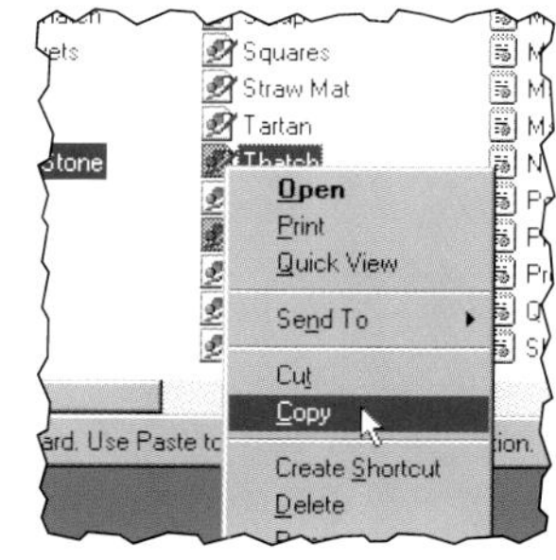

3 Move the mouse pointer into the *Magic* window and choose *Paste* from the *Edit* menu. You will see the copied files appear within the window.

To move instead of copy files to a new folder, follow the same procedure, but choose *Cut* instead of *Copy* from the pop-up menu in step 2.

Backtracking?
If you change your mind immediately after an operation such as copying, deleting, or renaming, you can reverse your action by choosing *Undo* from the active window's *Edit* menu. Alternatively, press Ctrl and Z together.

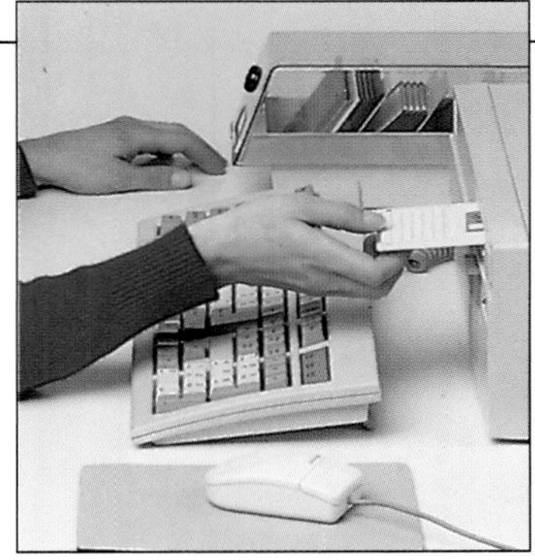

COPYING MULTIPLE FILES TO A FLOPPY DISK

Now try copying some files from your hard disk to a floppy disk. You might want to do this to transfer data between two PCs that are not connected via a network. First close all windows on your Desktop except for the *Magic* window and the *My Computer* window. Position these windows adjacent to each other. Place a formatted floppy disk into disk drive A, and do the following:

1 Select two files in the *Magic* window. Point at one of the selected file icons, press down on the mouse button and move the mouse pointer toward the *My Computer* window. You will see outlines of the two selected file icons move together across the screen.

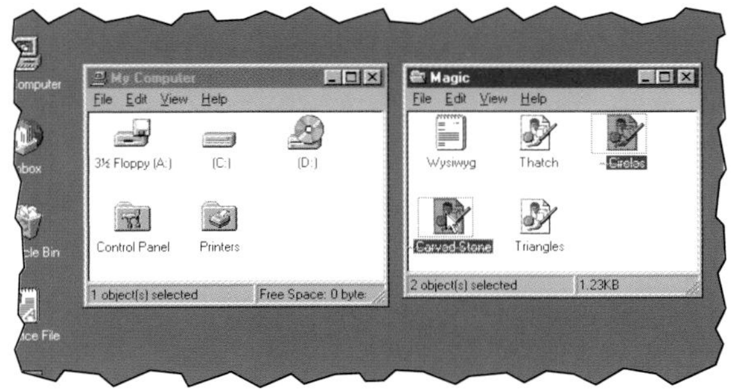

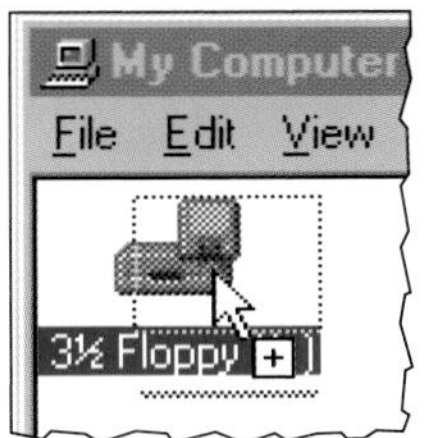

2 Place the pointer over the [A:] icon in the *My Computer* window until you see the icon change color. Then release the mouse button.

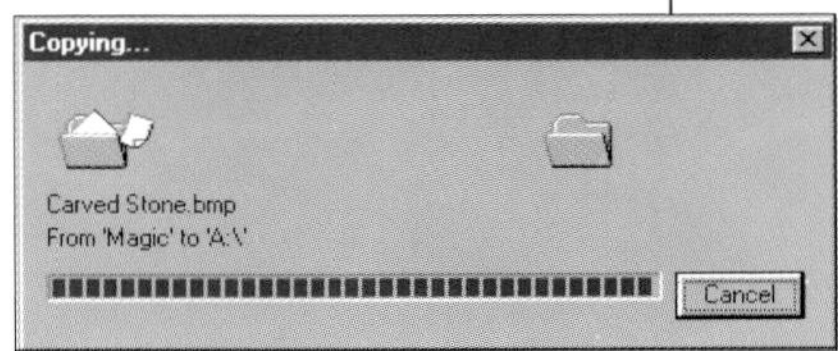

3 You'll see an animation representing the copying operation.

No Control?
When you use drag and drop to transfer files from one disk drive to another, they are always copied rather than moved. If you want to move rather than copy files, choose *Cut* in the source window followed by *Paste* from the destination drive window's *Edit* menu. Alternatively, you can hold down Shift while you drag the file.

Deleting Files

It's easy to remove files you no longer need. You just select the files and then use the *Delete* command. Try the following example.

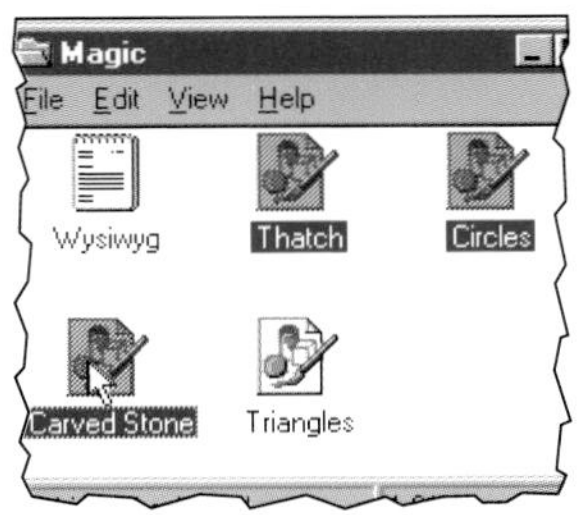

1 Select three files in the *Magic* window by activating this window, holding down Ctrl, and clicking on each file icon in turn. Do *not* select the **Wysiwyg** file.

2 Right-click on any of the icons and choose *Delete* from the pop-up menu. Alternatively, simply press Delete on your keyboard.

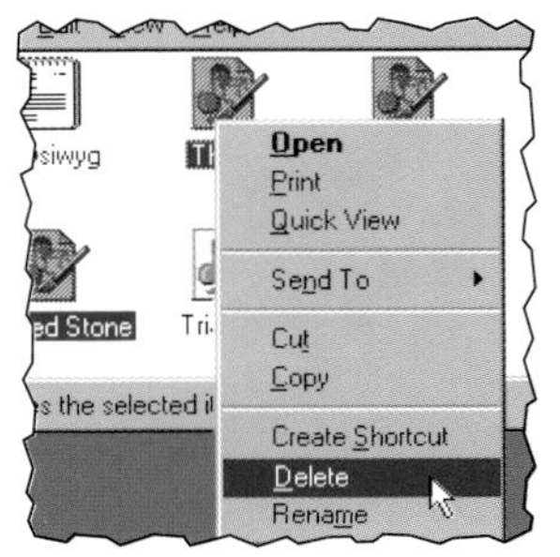

3 A message pops up asking you to confirm that you want to delete the items. Click on *Yes*. You'll see an animation as the files are deleted.

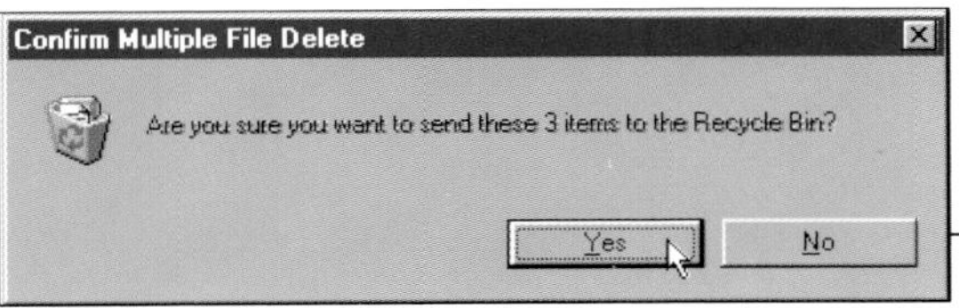

Take Care with Deletions!
For now, don't delete any files or folders except for files you have created yourself or have copied to new folders — otherwise you may delete something important. Also avoid moving any existing files (except those you have created yourself) to new folders — this could have an adverse effect on your PC's or Windows 95's performance.

Using the Recycle Bin

You might think that after you've deleted a file, it's been removed from your computer. But in fact, it hasn't — it's been moved to an area on your hard disk called the Recycle Bin, which is represented by an icon on the Desktop. While a file is in the Recycle Bin, it's still easy to retrieve. But once you've emptied a file from the Bin, it's gone forever. To see how this works, follow the steps starting at left:

1 Close all windows on your Desktop except for the *Magic* window and then double-click on the *Recycle Bin* icon.

2 Within the *Recycle Bin* window, you should see the files you recently deleted. Select two of these files and then click on *File* in the menu bar.

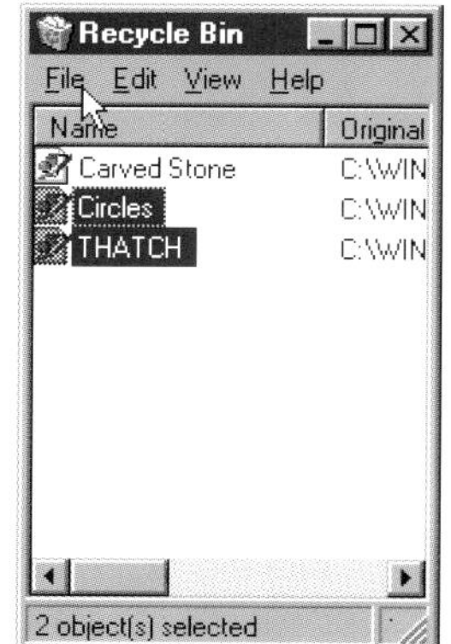

Restore
Choose this option if you want to restore selected files to their original locations.

Empty Recycle Bin
Choose this option if you want everything in the Bin to be removed irretrievably.

Delete
Choose this option if you want only the selected files removed from the Bin.

3 The *File* menu drops down. You now have three main options. In this instance, choose *Restore*. You should see the restored files reappear in the *Magic* window.

Bin It!
If you wish, you can drag any file (or folder) that you no longer want from a drive or folder window and drop it straight onto the *Recycle Bin* icon. This has exactly the same effect as deleting the file or folder — but it's a lot more satisfying! However, be careful when you are throwing away a folder. Make sure it's empty or that you really want to delete everything in it.

Object Properties

Any Windows 95 object, such as a document, folder, program, printer, even the Taskbar and Recycle Bin, has information about its individual characteristics and settings that can be displayed within a *Properties* dialog box. The *Properties* dialog box provides information you might like to know about a file, folder, or other object before you perform an operation on it, such as copying or deleting. Try the following:

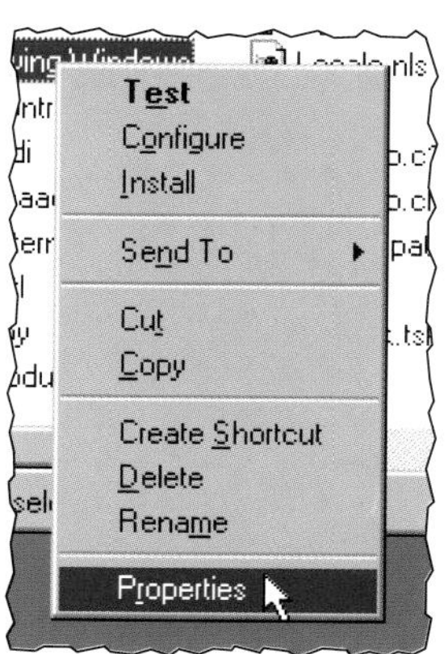

1 Open the **System** folder in the *Windows* window and locate the file labeled *Flying Windows*. What sort of file could that be? To find out, click on the icon with the right mouse button and choose *Properties* from the pop-up menu.

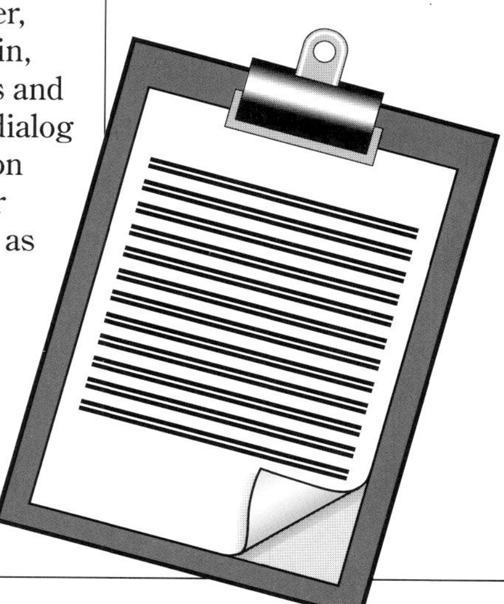

2 The *Flying Windows Properties* dialog box appears, giving several pieces of information about the file.

Flying Windows Properties

General | Version

Flying Windows

Type: Screen Saver
Location: SYSTEM
Size: 14.0KB (14,336 bytes)

MS-DOS name: FLYING~1.SCR
Created: (unknown)
Modified: Wednesday, May 10, 1995 5:00:00 PM
Accessed: Tuesday, May 23, 1995

Attributes: Read-only, Hidden, Archive, System

OK | Cancel | Apply

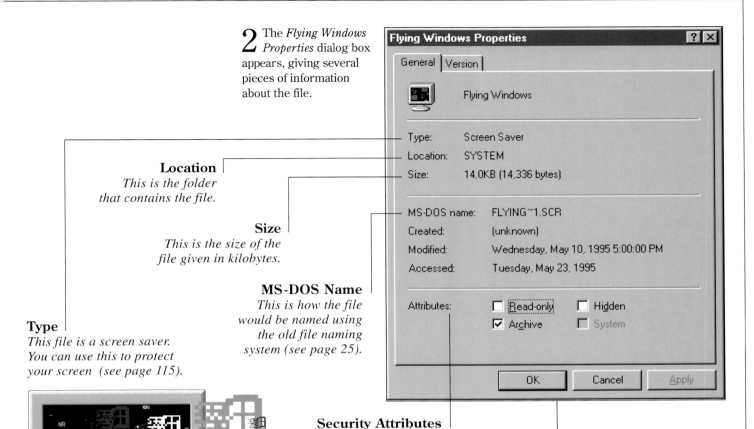

Location
This is the folder that contains the file.

Size
This is the size of the file given in kilobytes.

MS-DOS Name
This is how the file would be named using the old file naming system (see page 25).

Type
This file is a screen saver. You can use this to protect your screen (see page 115).

Security Attributes
This area defines various attributes that you can turn on or off. If a file is hidden, it usually won't be displayed in its folder window. A read-only file cannot have changes made to it. The archive attribute is set automatically by Windows 95 and indicates that a file has been changed since it was last backed up.

You might sometimes want to change a file's security attributes. For example, you might want to make an important data file read-only to prevent you, or anyone else, from changing it. With the **Flying Windows** file, you don't want to make any such changes, so just close its *Properties* dialog box.

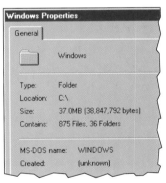

How Big Is Your Bin?

You can adjust the size of your Recycle Bin. To do so, right-click on the *Recycle Bin* icon, choose *Properties*, and set the size of the Bin, either for all drives or for a particular drive, in the *Recycle Bin Properties* dialog box. Note that if you delete a file when the Recycle Bin is full, Windows 95 will need to remove some of the existing Bin contents to create room. Files are removed on a "first in, first out" basis.

Windows Properties

General

Windows

Type: Folder
Location: C:\
Size: 37.0MB (38,847,792 bytes)
Contains: 875 Files, 36 Folders

MS-DOS name: WINDOWS
Created: (unknown)

What's in That Folder?
To find out how many files and subfolders are contained in a folder, and the total disk space occupied by the folder's contents, right-click on the folder icon and choose Properties *from the pop-up menu. You'll see the information about the folder's contents in the* Properties *dialog box.*

Windows Explorer

WINDOWS EXPLORER IS A POWERFUL TOOL that lets you look inside your PC. If you want to view the files and folders on your computer, it provides a convenient alternative to browsing individual drive and folder windows. Windows Explorer also helps you understand the drive and folder hierarchy on your computer and keep on top of general "housekeeping" tasks such as moving, copying, naming, or deleting files.

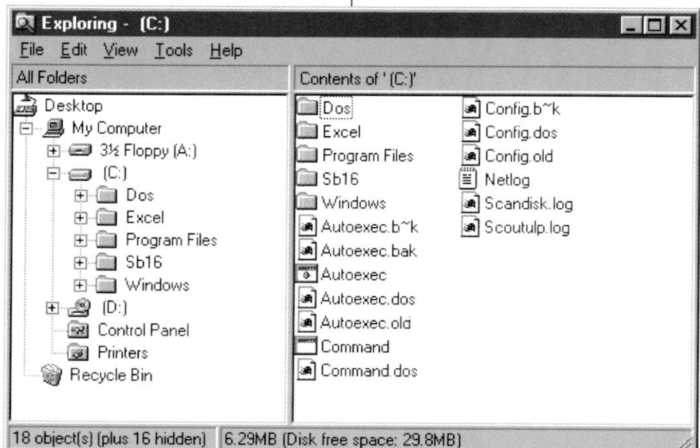

Viewing Files and Folders with Windows Explorer

Windows Explorer replaces the File Manager found in previous versions of Windows. Open Windows Explorer now by choosing *Programs* from the *Start* menu and *Windows Explorer* from the submenu. A two-pane window appears. The left-hand pane displays the drive and folder tree. This tree represents the structure of your computing environment. Imagine the computers and disk drives as the roots and trunk of the tree, folders as its branches, subfolders as progressively smaller branches, and files as the leaves on the tree.

The right-hand pane of the window displays the contents of whatever is highlighted in the left half. Follow the steps below to find out how to expand and collapse a "branch" of the folder tree and then how to show the contents of a folder in the right-hand pane.

Plus and Minus

If a plus sign is displayed next to a drive or folder icon, it means that the drive or folder contains subfolders that are not currently shown. A minus sign indicates that the drive or folder is expanded and its contents are listed below — indented to show that the subfolders are subordinate and joined by lines to reveal how they relate to each other.

Expanding and Collapsing the Folder Tree

1 At present, the main folders on your hard disk are listed below the hard disk icon, labeled *[C:]*. Click on the plus sign next to the **Windows** folder in the left-hand pane to expand the folder tree.

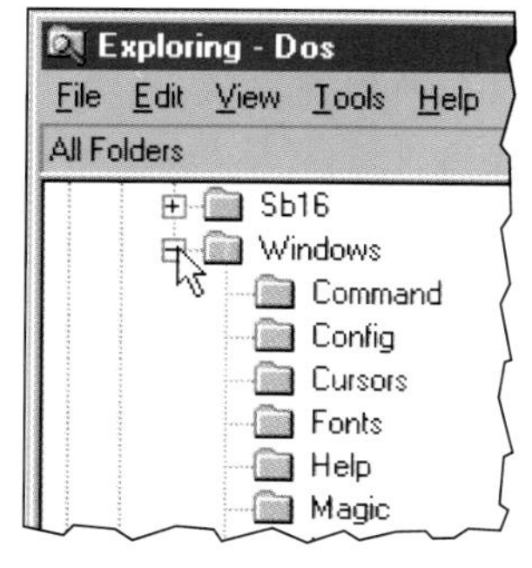

2 The subfolders of the **Windows** folder are now listed below it. To collapse the **Windows** folder, click on the minus sign next to it.

New Ways to Explore?

Rather than accessing Windows Explorer via the *Start* menu, you can open it by right-clicking on the *My Computer* icon, or on any drive or folder icon, and then choosing *Explore* from the pop-up menu that appears.

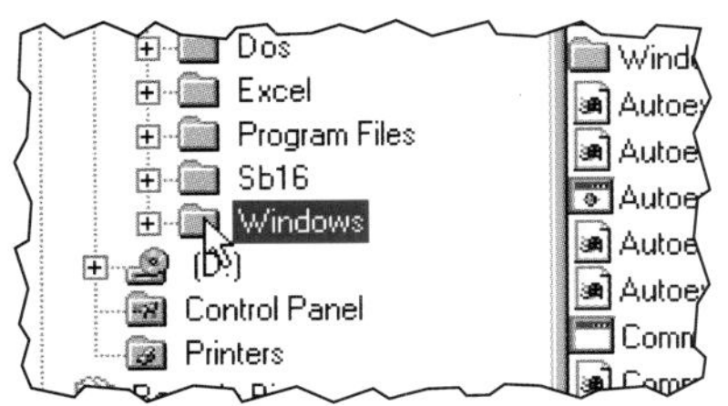

Viewing the Contents of a Folder

1 At the moment the right-hand pane displays the contents of your hard disk — folders as well as some "loose" files. This is indicated in the title bar as *Exploring - [C:]*. To view the contents of another folder, you click on the folder icon next to its name in the left-hand pane. Click on the icon for the **Windows** folder.

2 The right-hand pane now displays all the subfolders and files contained in the **Windows** folder. The title bar now reads *Exploring – Windows*. To look through the list of files, drag the scroll box within the scroll bar in the right-hand pane.

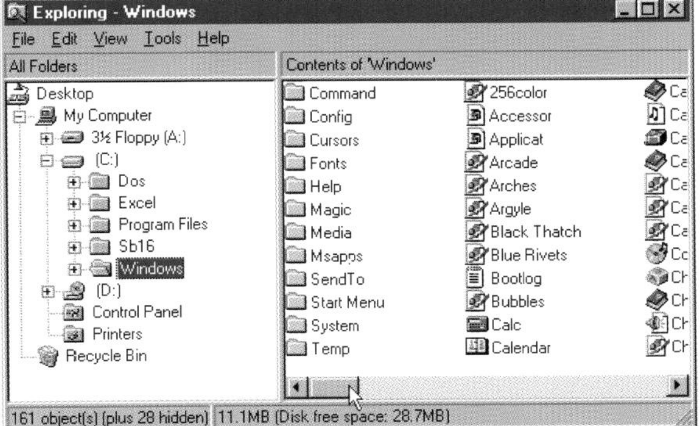

Drag It Out
To change the sizes of the panes in the *Exploring* window, move the mouse pointer over the bar that separates the two sides — the pointer will change to a vertical bar with two arrows. Hold down the mouse button and drag the bar in the desired direction.

File Management with Windows Explorer

Windows Explorer not only helps you browse through your files, it also enables you to carry out general housekeeping tasks. To build and maintain a folder structure that is tailored to your needs, you may need to move or copy files from one folder to another, change the name of a file or folder, or delete files you no longer need. You have already practiced a number of these file management techniques under "Organizing Files and Folders" on pages 50 to 55. The advantage of Windows Explorer is that it allows you to carry out operations such as moving and copying within a single window.

MOVING FILES OR FOLDERS

As described on pages 51 and 52, there are two methods that you can use to move files and folders: the drag and drop technique or the use of menu commands. In the steps starting on the next page you'll use the drag and drop method to move the **Wysiwyg** file, which you created on page 33, from the **Magic** folder, created on page 50, to the **Dos** folder. But first you'll practice another way of displaying the contents of a folder in the Windows Explorer.

Changing Your View?
By default, Windows Explorer lists the folders and files alphabetically in the right-hand pane (folders first, and then files). By choosing *Arrange Icons* from the *View* menu, you can also rearrange them by type, by size, or by date. Choosing *Details* from the *View* menu reveals the sizes and types of files and when they were last worked on.

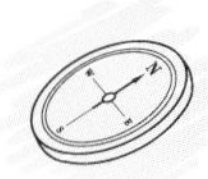

Moving a File from One Folder to Another Folder

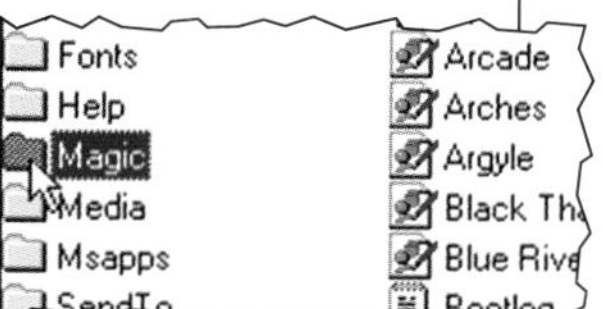

1 With the contents of the **Windows** folder still displayed in the right-hand pane, double-click on the icon for the **Magic** folder to show its contents.

2 The right-hand pane now shows the contents of the **Magic** folder, while the left-hand pane lists the subfolders of the **Windows** folder. To locate the **Dos** folder, drag the left-hand vertical scroll bar upward.

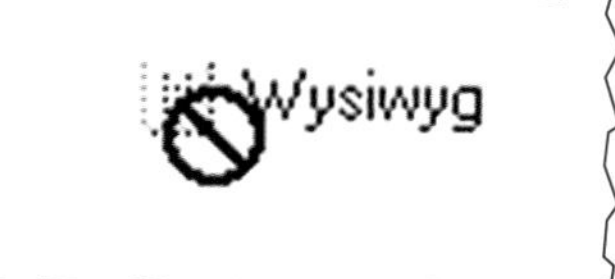

"No Go" Symbol
If you see this symbol appear below a file or folder icon when you are dragging it, it indicates that the item cannot be moved or copied to its current location on-screen.

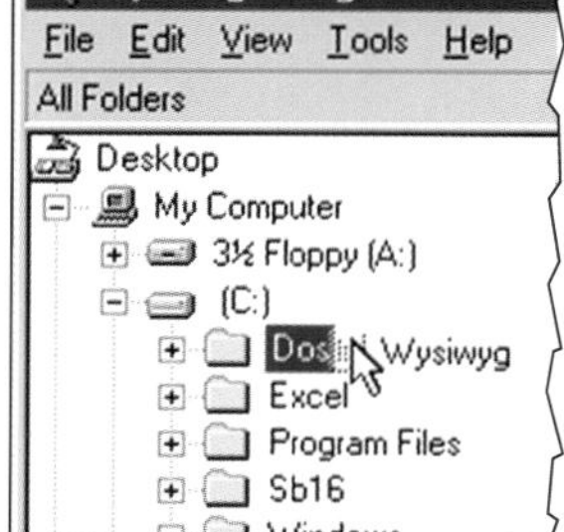

3 In the right-hand pane, click on the icon for the **Wysiwyg** file and hold down the mouse button. Drag the **Wysiwyg** file into the left-hand pane close to the **Dos** folder so that the folder becomes highlighted. Then release the mouse button.

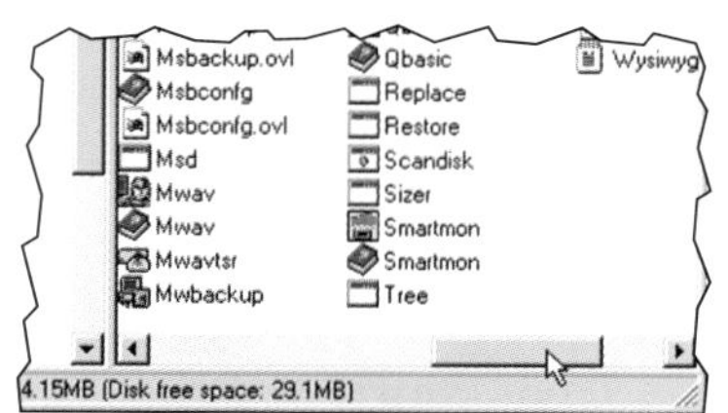

4 To verify that the **Wysiwyg** file is in the **Dos** folder, click on the icon for the **Dos** folder in the left-hand pane and then use the horizontal scroll bar in the right-hand pane to locate the **Wysiwyg** file.

To select more than one file or folder, hold down Ctrl and click the items you want to select. To select a group of adjacent items, hold down Shift and then click on the last item in the list (see also "Selecting Files and Folders" on page 51).

If you prefer to use menu commands, you can move a file or folder by right-clicking its icon and choosing *Cut* from the pop-up menu. Locate and select the folder to which you want to move the item and choose *Paste* from the Windows Explorer *Edit* menu.

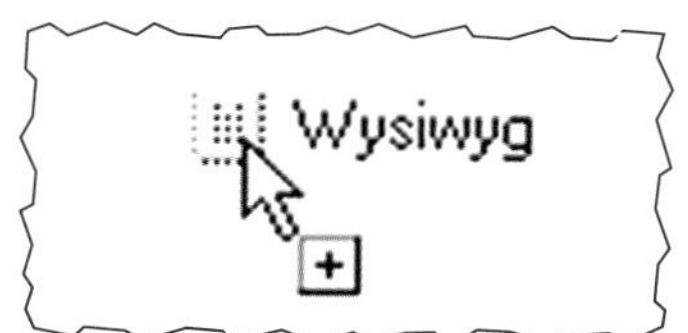

What's That Plus Sign?
When you drag a file or folder icon and you hold down Ctrl to effect a copy instead of a move, you'll see a plus sign appear below the icon. You might also see a plus sign if you drag a document icon over a program file icon. When you drop the icon, Windows 95 will start the program and attempt to load the document in that program.

COPYING FILES AND FOLDERS BY DRAG AND DROP

Copying by drag and drop in Windows Explorer is performed in the same way as moving by drag and drop, except that you need to hold down the Ctrl key. First locate the item you want to copy in the drive and folder hierarchy and make sure that the icon for the target drive or folder is also visible. Finally, click on the icon for the file or folder you want to copy, hold down Ctrl, and drag the icon to its new location.

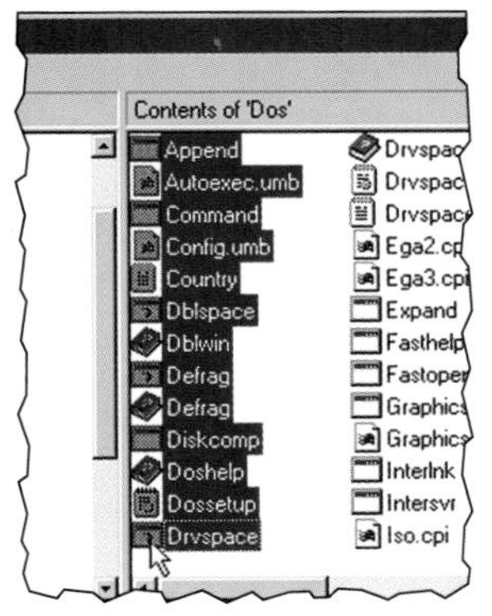

COPYING FILES USING MENU COMMANDS

Follow the steps below to practice copying files to a new folder using the *Copy* and *Paste* commands rather than the drag and drop method.

1 Open the contents of the **Dos** folder. Hold down Shift, click on the first file and then on the last file of the first column to select the entire column.

2 Choose *Copy* from the *Edit* menu. Alternatively, right-click on a selected file and choose *Copy* from the pop-up menu. In either case, take special care not to choose the *Cut* command.

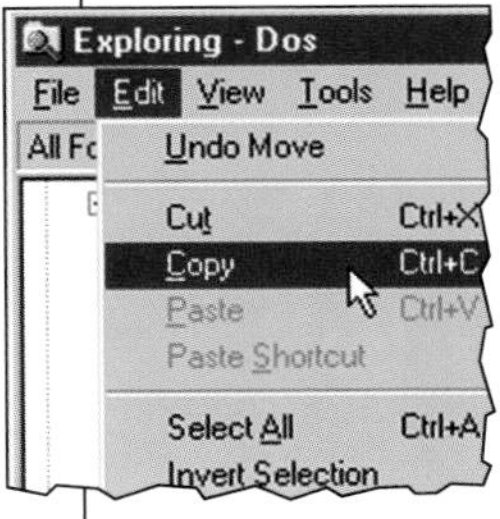

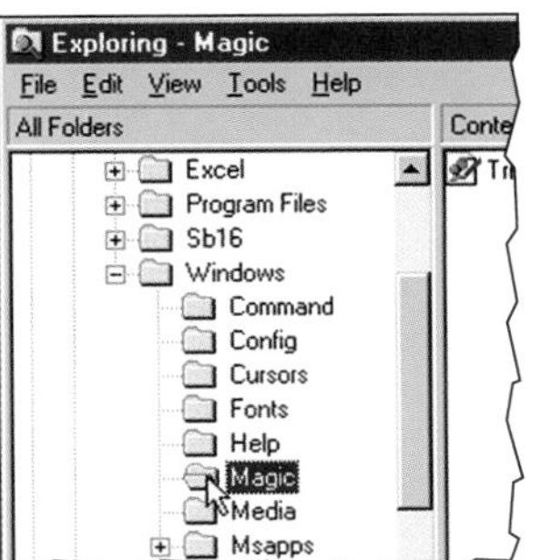

3 Drag the scroll box in the left-hand vertical scroll bar down until you see the **Magic** folder.

4 Choose *Paste* from the *Edit* menu. The files you have copied from the **Dos** folder will appear in the right-hand pane.

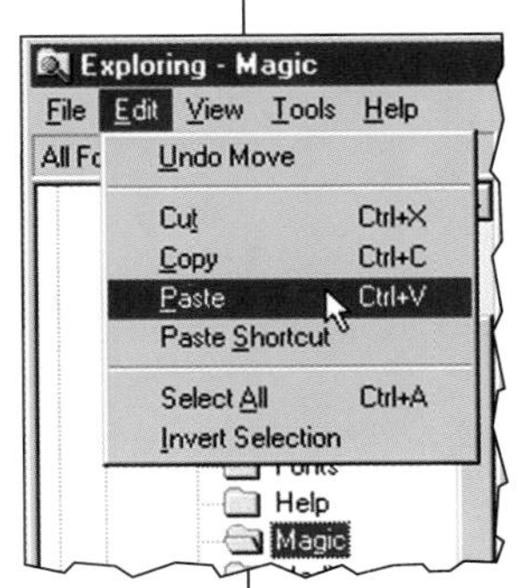

COPYING A FILE TO A FLOPPY DISK

Here is a quick way to copy a file to a floppy disk. First insert the floppy disk into the floppy disk drive, which is usually configured as disk drive A, and then follow the steps starting at left.

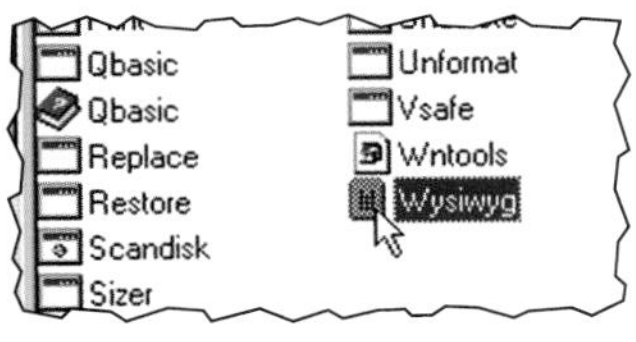

1 Click on the file you want to copy. In this case, click on the **Wysiwyg** file in the **Dos** folder.

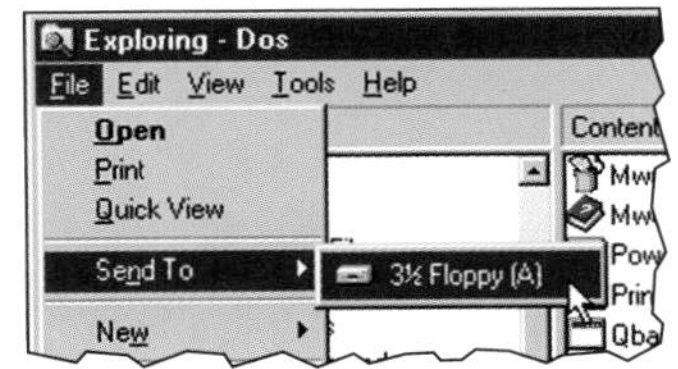

2 Choose *Send To* from the *File* menu and then *3 ½ Floppy [A]* from the submenu. The file is copied to the floppy disk. You'll see an animation representing the copying process.

Renaming a File or Folder

To rename a file or folder, click on the icon for the file or the folder whose name you want to change. Choose *Rename* from the *File* menu. Alternatively, click on the relevant icon and then click again on its name. A box will appear around the highlighted name and you'll see a flashing insertion point at the end of the name. Type the new name and press Enter. Now click outside the file or folder to deselect it. It's best to use obvious names that you'll remember easily. This will help you keep up with the management of your files and folders.

Avoid Litter!

To avoid cluttering your hard disk, delete files and folders you no longer need. To delete them with Windows Explorer, select the items and choose *Delete* from the *File* menu or drag their icons straight to the Recycle Bin.

The Magic of Multimedia

THESE DAYS, MOST NEW PCs are multimedia PCs — that is, they come with a CD-ROM drive and special sound facilities. If you don't have a multimedia PC, new tools in Windows 95 make easy work of installing the necessary hardware. This section starts off by describing how to add a sound card and a CD-ROM drive to your PC; if you already have these devices installed, turn to pages 62 to 67 to find out how to make use of them.

What Can I Do with a Multimedia PC?
Multimedia PCs open up a whole new world of games, educational, and reference software in the form of CD-ROM titles. You can also use your CD-ROM drive to listen to audio CDs. Budding musicians, meanwhile, can record and play their own sound files with a multimedia PC.

Sound Cards

Sound Card
Most sound cards provide microphone, speaker, and MIDI (musical instrument digital interface) connections for recording and playing sound files.

Nonmultimedia PCs have limited sound capabilities. To play CD-quality music or to record sounds on your computer, it is necessary to install a sound card. This is not a difficult task, but if you don't feel confident about doing it yourself, your dealer should be able to help you. A step-by-step guide to the process can also be found in *The Way Multimedia Works*, available in the WYSIWYG series of computer guides.

A sound card is a rigid fiberglass card bristling with electronic components. It fits into a free expansion slot on a PC's motherboard (the fiberglass circuit board that resides at the bottom of the system unit). The back of the sound card provides sockets for connecting a microphone and speakers.

Once the sound card is installed in the PC, it must be configured for use so that its settings don't clash with those for other hardware on your PC. The method for configuring your sound card depends on whether you have a Plug and Play PC or an older model that lacks Plug and Play capability. If you're not sure whether you have a Plug and Play PC, consult the owner's manual or ask your dealer.

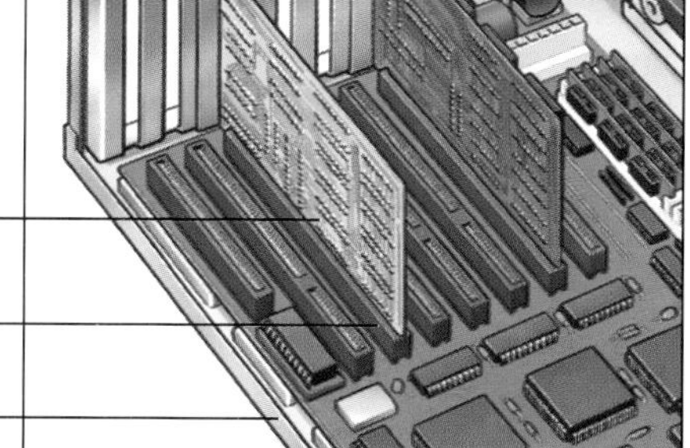

Sound Card

Expansion Slot

System Unit

Installing a Sound Card
The sound card is inserted into a free expansion slot in the motherboard while the PC's power is turned off.

PLUG AND PLAY

If you have a Plug and Play PC, installing a sound card couldn't be easier — you simply connect a Plug and Play sound card, switch on the computer, and you're ready to roll! Windows 95 automatically allocates system resources so that the sound card doesn't have to compete with other hardware components in your PC.

CONFIGURING A SOUND CARD FOR COMPUTERS WITHOUT PLUG AND PLAY
Even if you have an older PC with no Plug and Play capabilities, Windows 95 can identify most types of sound cards and will automatically fine-tune system settings so that there is no clash with other devices.

To begin configuring a newly installed sound card, click on *Start* and then choose *Control Panel* from the *Settings* menu. Double-click on the *Add New Hardware* icon, click on *Next* in the box that appears, and follow the steps starting at the right.

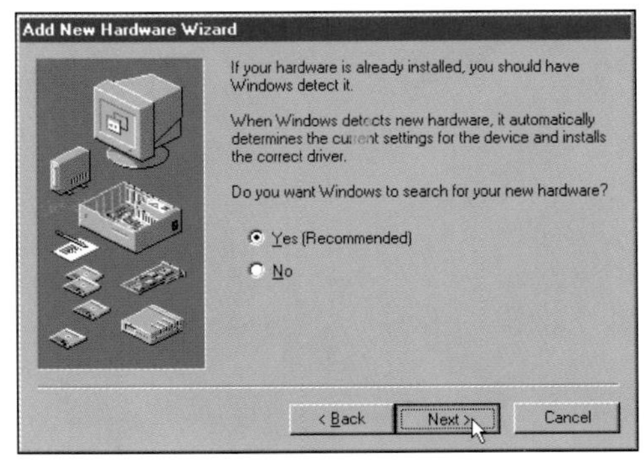

1 In the *Add New Hardware Wizard* box, you are offered two choices for setting up the sound card. Make sure the *Yes (Recommended)* option is checked, and click on *Next*. Read the warning that appears in the dialog box and click *Next* again.

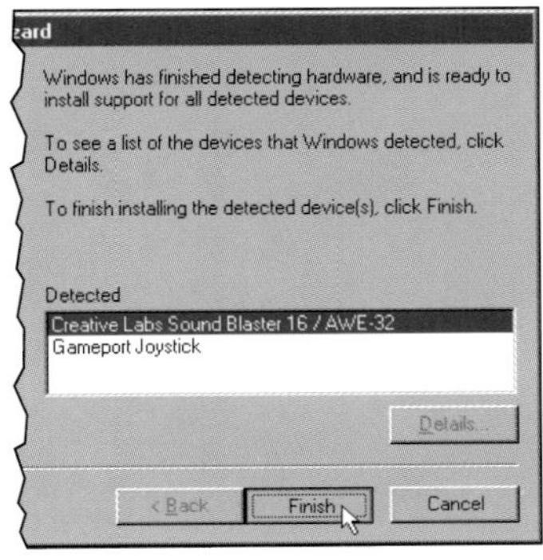

2 Windows 95 will scan your system to detect new hardware. When the scan is completed, you can view a list of the detected hardware by clicking on *Details*. When you have done so, click on *Finish*. (Windows will now ask you to verify the type of sound card you have installed. Click *Change* if you need to modify any details.) Click *Next* to complete the configuration of the sound card.

3 To check that the sound card has been installed correctly, double-click on the *System* icon in the Control Panel. In the *System Properties* dialog box, click on the *Device Manager* tab.

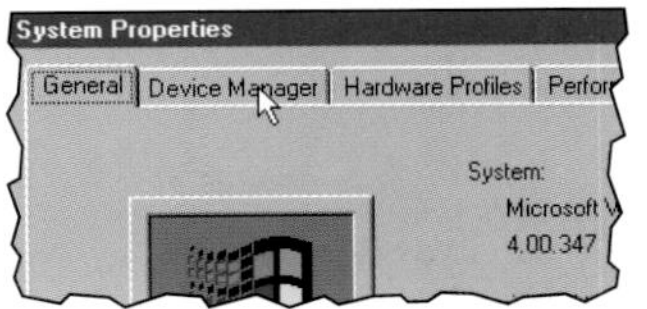

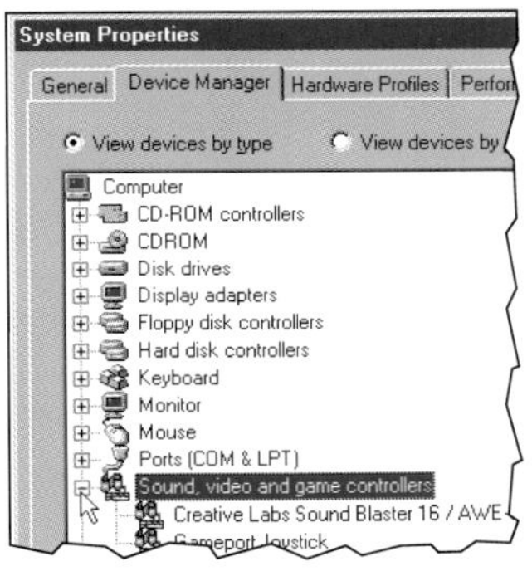

4 A list of hardware connected to your PC appears. In this list, you'll see *Sound, video and game controllers*; click on the plus sign next to the icon and you'll see the name of the sound card you've just installed. Click on *OK* to close the dialog box.

CD-ROM Drives

As with sound cards, adding a CD-ROM drive to your PC is easy with Windows 95. With the PC's power turned off, you first insert the drive into a spare drive bay in your system unit. You then connect one end of a data cable to the CD-ROM drive. The other end of the data cable connects either directly to the sound card (if it has a built-in CD-ROM interface) or to a special interface card (normally a Small Computer Systems Interface or SCSI card) that you must install in a free expansion slot. You must also plug one of the PC's power cables into the back of the CD-ROM drive, and in some cases you may need to connect an audio cable between the CD-ROM drive and sound card. (Once again, detailed instructions for installing a CD-ROM drive appear in *The Way Multimedia Works*.)

Once the CD-ROM drive is installed, launch the Add New Hardware Wizard from the Control Panel. Windows 95 will automatically detect and configure the drive for use with your PC.

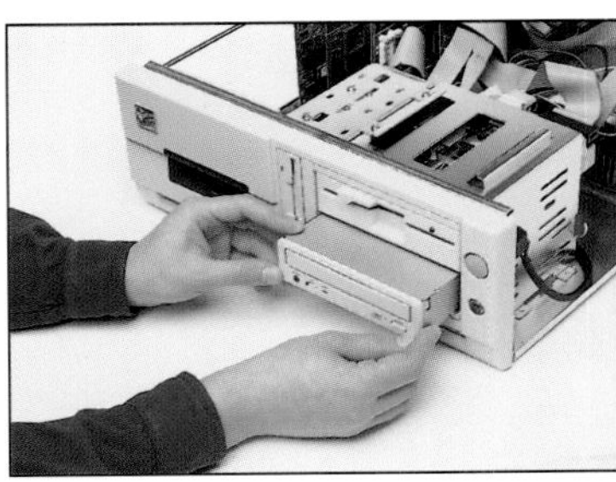

Perfect Fit
You install the CD-ROM drive into a spare drive bay in the system unit while the PC's power is turned off.

Multimedia Setup

Before experimenting with the multimedia tools described over the next few pages, you should check that all Windows 95's multimedia components are installed on your system. Do so by using the *Windows Setup* flipcard in the *Add/Remove Programs Properties* dialog box (see page 123). After highlighting *Multimedia* under components, click on the *Default* button, make sure all the multimedia components are checked, and click on *OK*.

Musical Choices
The Sounds Properties *dialog box lets you assign sounds to Windows events.*

Sound Schemes

Windows 95's Sounds feature lets you assign sounds to Windows 95 events. To see how it works, double-click on the *Sounds* icon in the Control Panel to open the *Sounds Properties* dialog box. There are three main parts to the dialog box. Under *Events*, you can select the Windows 95 event to be linked to a chosen sound. Under *Sound*, you select and preview the sound you would like to link to an event. Under *Schemes*, you select an existing Windows 95 Sound Scheme or you can create and save your own sound arrangement to use for your Windows 95 computing sessions. To set up your own scheme, follow these steps:

Sounds like a doorbell chime

Sounds like a single note on a xylophone

Sounds like a single chord on a piano

Sounds like a horn fanfare

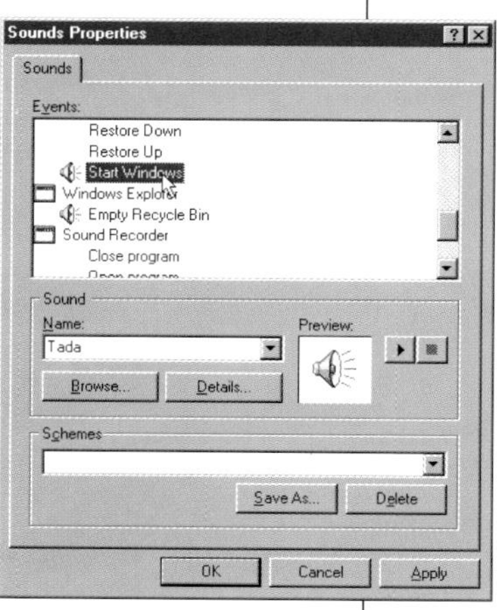

1 Use the scroll bar on the right of the *Events* box to view the options. Click on the *Start Windows* option to highlight it. The sound currently associated with starting Windows appears in the *Name* box.

2 Change the sound associated with starting Windows to *Robotz Windows Start* by choosing this option from the drop-down list box under *Name*. Under *Preview* is an icon of a loudspeaker; click on the Play button next to this icon to preview the sound. (You can preview any of the sounds listed by clicking on a sound so that it appears in the *Name* box and then clicking on the Play button.)

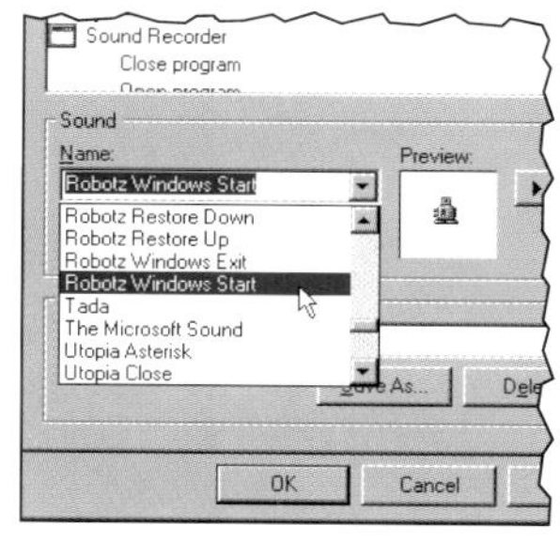

3 Repeat steps 1 and 2 for each event you wish to link with a sound. Then click on *Save As*, and in the *Save Scheme As* dialog box, name your scheme **Sound Symphony**. Click on *OK*, and then on *OK* again to close the *Sounds Properties* dialog box. The new sound scheme will be used until you change it.

Recording Sounds

If you have a sound card and a microphone, you can use Sound Recorder to record your own sound files. You can then assign these sound files to Windows 95 events. You can also insert sound files into documents (see page 69). Make sure your microphone has an $\frac{1}{8}$-inch jack for connection to the sound card. (You can buy an adapter if necessary.)

How to Record Sound

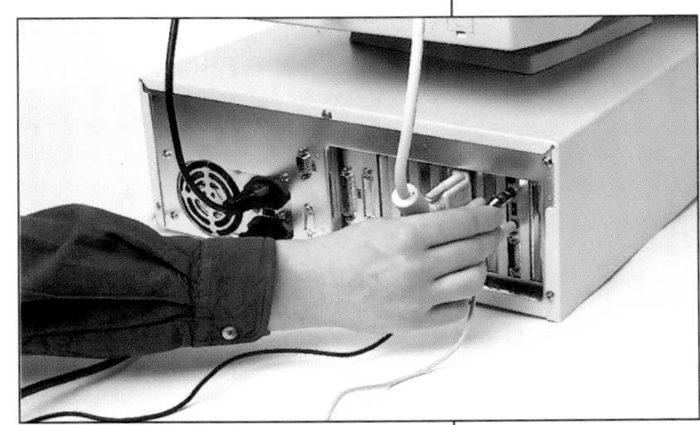

1 With your PC's power turned off, plug your microphone into the "Mic" port on the back of the sound card and switch the microphone on (if it has a switch). Now turn on your PC. Once the Windows 95 opening screen appears, open Sound Recorder from the *Start* menu (it's in the *Multimedia* group within the *Accessories* group on the *Programs* menu).

2 Click on the Record button in the *Sound Recorder* window. After a brief pause, the slide on the scroll bar starts moving, and the *Position* counter begins to increment. The *Length* counter tells you how much recording time is available to you. Keeping the microphone about eight inches from your mouth, speak or sing "Happy Birthday," and you'll see the sound waves displayed. Then click on the Stop button.

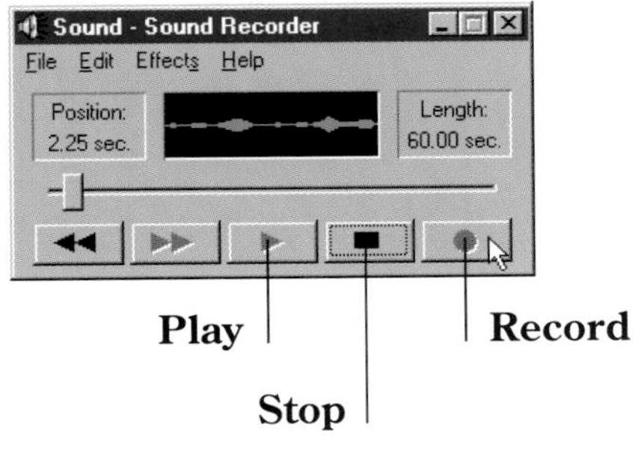

Play

Stop

Record

3 Choose *Save As* from the *File* menu. In the *Save As* dialog box, navigate so that the **Media** subfolder of the **Windows** folder appears in the *Save in* box. When **Media** is the current folder, type the name of your file (**Happy Birthday**) into the *File name* box and click on *Save*. Close Sound Recorder. If you wish, you can now use the *Sounds Properties* dialog box to assign your new sound file to an event of your choice.

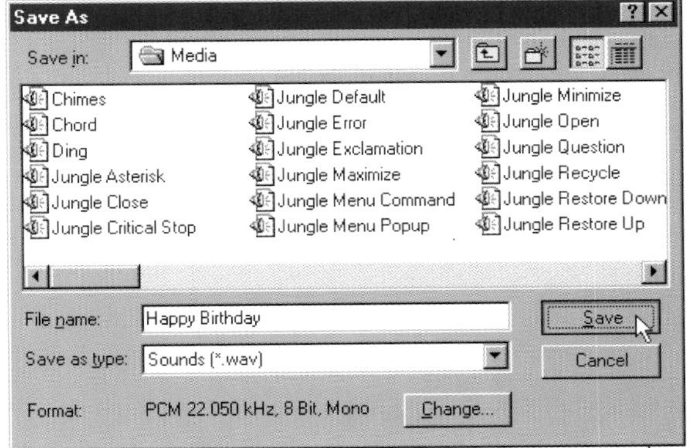

Other Sound Recorder Facilities

Sound Recorder offers a number of editing and special effects options. Using commands in the *Edit* menu, you can delete portions of a file, insert another sound file, or even mix two sound files together. Commands in the *Effects* menu offer options to turn the volume up or down, change the running speed, add an echo, and even reverse the sound. If you want to experiment with these options, remember that you can always choose *Revert* from the *File* menu to return to the last saved version of your file.

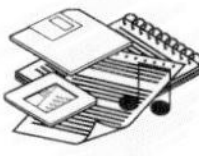

Multimedia and CD-ROM

As with other types of computer disks, CD-ROM discs store program and data files. Unlike other storage devices, however, a CD-ROM disc cannot be used to save your data; information is stamped into the disc during manufacture, and after that you cannot alter it.

CD-ROM discs are used to store games, encyclopedias, training programs, and educational software titles. If you have a CD-ROM drive, you can also use it to play your audio CDs (see page 66).

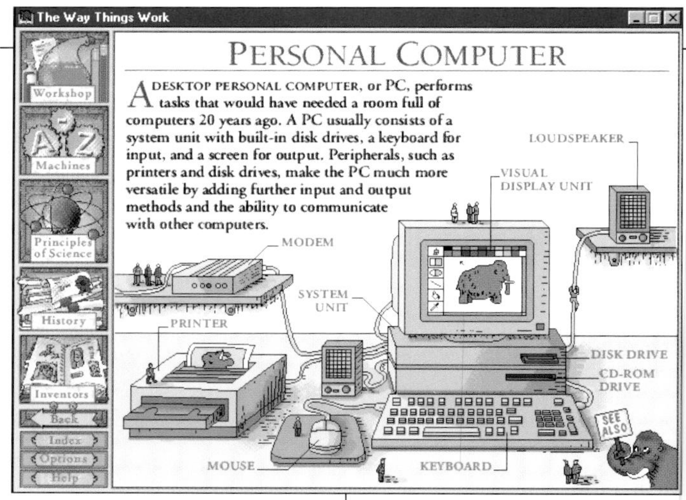

Look and Learn
CD-ROM software is usually packed with sound and graphics; Dorling Kindersley's The Way Things Work, *for example, uses sound and animation clips to explain the workings of 150 machines and inventions.*

USING A CD-ROM DISC

The first time you use a CD-ROM title, you will probably have to run an install program.

When you first insert a disc into the CD-ROM drive, the label for the D drive in the *My Computer* window changes to display the name of the CD-ROM disc. If you can find a *Setup* or *Install* icon in this window, you can begin installing the program by double-clicking on the icon. However, it's usually easier to use the *Add/Remove Programs* icon in the Control Panel.

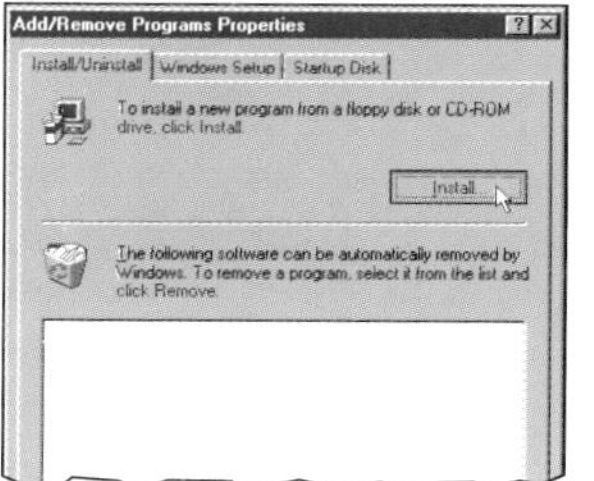

1 In the Control Panel, double-click on the *Add/Remove Programs* icon, click on the *Install/Uninstall* tab, and click on the *Install* button. Click *Next* in the box that appears.

2 Insert the disc for the title you want to set up into the CD-ROM drive and then click on *Next*. Windows 95 will scan the disc for the necessary setup file. Once Windows 95 confirms that it has found the setup program, click on *Finish*.

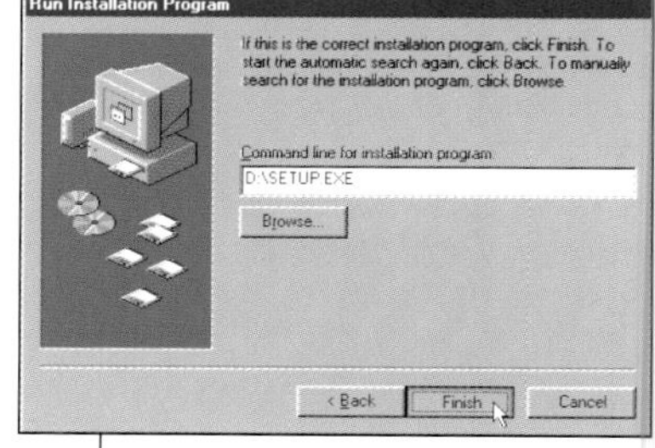

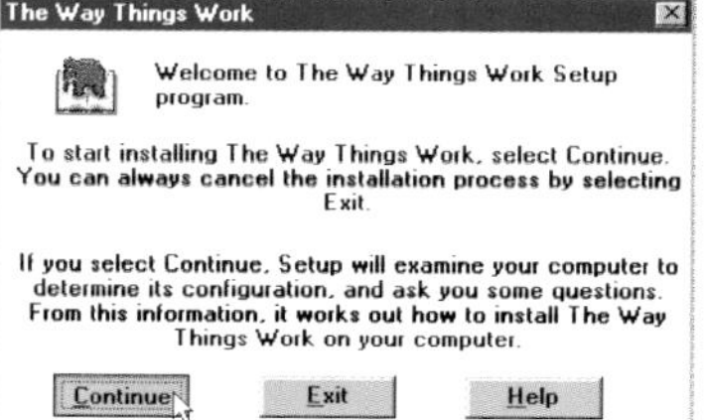

3 The CD-ROM title's setup program will appear on the screen; click *Continue* and simply follow the instructions on the screen to install the title.

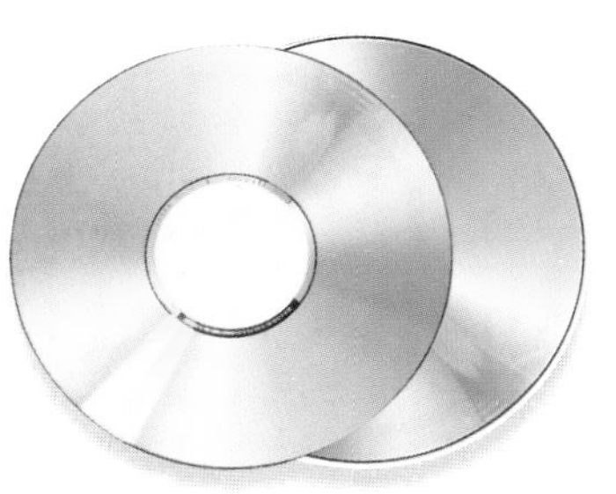

After you've installed the new software, a new program group will usually appear in the *Programs* menu, representing the title or the group to which the software belongs. You can launch the title from the *Programs* menu. Just make sure that you've first inserted the disc into the CD-ROM drive.

Media Player

You use Media Player to play individual media clips such as video, music, or animation files. It also controls your PC's multimedia hardware. Open Media Player now. (You'll find it in the *Multimedia* group within the *Accessories* group on the *Programs* menu.)

To play a media clip, you first need to specify the Windows 95 program or software "device" to use. Some programs, such as the one for playing video clips, are included with Windows 95 and don't require special hardware to run. Other programs, such as the one for CD Audio, are available only if you have the relevant hardware installed in your PC. If you have access to any video files with the .avi extension you can use Media Player to view them.

Playing a Media Clip

1 To view a video clip, choose *Video for Windows* from Media Player's *Device* menu. In the *Open* dialog box, navigate to the folder that contains the video clip you want to view (see page 31 if you've forgotten how to navigate folders). Click on the relevant video file and then click on *Open*.

Play/Pause Button

2 The first frame of the video clip will appear in a window below the *Media Player* window. Click on the Play button to view the clip. When the clip is running the Play button becomes the Pause button. Click on this to freeze the action.

Filling the Whole Screen

To switch to full screen mode when using Video for Windows, choose *Configure* from the *Device* menu. In the *Video Properties* dialog box, check *Full Screen* under *Show video in*, and then click on *OK*. Now when you view the clip, it is played on the full screen. You can choose other viewing options from the drop-down list next to *Window* in the *Video Properties* dialog box.

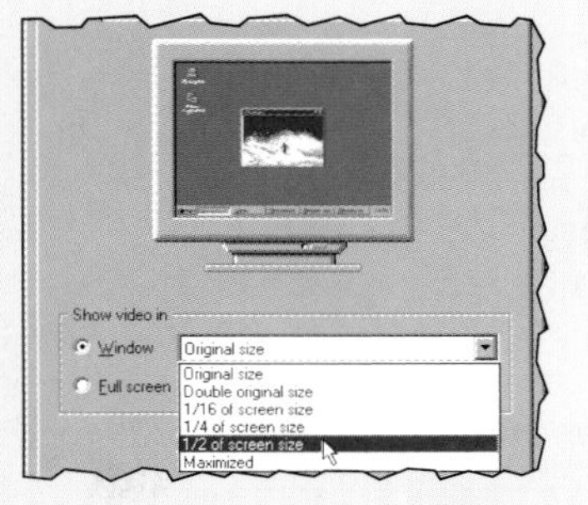

LEAVING MEDIA PLAYER

How you exit Media Player depends on the type of program you are using to play the media clip.

Some programs, such as CD Audio, run automatically — you don't need to specify a file to open (see right). When you exit Media Player after using one of these programs, first stop the media clip by clicking on the square Stop button, or it will keep playing even after you exit Media Player.

For other programs, such as Video for Windows, just choose *Exit* from the *File* menu to close both the media clip and Media Player itself.

A Simple Device
Programs like CD Audio that launch automatically do not have an ellipsis (...) next to their names. The ellipsis indicates that you need to specify a file to open.

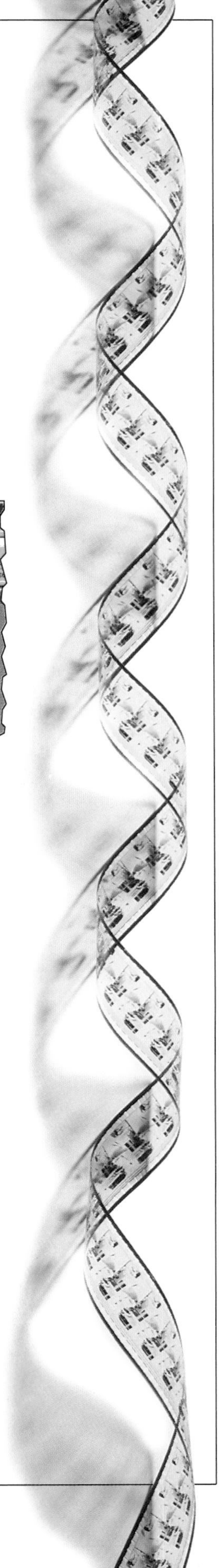

Sound File Formats

If you browse through the **Media** folder within the **Windows** folder, you can quickly identify different media clips by their file icons. Sound files fall into two types — waveform files and MIDI files. Waveform files are represented by speaker icons and consist of sound waves that have been digitized (turned into numbers) by the process of sampling (see opposite page). MIDI files, which have icons representing musical notes on a staff, contain instructions for a synthesizer to make music. While you can play waveform files on any PC that has a built-in speaker, MIDI files can be played only on PCs with sound cards that incorporate a synthesizer.

Waveform Files
The waveform format is used to store sound files that were recorded with a microphone. Waveform files can store any type of sound — voices, music, and special effects.

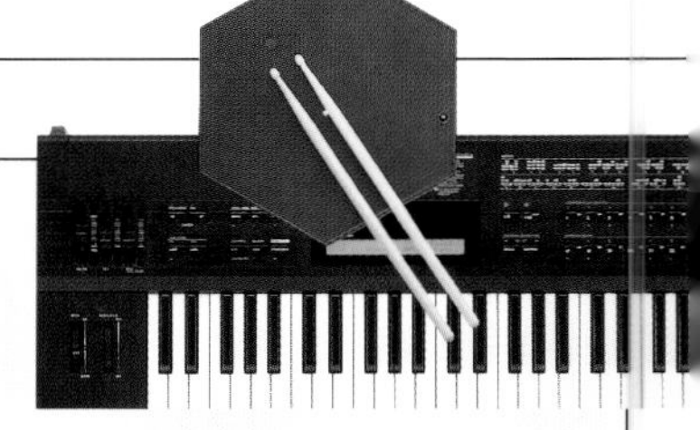

MIDI Files
The MIDI format can be understood only by a PC with a sound card that incorporates a synthesizer (a standard sound card component today). MIDI files store instructions for making music rather than sounds themselves.

Listening to Audio CDs

If you have a CD-ROM drive, one of the devices available in Media Player will be CD Audio. If you want to whistle while you work, however, Windows 95 offers a far more sophisticated program for listening to audio CDs: CD Player. CD Player can be found in the *Multimedia* group within the *Accessories* group within the *Programs* menu.

To listen to an audio CD, insert the disc into your CD-ROM drive and the CD Player will launch automatically. You can use the program's controls to navigate the tracks on the disc. You can also create a play list for individual discs, as described here.

Pump Up the Volume!
To adjust the volume of sound emanating from your multimedia PC, just click on the speaker icon at the right-hand end of the Taskbar and then drag the slider in the box entitled *Volume* that pops up.

How to Create a Play List

1 Select *Edit Play List* from the *Disc* menu.

2 In the *Disc Settings* dialog box, click on *Clear All* to remove the tracks currently listed under *Play List*. In the *Available Tracks* list, click on the first track you would like on your play list, and then click on *Add*. The track number will appear at the top of the *Play List* box.

3 If you want to name the track, make sure the track is highlighted under *Available Tracks*, type its title in the *Track* box, and click on the *Set Name* button. The track will now appear under its name.

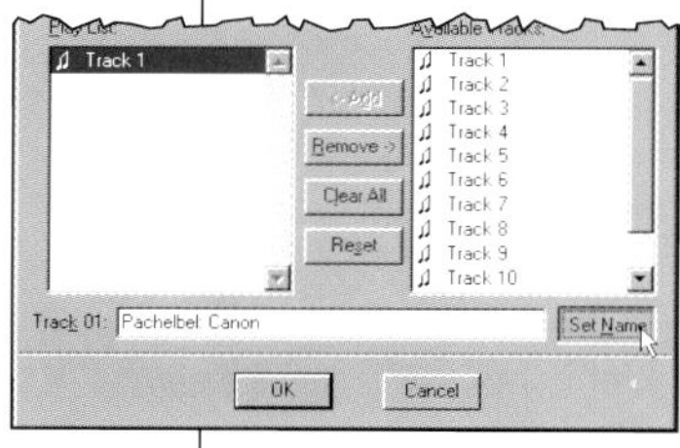

4 Continue adding the tracks you would like in your play list. If you add the wrong track, simply select the entry in the *Play List* box and then click on *Remove*. When you've finished creating the list, type in the name of the artist within the *Artist* box. Type in the title of the disc under *Title*, and then click on *OK*.

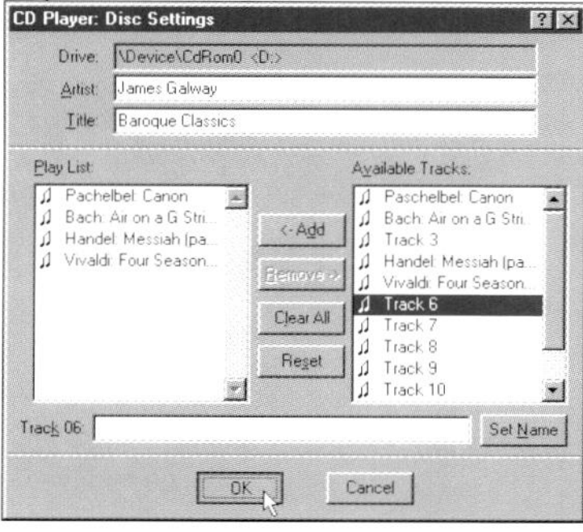

Once you've set up a play list, CD Player will automatically offer it for use every time you insert that disc into the CD-ROM drive and launch CD Player. Your disc will play on, uninterrupted, while you continue with other work on your PC. If the *CD Player* window clutters up your screen, use the Minimize button to shrink it to a button on the Taskbar.

Multimedia Properties

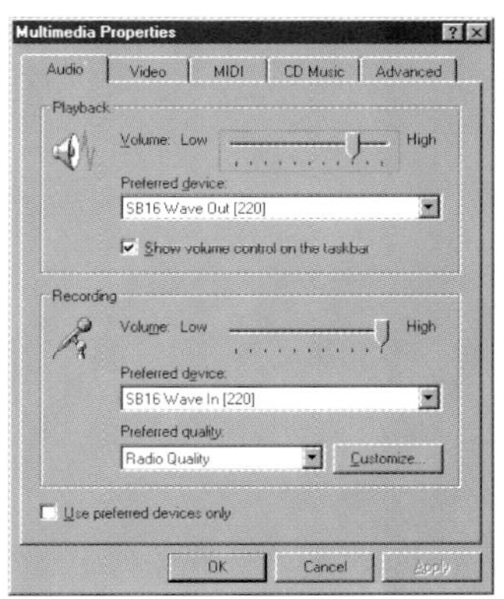

Record Levels
The Audio *flipcard is where you set your playback and recording preferences.*

You can change many of the settings that control multimedia devices from the *Multimedia Properties* dialog box. As an example, let's look at the settings used for sound recordings.

Open the *Multimedia Properties* dialog box by double-clicking on the *Multimedia* icon in the Control Panel. The dialog box opens with the *Audio* flipcard displayed by default.

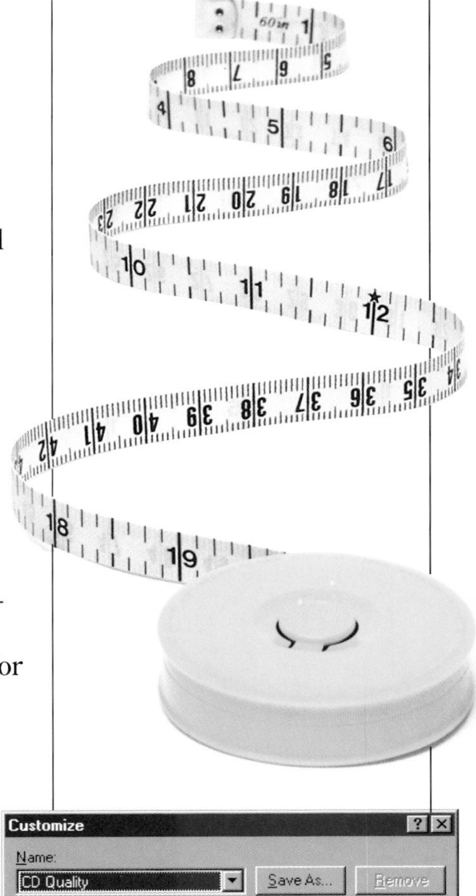

UNDERSTANDING SAMPLING RATES

Sound files recorded with a microphone are stored in the waveform format. A waveform file is produced by a process known as sampling, whereby the sound card makes thousands of measurements of the strength of the sound wave at fixed time intervals.

The number of samples recorded every second is known as the sampling rate, and the higher the sampling rate, the better the quality of the recording.

Windows 95 offers three different sampling rates for recording sound files (and options for setting your own). To see what these are, follow these steps:

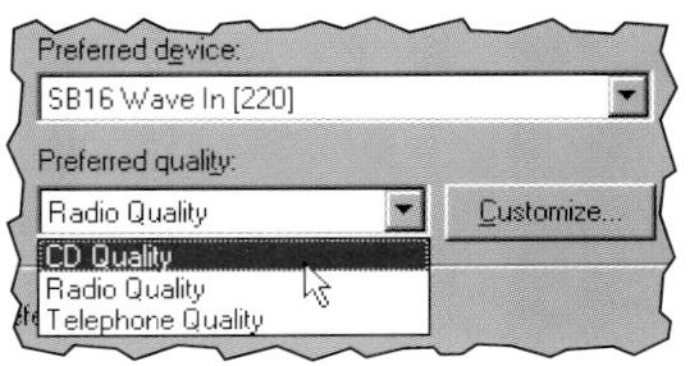

1 Click on the down arrow next to *Preferred quality* in the *Audio* flipcard and you will see three options listed: *CD Quality*, *Radio Quality*, and *Telephone Quality.*

2 To see the sampling rates associated with these options, click on *Customize* to open the *Customize* dialog box. Click the down arrow next to *Name* and choose *CD Quality*. Under *Attributes*, you can now read the sampling rate as 44.100 kHz (kilohertz). This means that a sound recorded at CD Quality will be sampled at 44,100 times per second. (*Format* indicates the *codec* used to store the file — see right.)

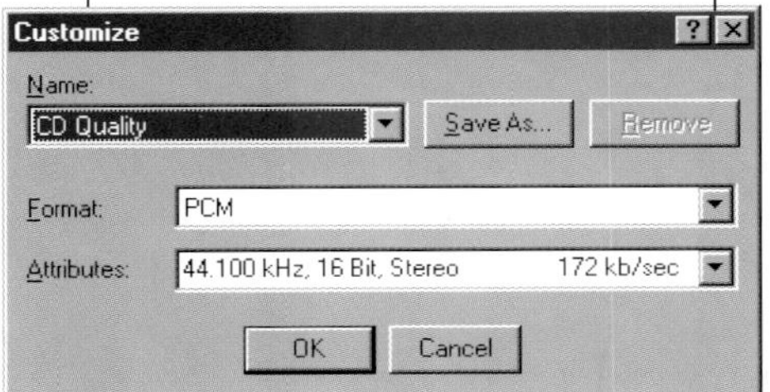

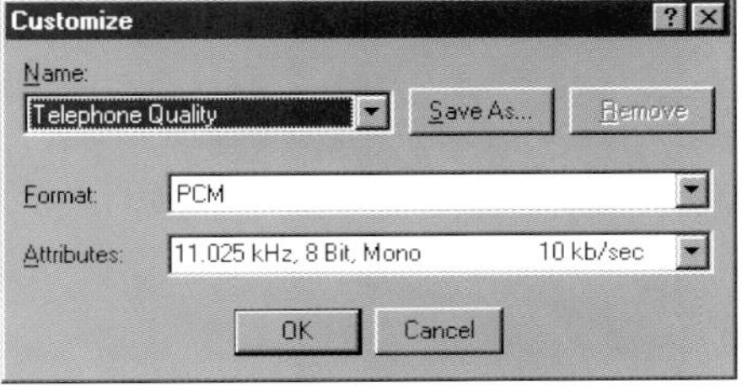

3 Now use the down arrow under *Name* to choose *Telephone Quality*, and read the sampling rate for this option — 11.025 kHz, or just over 11,000 times per second.

SIZING UP THE QUALITY

A sound file recorded at a high sampling rate will require more disk storage space than a file recorded at a lower rate. You can compare the difference between the size of CD Quality and Telephone Quality files by reading the kb/sec figure in the *Attributes* box. CD Quality files require 172 kb (kilobytes) of disk space per second of recording, while Telephone Quality only takes up 10 kb per second.

What Are Codecs?
Sound files are very demanding on disk storage space. To lighten the burden, Windows 95 includes a set of sound compression technologies (*codecs*) that can process sound files to reduce their size for storage on disk.

Using OLE to Exchange Data

YOU CAN TRANSFER OR SHARE "objects," or collections of data (such as text, pictures, or audio data), between different Windows documents using OLE (pronounced "olé"). OLE describes the process of taking data from a document created in one application, such as a picture you create in Paint, and integrating it into a document created in the same or a different application, such as a letter you write in WordPad. You can usually edit the imported data from within the compound document you have created.

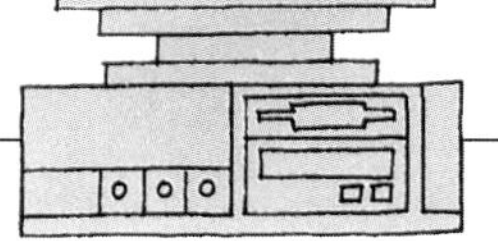

Using Paste Special
To create a link between two documents, you simply copy information from one document (the source) and paste it into another document (the destination)using the *Paste Special* command. If you then make changes to the information in the source document, Windows 95 updates the destination document.

Linking and Embedding

Linking and embedding are ways in which data from one document can be integrated into another document. Linked data remains in the source document and only a representation of it is put in the destination document. Any changes that you subsequently make to the linked data appear in both documents.

Embedded data is copied into the destination document, with no link to the source document. Changes that you subsequently make to the data in the source document are not transmitted to the destination document, and vice versa.

Try embedding a sound file into a text document. Open **Jenny Birthday Letter**, the WordPad document you created on page 45, and follow the steps below:

Embedding an Object

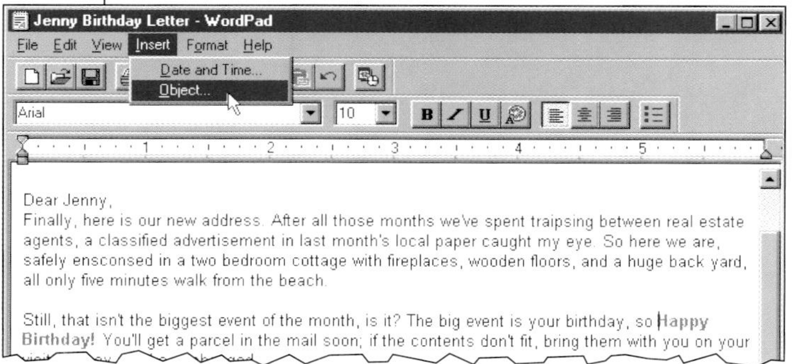

1 In the *Jenny Birthday Letter - WordPad* window**,** place the insertion point immediately before the words **Happy Birthday**. Choose *Object* from the *Insert* menu.

Missing Link!
Not all applications allow you to link data. If a linking option isn't available, the *Paste Special* command on the *Edit* menu will be unavailable.

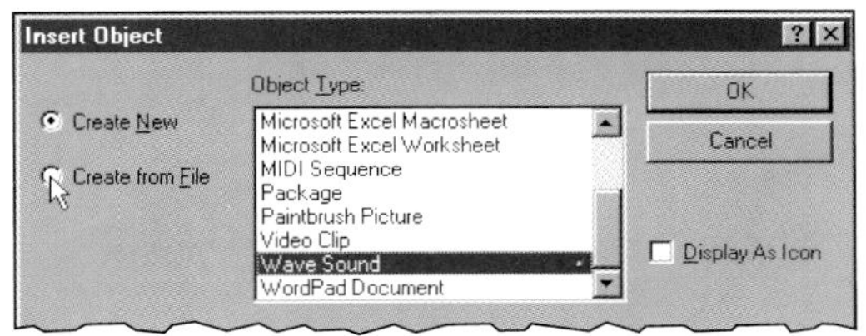

2 In the *Insert Object* dialog box, click on *Wave Sound* and check the *Create from File* option.

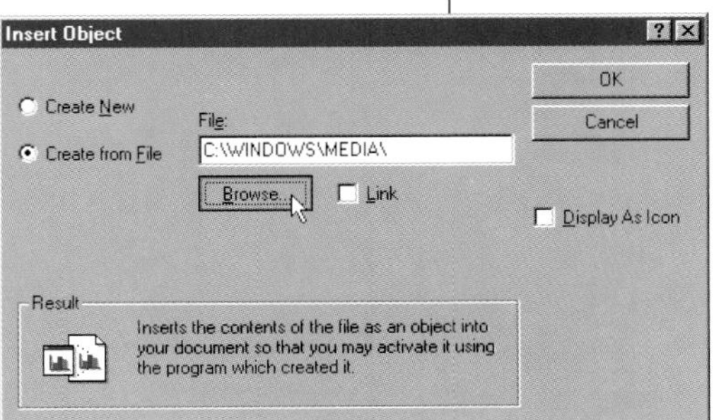

3 Click on the *Browse* button. In the *Browse* dialog box, navigate to the **Media** folder in the **Windows** folder.

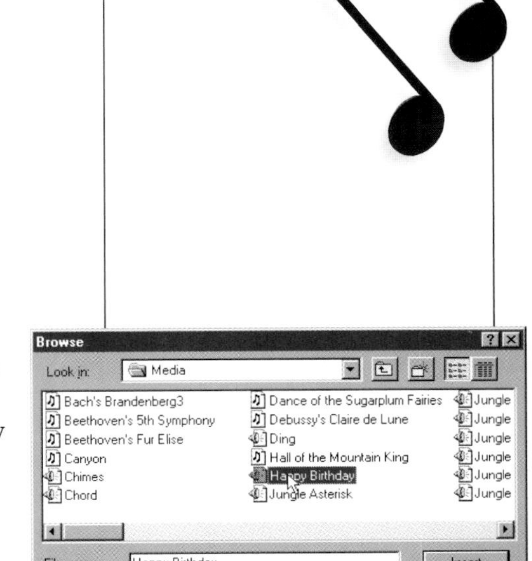

4 Click on *Happy Birthday* to select it, then click on the *Insert* button. You now return to the *Insert Object* dialog box.

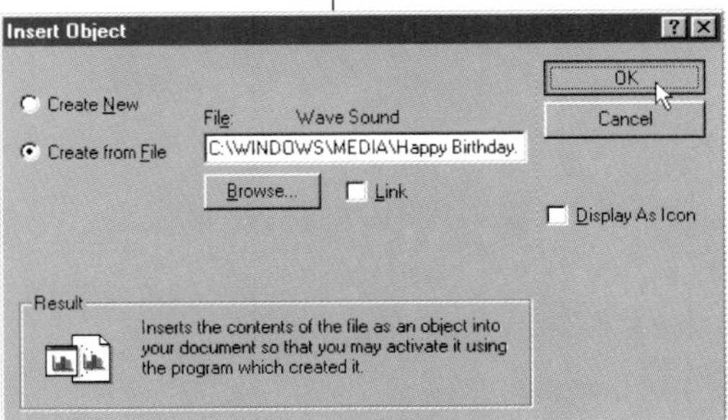

5 The name and path of the **Happy Birthday** sound file will now appear under *File: Wave Sound*. Click *OK*.

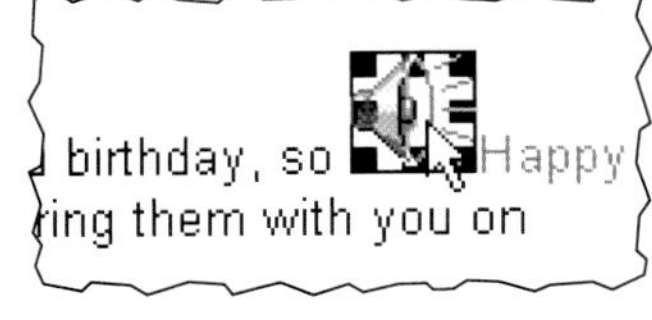

6 A sound icon appears in the WordPad document where your insertion point was placed. If you double-click on this icon, your birthday greetings will be conveyed audibly.

LINKING AN OBJECT

To link an object, simply follow the same procedure as for embedding an object described in steps 1 through 6 above; except in Step 4, check the *Link* box. Remember, if you make any changes to linked data in the destination document and save those changes, the changes will also be saved to the source document.

Want to Change?
To edit the birthday sound clip in the example, right-click on its icon. Choose *Sound Recorder Document Object* from the pop-up menu and *Edit* from the submenu. You can now make changes to the sound file in the *Sound Recorder* window. To save your changes and return to the letter, choose *Update* and then *Exit & Return to Jenny Birthday Letter* from the *File* menu.

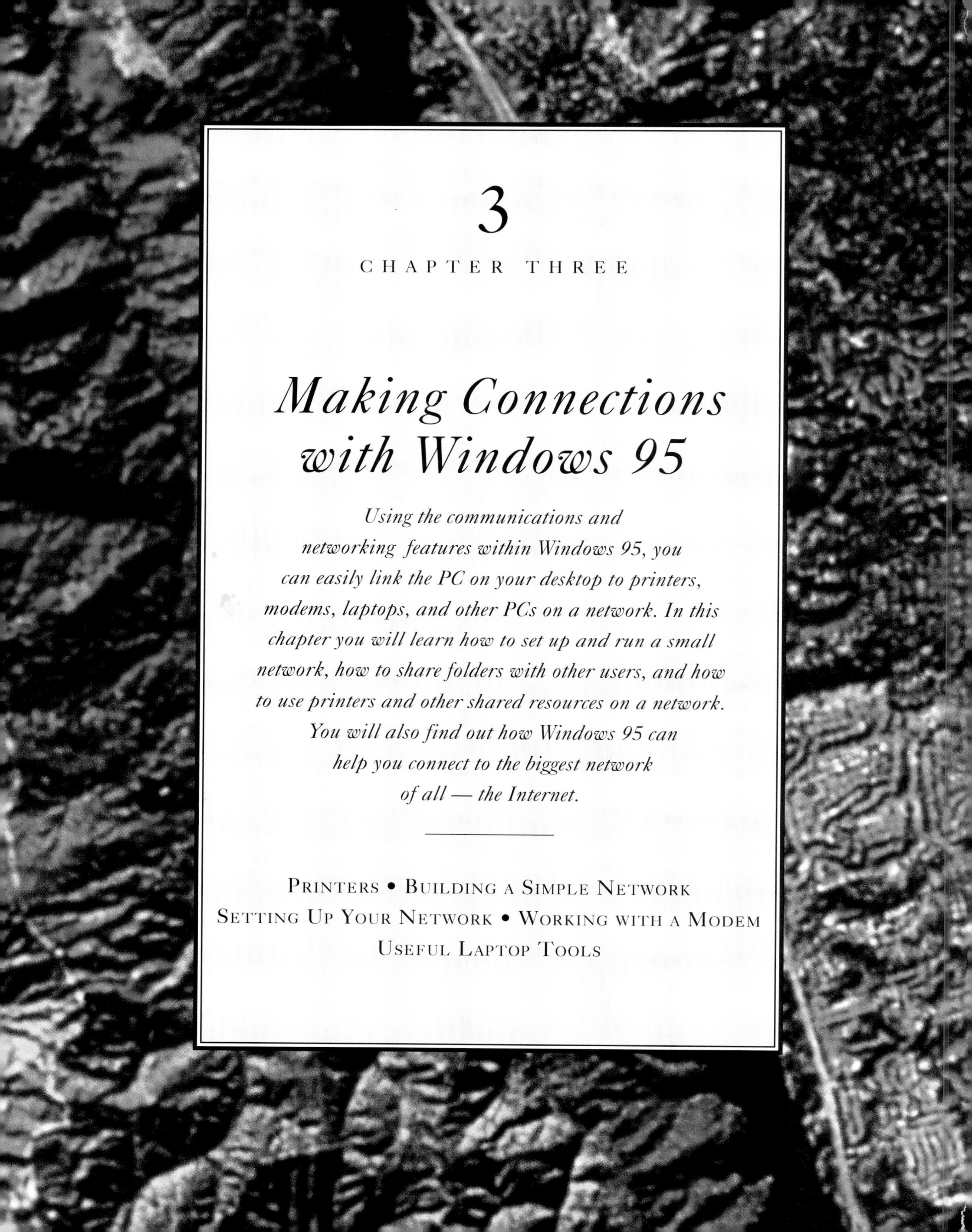

3

CHAPTER THREE

Making Connections with Windows 95

Using the communications and networking features within Windows 95, you can easily link the PC on your desktop to printers, modems, laptops, and other PCs on a network. In this chapter you will learn how to set up and run a small network, how to share folders with other users, and how to use printers and other shared resources on a network. You will also find out how Windows 95 can help you connect to the biggest network of all — the Internet.

PRINTERS • BUILDING A SIMPLE NETWORK
SETTING UP YOUR NETWORK • WORKING WITH A MODEM
USEFUL LAPTOP TOOLS

PRINTERS 72

Find out how different types of printers work, how to set up and use a local printer (attached directly to your PC) and a network printer (attached to another PC on your network), and how to change your printer's settings.

BUILDING A SIMPLE NETWORK 76

Windows 95 has a wealth of features for users of existing networks and for anyone setting up a new network. This section shows you how to build a simple three-computer network using a network adapter card, a few lengths of cable, and some connectors.

SETTING UP YOUR NETWORK 78

Learn how to set up and manage the network that you put together in the previous section, how to set up a network postoffice, and how to use Microsoft Exchange for sending, collecting, and managing all your electronic mail messages.

WORKING WITH A MODEM 88

Before you can start surfing the Internet you need a surfboard! This section shows you how to connect and set up a modem, how to send your first fax from your PC, and how to dial up bulletin boards. Finally, you get to catch a wave or two!

USEFUL LAPTOP TOOLS 96

Keeping track of which version of a file is the current version is always important — especially if you are regularly using the same programs and files on a laptop as well as on a desktop PC. This section shows you how a cable connection and a Windows 95 component called Briefcase can make life a lot simpler.

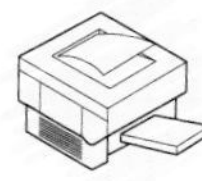

Printers

WINDOWS 95 MAKES IT VERY EASY TO PRINT documents from your PC. The Add Printer feature helps you install the software for a new printer that you have connected directly to your PC. If you have access to a network, this feature can also help you install the necessary software for accessing any shared network printer.

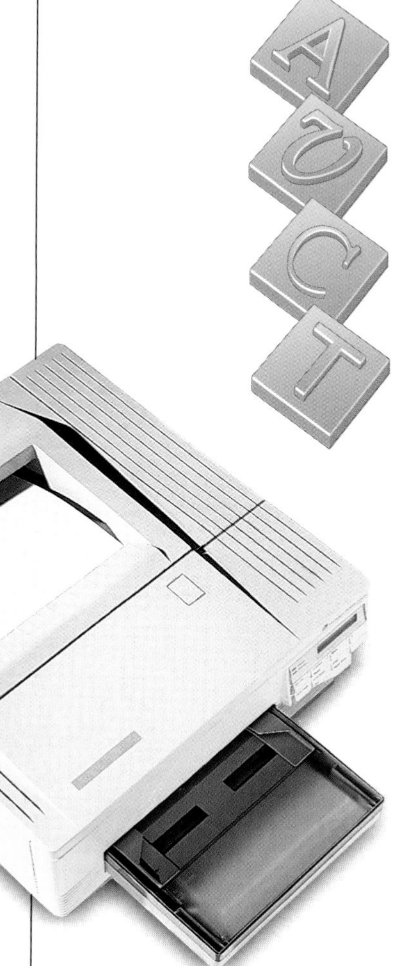

Types of Printers

Let's look at the types of printers available. All printers create patterns of dots on a sheet of paper. The smaller the dots and the greater the number of dots produced per inch, the better and clearer will be the resulting printout. There are three basic printer types that can be used with computers: laser, ink-jet, and dot-matrix printers. Laser printers provide the best quality output and are the fastest; however, they are also the most expensive. Ink-jet printers provide output whose quality is similar to that of a laser printer, but they are slower. Last, dot-matrix printers are relatively inexpensive, but the dots they produce are the largest, resulting in a lower-quality output; they are also noisier than other types of printers.

Viewing Installed Printers

If the software for a printer has already been installed, you will find an icon for the printer in the *Printers* window. To view the window for this folder, choose *Settings* from the *Start* menu and *Printers* from the submenu. In the *Printers* window, you can see the icon(s) representing your printer(s). If you can't see a printer icon in the *Printers* window, no printer has been set up for use by your PC.

The Printers Window
In this window, a network printer is represented by a printer icon placed on top of a cable, as is shown here for the Apple LaserWriter.

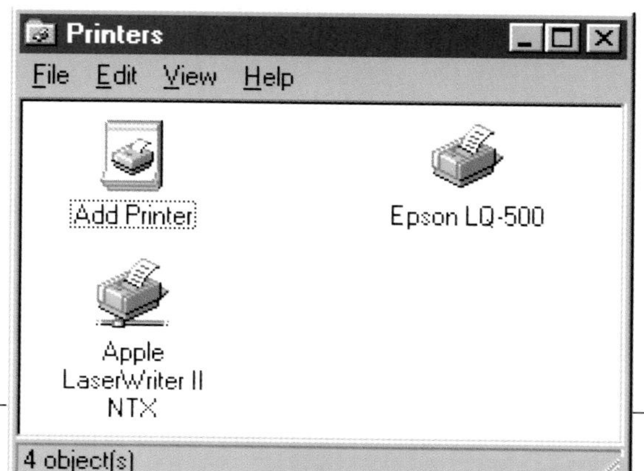

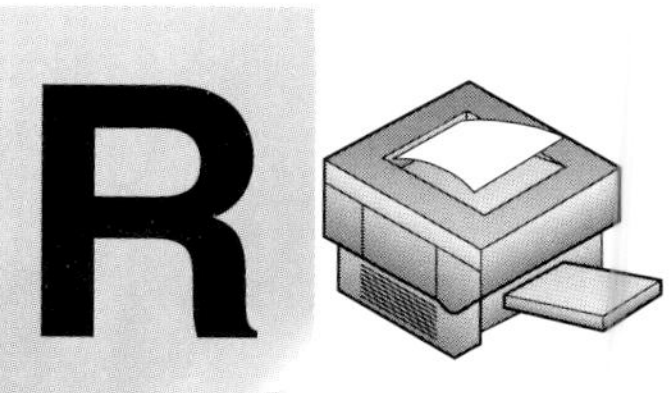

Laser Printer
A laser printer uses a laser to "draw" the entire image of a page onto an internal drum. Where the laser touches the drum, the drum becomes charged and attracts fine toner powder, which is then transferred onto a sheet of paper. Laser printers provide a high quality printout.

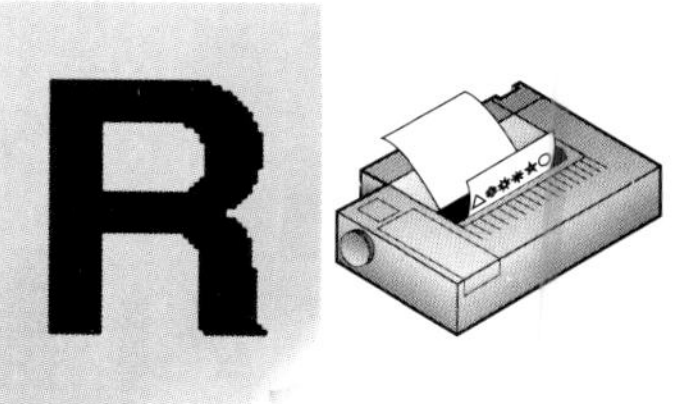

Ink-Jet Printer
An ink-jet printer creates images by depositing tiny drops of ink onto the paper. The dots, though visible, are much smaller than those of a dot-matrix printer.

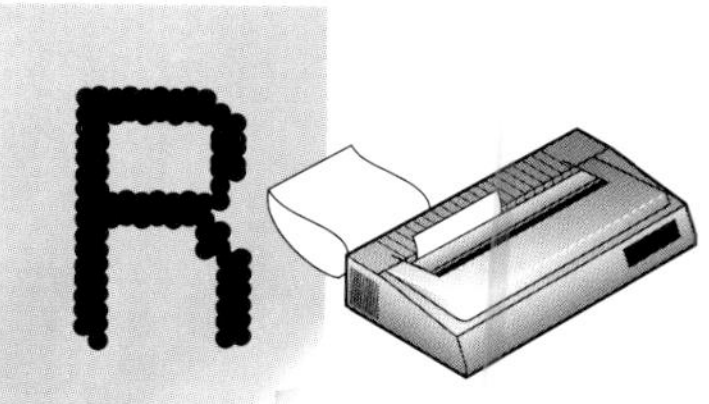

Dot-Matrix Printer
A dot-matrix printer has a vertical row of tiny metal pins that strike an inked ribbon against a sheet of paper. The individual dots that make up each character are easily seen.

Setting Up a Local Printer

To set up a local printer (one directly attached to your PC), you first need to connect the printer to the parallel port (usually labeled "LPT1") at the back of your system unit. Make sure that the printer is plugged into the electrical outlet and that it contains paper and toner. Before you can use the printer, you must also describe the printer to Windows 95 by installing a piece of software called a printer driver. To perform these tasks, you use the Add Printer wizard.

1 In the *Printers* window, double-click on the icon labeled *Add Printer*. The first *Add Printer Wizard* window appears. Click on *Next*.

2 When the window at right appears, make sure the *Local printer* option is selected and click on *Next*.

3 In the next window, under *Manufacturers*, click on the name of the company that produced your printer. If necessary, use the scroll bar to look through the list. Under *Printers*, you'll find a number of models manufactured by the company. Scroll through the list if necessary, and click on the correct model. Then click on *Next*.

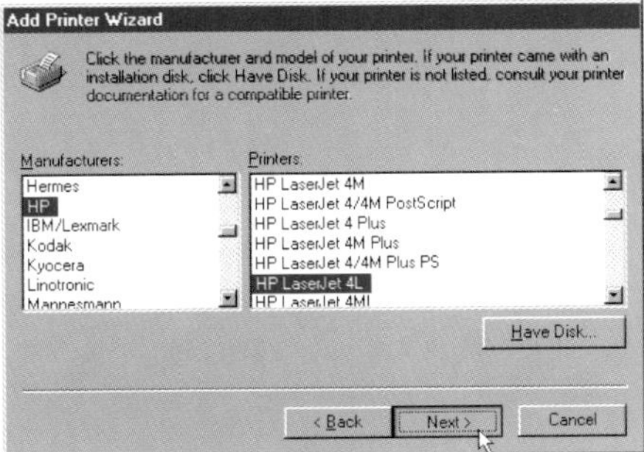

4 In the next window, make sure that the *LPT1* line is highlighted and click on *Next*.

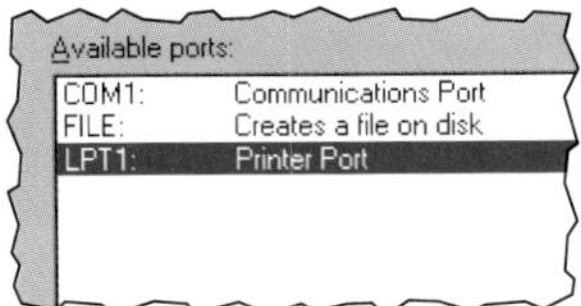

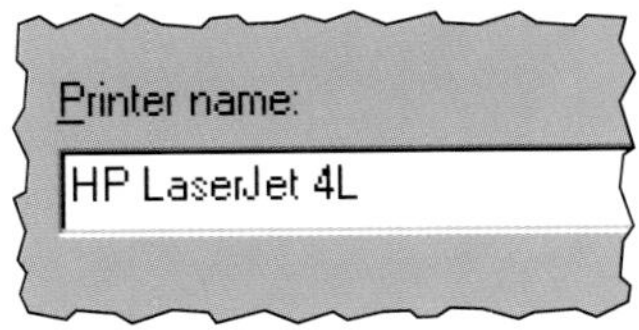

5 If you want to use a name other than the printer's brand name, you can type it under *Printer name*. Click on *Next*. In the next window, you will be asked whether you wish to print out a test page. Make sure the *Yes* option is selected, and click on *Finish*.

6 You may now be asked to insert the Windows 95 installation CD or floppy disk so that the printer driver software can be loaded. Do so and click on *OK*.

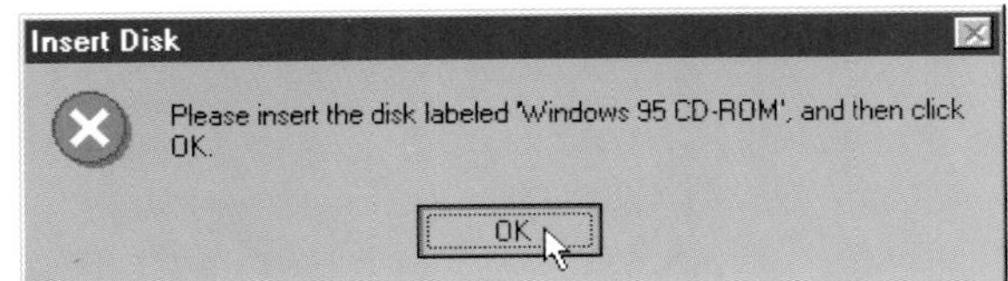

Once the printer driver is loaded, a test page should appear in the tray of your newly installed printer.

Drag and Drop to Print!

To set up a Desktop shortcut to a printer, drag the printer's icon from the *Printers* window to the Desktop, release the mouse button, and choose *Yes* in the *Shortcut* dialog box. You can then print any document by dragging the document icon from its folder window and dropping it straight onto the Desktop printer icon.

My Printer's Not Listed!

If your printer isn't listed in step 3, check the documentation that comes with your printer. It will either give you an alternative name for the printer or will provide you with a floppy disk containing a printer driver. In the latter case, insert the disk into the floppy disk drive, and then click on the *Have Disk* button.

Name It Well!
Give your network printer a useful name, such as "Laser printer beside Bill, Floor 1," or you might soon get confused if your office has several printers connected to the network.

Network Printers

If your PC is attached to a network, you can use any shared printer on the network. Because several people may want to print files at the same time, a queue is needed to temporarily hold the information about each file until the printer is free to deal with it.

Each printer on a network has a name (called the queue name) that Windows 95 needs to know before you can print to that printer. If you don't know the exact name, you can usually discover it during the connection procedure by using the *Browse for Printer* dialog box and typing in the network path where the printer queue is stored. If the network is large, you may need some help from your network administrator.

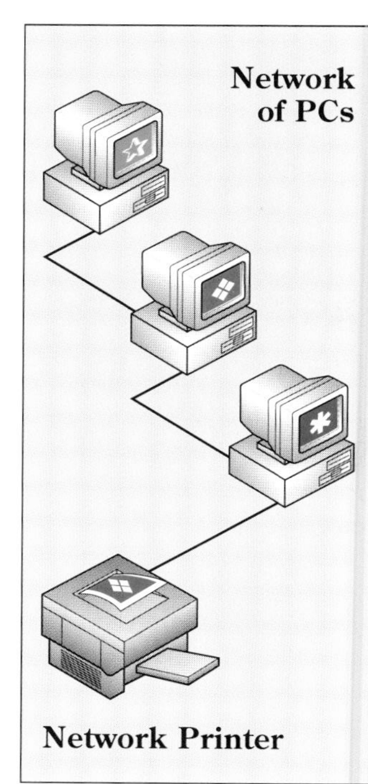

CONNECTING TO A NETWORK PRINTER

To connect to a network printer, start with the same steps as for setting up a local printer (see page 73) but in step 2, click on the *Network printer* option button before clicking on *Next*. Then do the following:

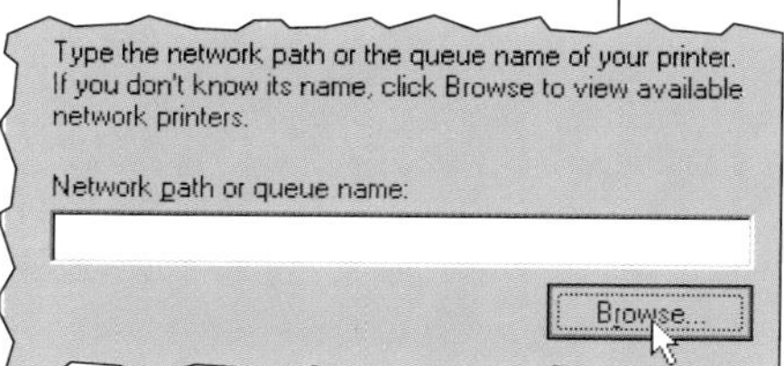

1 Type the name of the network path or queue for your printer, or, if you don't know the name, click on the *Browse* button.

2 In the *Browse for Printer* dialog box, navigate through your Network Neighborhood (see pages 86 to 87) and choose the printer to which you want to connect. Then click on *OK*.

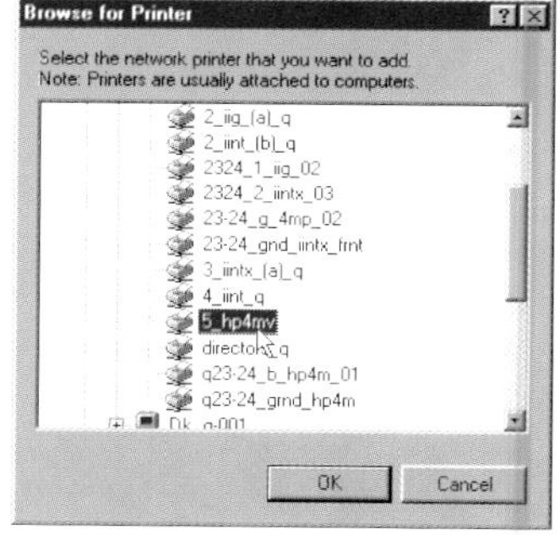

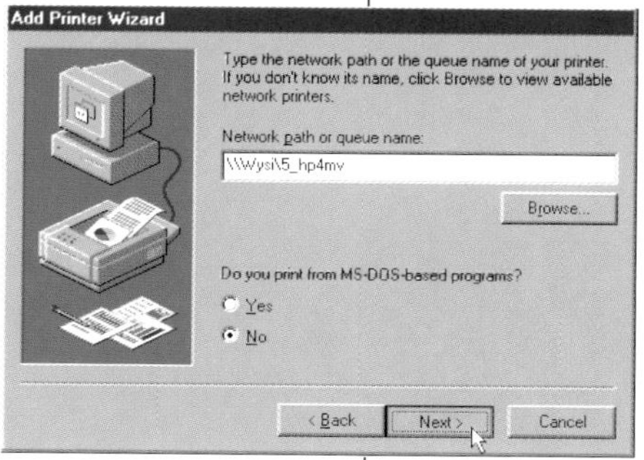

3 In the *Add Printer Wizard* window, the network path or queue name is now displayed. Click on *Next*. Now follow steps 3, 5, and 6 on page 73. Step 4 (specifying a printer port) is not needed for network printers.

Changing the Default Printer

If your PC is set up for printing to a choice of printers, at any one time one of these is the default printer. You can change the default printer by opening the **Printers** *folder, right-clicking on the printer that you want to set as the default, and choosing* Set As Default *from the pop-up menu.*

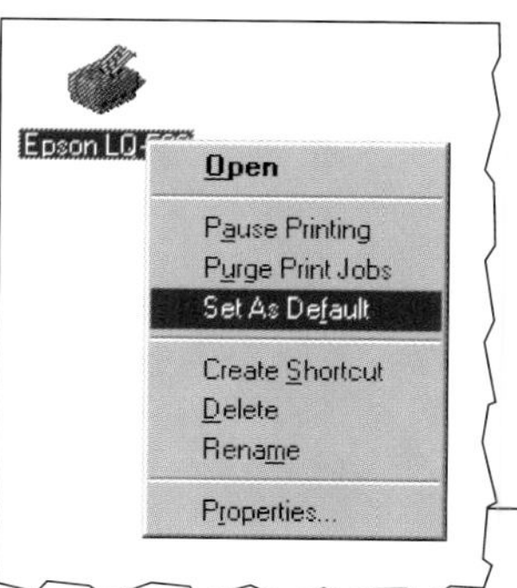

1 In the *Printers* window, double-click on the icon for the printer to which you've sent your document.

THE PRINT QUEUE

When you print a file to a network printer, it is stored temporarily in a queue. Your document will stay in the queue until the printer is ready to run it out. Even if the printer runs out of paper or is not switched on, your document won't get lost; it will be held in the queue until you refill the printer's paper tray or switch on the printer. If nothing appears for a while after you've instructed a file to print, you may get nervous and may want to view the queue to see if your document is waiting to be printed. First open the **Printers** folder and then follow the steps starting at left.

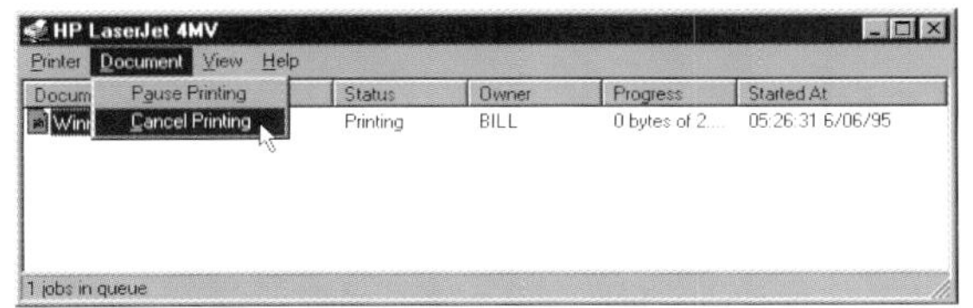

2 The print queue appears with all the print jobs listed. Each print job is described with the document's name, its status, the name of the sender, what stage of the printing process it has reached, and when it was started. If you want to cancel or pause any of your own documents that are being printed, click the document and then choose a command on the *Document* menu.

Change Your Printer Settings For One or For All Documents!
Note that when you change the printer settings using the *Properties* dialog box for a printer using Windows 95, you are changing the default settings for everything you will print with that printer. If you want to change the printer settings for just one document, you should do so from within that document.

Shortcut to Printers Folder
When any of your documents is in a print queue, a small printer icon appears at the right end of the Taskbar, next to the time display. Double-clicking on this icon opens up the Printers *window.*

Changing Printer Settings

For most of your print tasks, you can keep the same settings for the type of paper, number of fonts, and model of printer. On occasion, you might need to make changes to the default printer's settings — in case you want to print on a different size of paper or install extra fonts. For example, if you have usually printed on portrait U.S. letter size but want to switch to printing on landscape U.S. legal size, you would change the default printer settings.

1 Right-click on the printer's icon in the *Printers* window and choose *Properties* from the pop-up menu.

2 Click on the *Paper* tab, and in the *Paper* flipcard, click on the *Legal* icon from the row of paper sizes displayed.

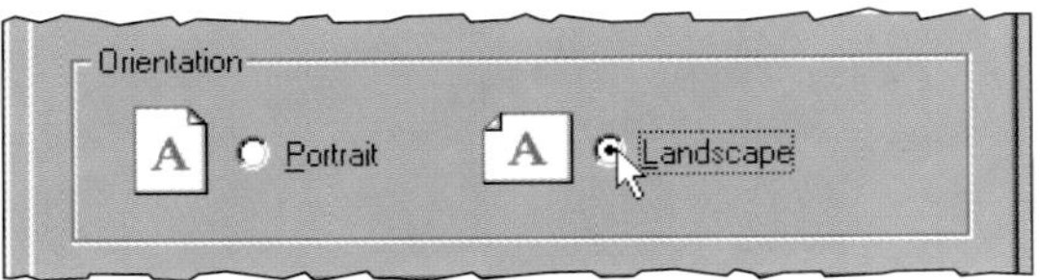

3 Click on the *Landscape* option button to select the orientation, and click on *OK*.

Network Adapter Card

Building a Simple Network

A NETWORK IS MADE UP OF TWO OR MORE COMPUTERS linked together so that users can send files and electronic mail to each other and can share folders and peripherals, such as printers. Network users can also "chat" to each other and even play network games (during approved recreation periods, of course).

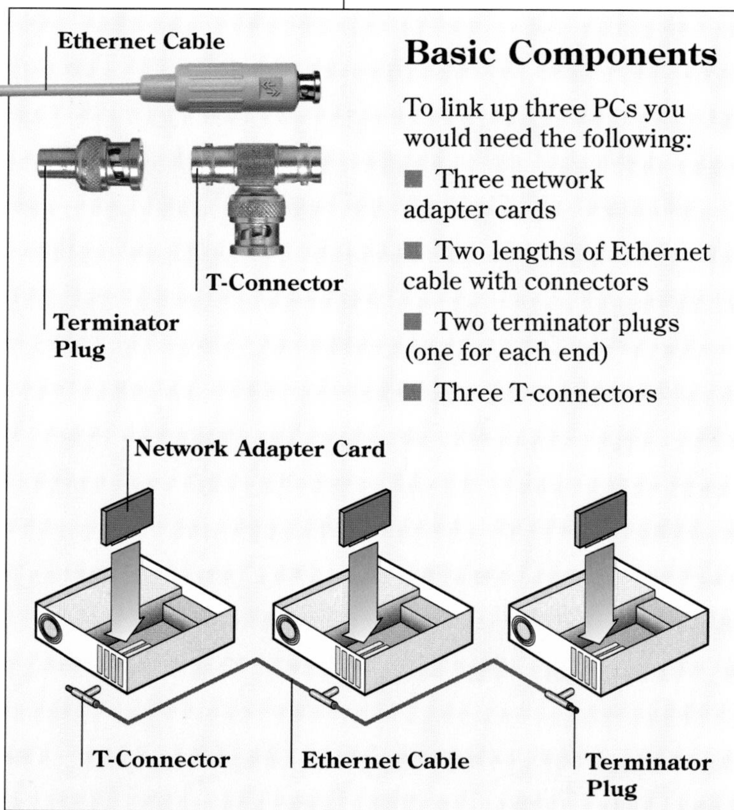

Basic Components

To link up three PCs you would need the following:

- Three network adapter cards
- Two lengths of Ethernet cable with connectors
- Two terminator plugs (one for each end)
- Three T-connectors

In this section, we describe how you can put together the simplest form of network by using network adapter cards, a few connectors, and some lengths of cable. Windows 95 has all the software you need for setting up a network. All you need is a network adapter card for each PC and network cables to connect them all together.

Collect Your Components

To set up a network, first make sure that you've got all the right parts. There are various types of network adapter cards, such as Ethernet, Token-Ring, and 10Base-2. We will use Ethernet in our example because it tends to be the least expensive and the most common in small offices.

INSTALLING A NETWORK CARD

Follow these steps to install a network card in your PC's system unit. Some precautions are needed to prevent damage to yourself and the electronics.

1 Turn off your PC and unplug the power cord and all other cables from the back of your system unit. Unscrew the chassis screws for the system unit's casing and remove the case. (Refer to the PC's manual for detailed instructions.) Before touching anything inside the system unit, ground yourself by touching a metal object outside the computer.

2 Find an appropriate expansion slot on your motherboard (consult your computer support person if you're not sure) and remove the small metal plate on the back panel. Push the network adapter card firmly into the slot and secure it with a screw to the back panel.

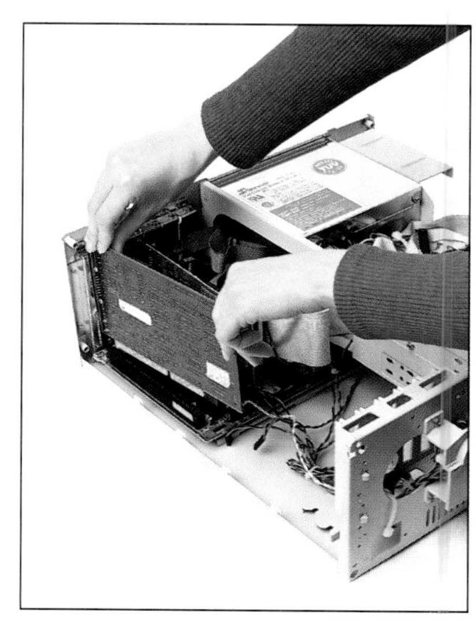

3 Replace the cover and the screws. Now take the T-connector and cable and a terminator plug if the PC is at either "end" of your network (see the "Basic Components" box on page 76), assemble them, and plug the T-connector into the back of your PC, in the socket in your network adapter card.

CONFIGURING YOUR SYSTEM FOR NETWORKING

Once you have installed the card into your PC, you need to configure it by running the Add New Hardware wizard from the Control Panel.

The example below shows how a typical network adapter card is configured, but the procedure may be slightly different on your PC, depending on the settings used by your PC and the make and model of your network adapter card. If you are unsure about how to answer any of the questions in the various dialog boxes that appear during the configuration procedure, simply click the Cancel button of the active dialog box and consult your computer support person.

Add New Hardware

1 In the Control Panel, double-click on the *Add New Hardware* icon.

2 In the *Add New Hardware Wizard* box that appears click on *Next*, make sure the *Yes (Recommended)* box is checked and click on *Next*. Click *Next* again in the next box and a progress indicator will show the progress of detection.

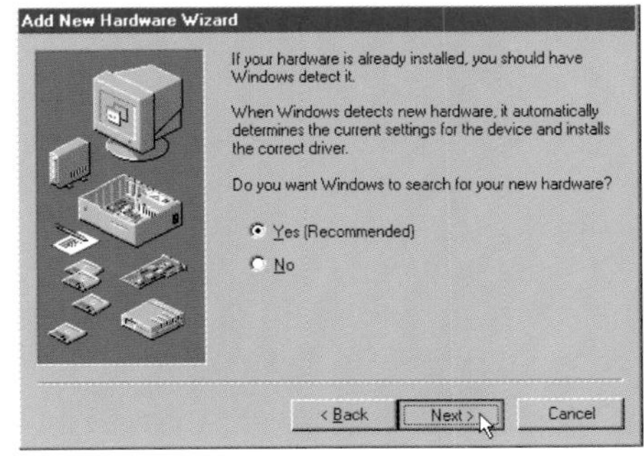

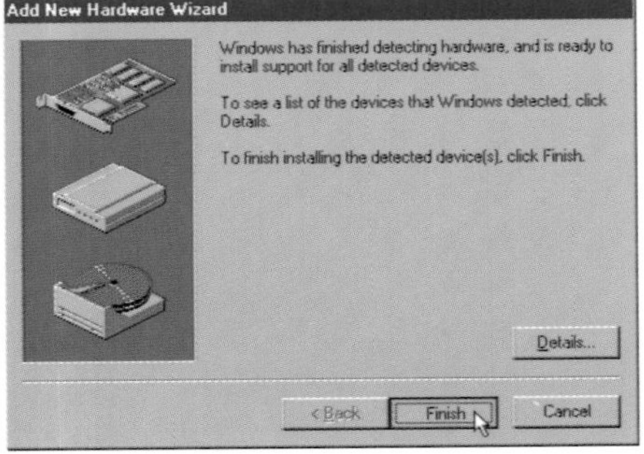

3 When detection is complete, click on the *Details* button. Windows should have detected your new hardware. If you are satisfied that all is correct, click *Finish*. In the *Network* warning box click *OK* and then in the *Identification* page of the *Network* dialog box supply the necessary details for your computer name, workgroup, and computer description in the appropriate boxes. (If you're not sure what a workgroup is, see the tip box on page 86). Click *Close* when you are ready.

4 In the *System Settings Change* box click *Yes* to restart your computer to finish setting up your hardware.

Be Careful in There!

Inside your PC are a number of electronic components that are sensitive to static electricity. Similarly, a network card could be damaged by a discharge of static electricity. The object of grounding yourself before you pick up your network card or start delving inside your PC is to discharge any static that may have built up on you.

Setting Up Your Network

BEFORE YOU CAN SET UP A NETWORK YOU WILL NEED TO make sure that the Windows 95 component called Microsoft Exchange is installed on your system. (See page 80 for a description of Microsoft Exchange.) To install this component, double-click on *Add/Remove Programs* in the Control Panel, access the *Windows Setup* flipcard, make sure the *Microsoft Exchange* box is checked, and click *OK*.

If you have checked the box, Windows prompts you for your Windows 95 installation disks or CD. Follow any further instructions that appear onscreen. When the Inbox Setup wizard appears, asking whether you have used Microsoft Exchange before, click *Cancel* for now and then click on *Yes* in the *Microsoft Exchange Setup Wizard* dialog box that pops up.

Spot the Difference?
If you have just installed the Microsoft Exchange software on your PC you will notice a few changes to the appearance of your Desktop. For example, two new icons — *Microsoft Mail Postoffice* and *Mail and Fax* — appear in the Control Panel, *Microsoft Exchange* appears on the *Programs* menu available via the *Start* menu, and the *Send To* submenu that you see when you right-click on a file now includes *Mail recipient* as an option.

Setting Up the Postoffice

You will return to the Inbox Setup wizard shortly, but first you need to set up a network postoffice. Any Windows 95 network needs an administrator and a network postoffice. The administrator assigns folders and passwords for all users and generally looks after the running of the postoffice, which is at the heart of a Windows 95 network. In this example, we will set up a network for three users called Bill, Anna, and Dave. (You will obviously substitute these names as appropriate.) Throughout the next few pages you are going to be Bill, the network administrator.

First you need to decide where you want to install the network postoffice. In this example you will install it on your (Bill's) PC.

How to Set Up the Postoffice

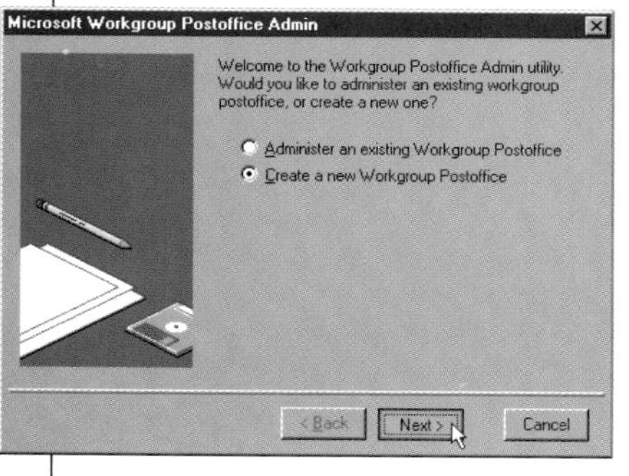

1 Double-click on *Microsoft Mail Postoffice* in the Control Panel. In the dialog box that appears, click on the button for *Create a new Workgroup Postoffice* and click *Next*.

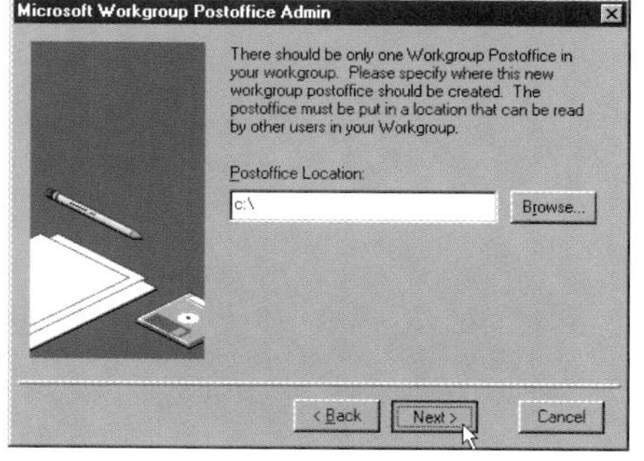

2 Type the location where you want the postoffice folder to be created. Type **c:** (indicating that the folder will be a main folder on the PC's hard disk) and click *Next*. The name for your postoffice folder (**C:\wgpo0000**) will appear in a "grayed out" box. Click on *Next*.

3 In the next box, enter **Bill** in the *Name* and *Mailbox* boxes, and use the default password **(PASSWORD)** for now. Fill in the other details as required and click on *OK*. A window called *Mail* pops up to confirm this action. Click on *OK*.

You must now make your postoffice folder a shared folder so that other users on the network can access it.

SHARING THE POSTOFFICE FOLDER

You won't be able to share any folders unless the *File and Print Sharing* option in Windows 95 is active. You can easily check its status by right-clicking on any folder in the window for your C drive. If *Sharing* doesn't appear on the menu, double-click on the *Network* icon in the Control Panel and, in the *Configuration* flipcard, click on the *File and Print Sharing* button. Check both the boxes in the *File and Print Sharing* dialog box and click *OK*. Then click *OK* in the *Network* dialog box.

Follow the instructions that appear onscreen and restart your PC when prompted. Now locate your postoffice folder in the C window and make it a shared folder by right-clicking on the icon and selecting *Sharing* from the list. In the *Sharing* tab of the postoffice *Properties* dialog box, check the box next to *Shared As* and then click on the *Add* button. In the *Add Users* dialog box, select *The World* to share your folder with everyone who has access to your network, and click on the *Full Access* button. Then click on *OK*, and in the postoffice *Properties* dialog box click on *OK* again. The icon will now change to indicate that the folder is now a shared folder.

MANAGING THE POSTOFFICE

Having set up the postoffice and the details for your own account, you need to do the same for all the other users who will be on the network. From your (Bill's) PC, follow the steps starting at left:

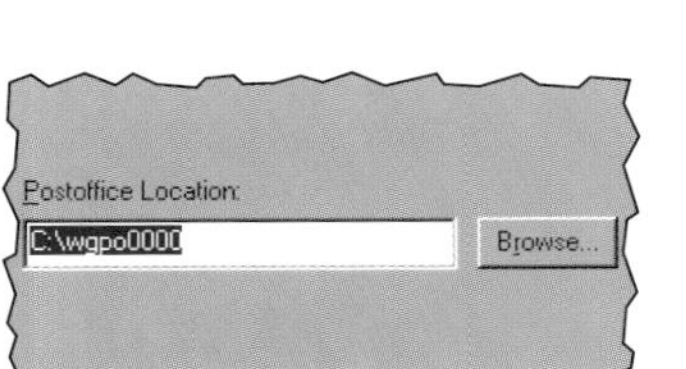

1 Double-click on the *Microsoft Mail Postoffice* icon in the Control Panel. In the *Microsoft Workgroup Postoffice Admin* dialog box, check the *Administer an existing Workgroup Postoffice* box and click on *Next*. The location of your postoffice should appear. Click on *Next*.

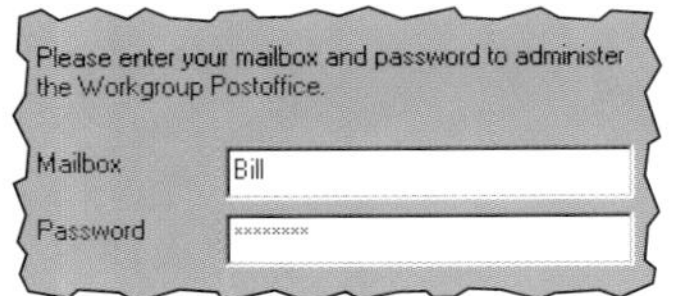

2 Type **Bill** for the name of your mailbox and **PASSWORD** for the password. You will see only an asterisk for each character you type. Click on *Next*.

3 In the *Postoffice Manager* dialog box, click on *Add User*.

4 In the *Add User* box, type the details for the other users who will be on your network. In this case, type **Anna** in the boxes for *Name* and *Mailbox* and accept **PASSWORD** for *Password*. Follow the same procedure to set up Dave. Then click *OK*. Finally, in the *Postoffice Manager* dialog box, click on *Close*.

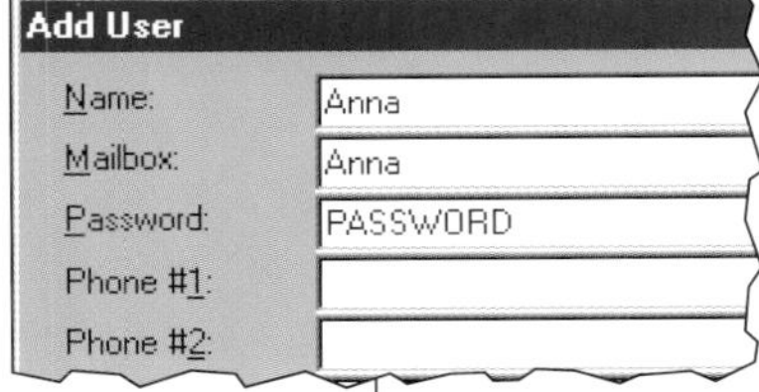

Microsoft Exchange

Now that you have set up the network postoffice and assigned mail boxes and passwords to the other users on your network, you are ready to set up Microsoft Exchange.

Microsoft Exchange acts as the communications center for your PC. It allows you to use the network postoffice to send and collect your electronic mail, faxes, and messages from the Internet. It also helps you manage all your mail messages by storing them automatically in several folders. There are initially four folders (see the box at the bottom of page 81).

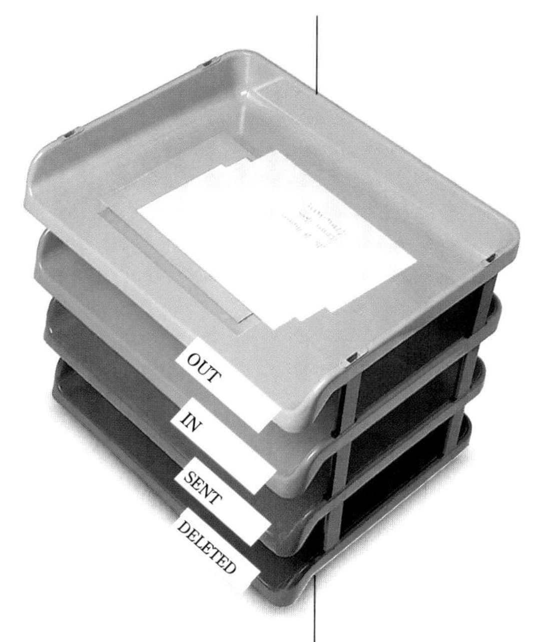

Setting Up Microsoft Exchange for the First Time

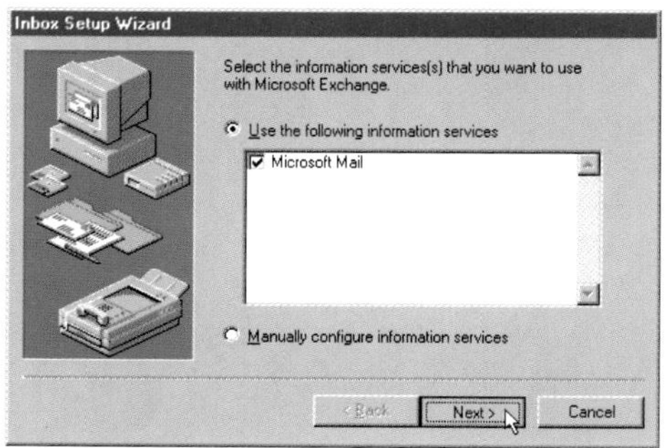

1 Double-click on the *Inbox* icon on your Desktop. In the first *Inbox Setup Wizard* box, check the *Use the following information services* button and check the box next to the *Microsoft Mail* option. Click *Next*.

2 In the next box, the path for your postoffice (**c:\wgpo0000**) should appear. (If it doesn't, click *Browse*, locate the folder in the *Browse for Postoffice* dialog box, and then click *OK* to return to the Inbox Setup wizard.) When you are ready to continue, click *Next*.

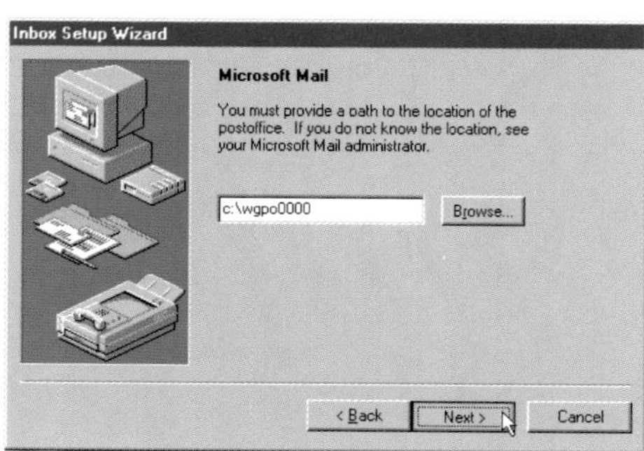

3 In the next dialog box, choose your name (i.e., **Bill**) from the list and click *Next*. Type your password when prompted and click *Next*.

Password Protect Your Mailbox!

To prevent others from reading your e-mail, do the following. Right-click on the *Inbox* icon on your Desktop and choose *Properties*. In the *MS Exchange Settings Properties* dialog box, choose *Microsoft Mail* and click on *Properties*. Then uncheck the *When logging on, automatically enter password* box in the *Logon* page of the *Microsoft Mail* dialog box and click *OK*. You'll now need to type your password every time you start Microsoft Exchange.

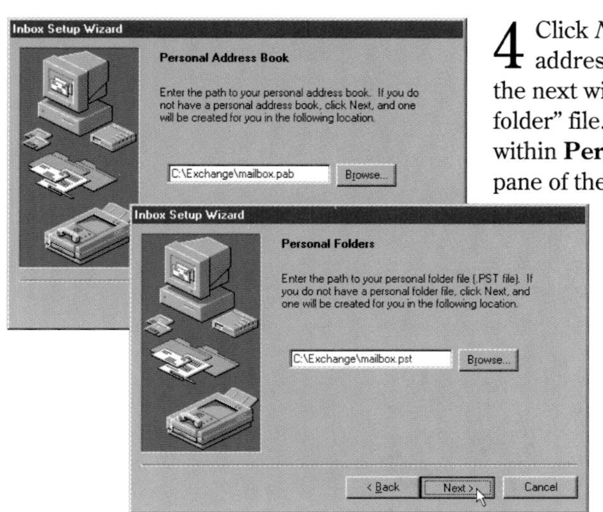

4 Click *Next* to create a "personal address book" and do the same in the next window to create a "personal folder" file. You will see these folders within **Personal folder** in the left-hand pane of the Microsoft Exchange window.

5 In the next box, choose one of the available options and click *Next.* (If you choose *Do not add Inbox to the StartUp group* you can always start Microsoft Exchange at any time by double-clicking the *Inbox* icon on your desktop.)

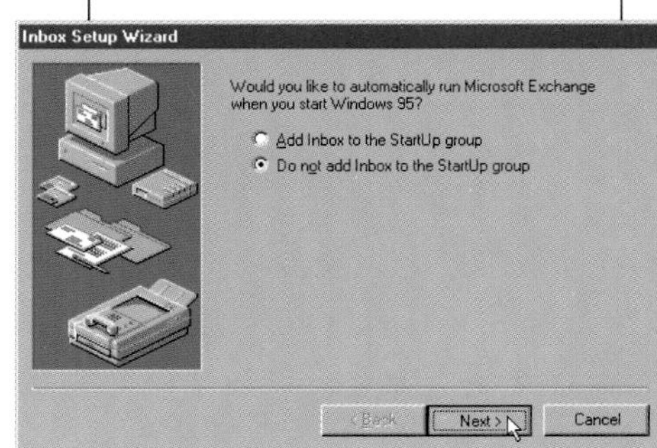

6 The final I*nbox Setup Wizard* box appears, telling you that Microsoft Exchange is now ready to use. Click *Finish.*

7 After a few seconds, Microsoft Exchange opens automatically. To read the message of welcome in your Inbox simply double-click it.

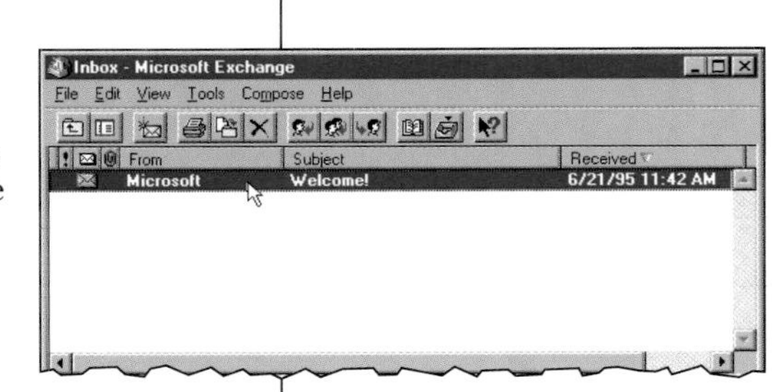

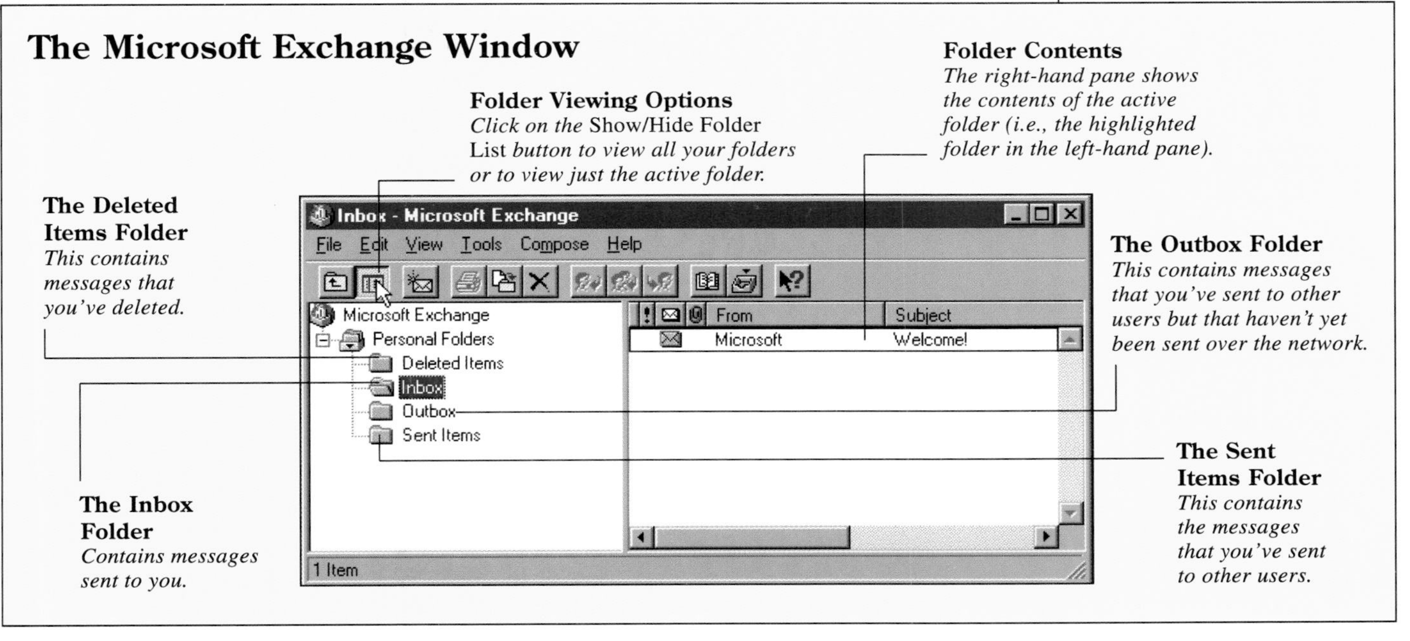

The Microsoft Exchange Window

Folder Viewing Options
Click on the Show/Hide Folder List *button to view all your folders or to view just the active folder.*

Folder Contents
The right-hand pane shows the contents of the active folder (i.e., the highlighted folder in the left-hand pane).

The Deleted Items Folder
This contains messages that you've deleted.

The Outbox Folder
This contains messages that you've sent to other users but that haven't yet been sent over the network.

The Inbox Folder
Contains messages sent to you.

The Sent Items Folder
This contains the messages that you've sent to other users.

HOW TO CONNECT OTHER USERS TO THE NETWORK

Your next task as network administrator is to set up Microsoft Exchange on each PC on the network. In the following example you will set up Microsoft Exchange on Anna's PC. First check that the Microsoft Exchange Windows 95 component is installed (see the instructions at the top of page 78) and that "file and print sharing" is set up on Anna's PC (see the instructions under "Sharing the Postoffice Folder" on page 79; then follow the steps starting at left.

How Many Address Books Do I Need?
Although there's normally only one Public Address List on a network, each user can have his or her own personal address book that contains private fax numbers or Internet addresses for users that are your personal contacts. If an address is in your personal Address Book but not in the Public Address List, only you can send the person a message.

How to Set Up Microsoft Exchange on Anna's PC

1 Double-click on the *Inbox* icon on Anna's PC. When the Inbox Setup wizard appears, choose *Use the following information services* and check the box next to the *Microsoft Mail* option. Click *Next.*

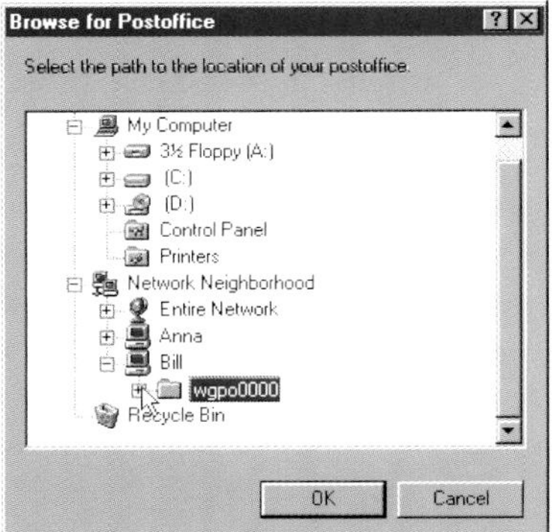

2 In the *Browse for Postoffice* dialog box, navigate to the **wgpo0000** folder — you will find it in the folder called **Bill** in the **Network Neighborhood** folder.

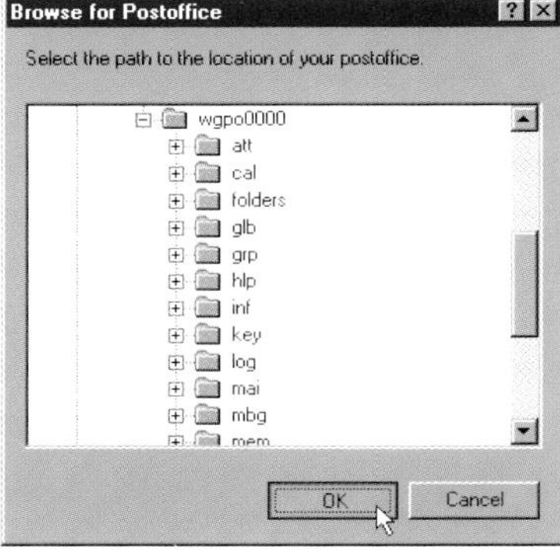

3 Click on the **wgpo0000** folder, then click *OK.*

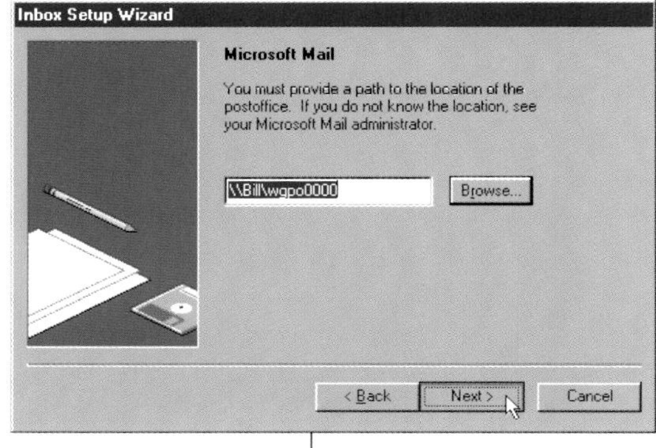

4 The path for the network postoffice (on Bill's PC) now appears. Click *Next.*

Now simply follow steps 3 through 7 on pages 80 and 81, choosing the name "Anna" instead of "Bill" in step 3, to finish setting up Microsoft Exchange on Anna's PC. You now need to repeat this procedure for Dave's PC (in other words, for every other PC and user that will be connected to the network). Remember, you need to tell users their passwords (in this example we simply used the default "PASSWORD") to allow them to access their mailboxes.

How to Send Electronic Mail

Now that you have finished setting up Microsoft Exchange on your network, you can begin to use it. One of the best features of a network is that you can send electronic mail (e-mail) messages to your colleagues. E-mail can be a simple "Are you free for lunch?" message or a message with a data file or files embedded within it. (See pages 68 and 69 for information on how to link and embed files).

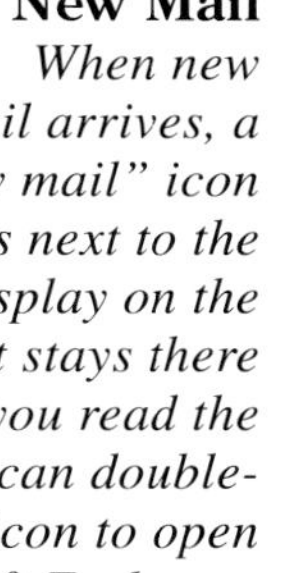

Reading New Mail

When new mail arrives, a "new mail" icon appears next to the time display on the Taskbar. It stays there until you read the message. You can double-click on this icon to open the Microsoft Exchange window. In the right-hand pane of the Microsoft Exchange - Inbox *window, the subject of any new mail message will appear in bold until you have read it.*

How to Send a Mail Message

1 Click the *Start* button and choose *Microsoft Exchange* from the *Programs* menu.

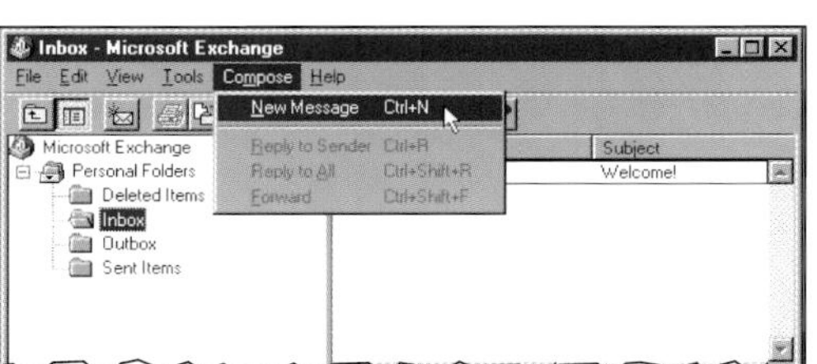

2 From the *Microsoft Exchange* window, choose *New Message* from the *Compose* menu.

3 Type the name of the person you want to send your message to in the *To* box and a brief description of the message in the *Subject* box. Click in the large white space of the screen and type your message.

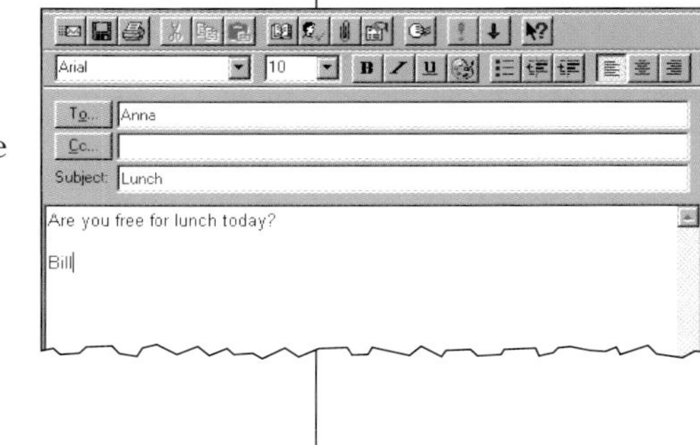

4 To send the message, click on the Send button on the toolbar. A "Sending" message will appear at the bottom of the window.

5 Check in the **Sent Items** folder. A record of the message to Anna should appear in the right-hand pane. Simply double-click on the message to see its contents.

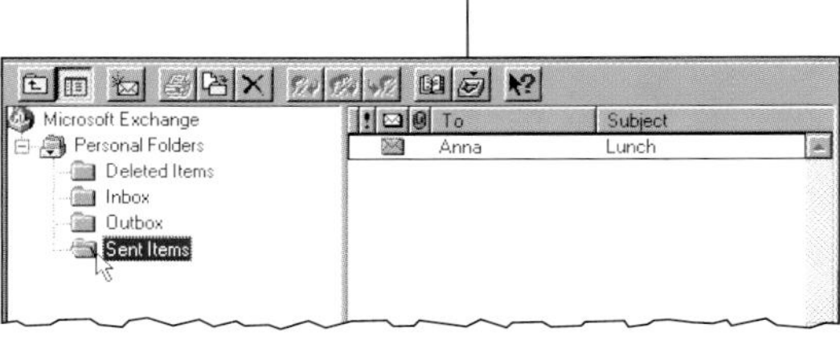

Slow Delivery?
If your mail seems to take too long to arrive, access the *Delivery* flipcard of the *Microsoft Mail* dialog box. In this flipcard you can adjust how often Windows 95 checks the postoffice for your new mail. To access the *Microsoft Mail* dialog box, choose *Options* from the *Tools* menu in the *Microsoft Exchange* window, click on the *Services* tab in the next dialog box, highlight *Microsoft Mail* and then click on the *Properties* button.

Replying to Mail Messages

You may want to reply to an e-mail message by sending the original message back to the sender as well as your reply. This can be helpful for the recipient, who may have a very busy Inbox. You can make an immediate reply to an e-mail message from the same window in which you are reading it by choosing *Reply to Sender* from the *Compose* menu, or you can reply later by following the steps below:

1 In the *Inbox - Microsoft Exchange* window, select the message you want to reply to from the list and click on the Reply to Sender button as shown at right. The message appears in a window that has the same title as the original message but with the abbreviation "RE:" in front of it.

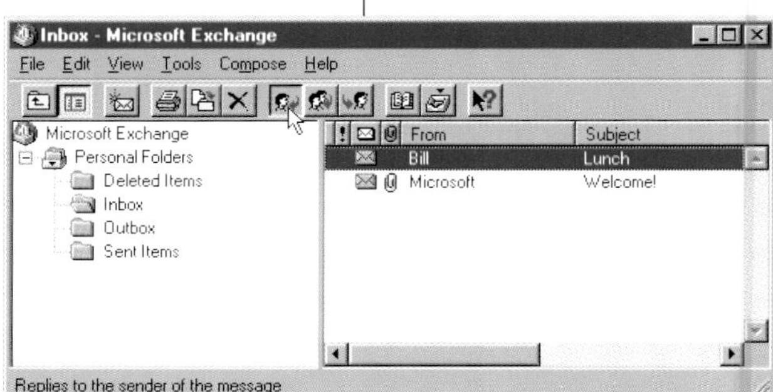

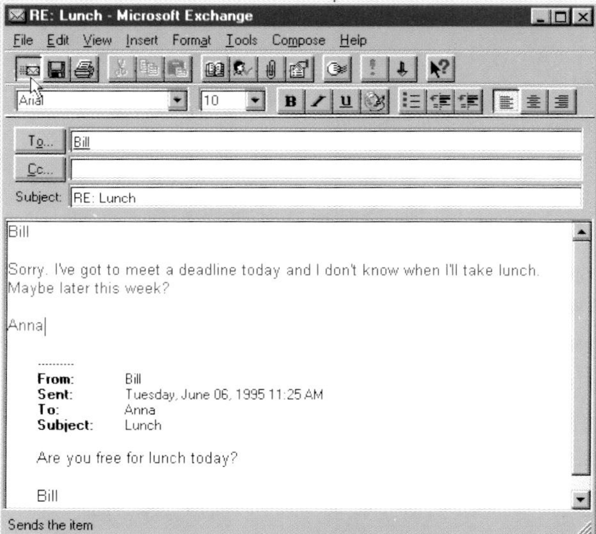

2 Type your reply. This will appear in a different color than the original message. Click the Send button when you have finished.

Customizing Your Toolbar

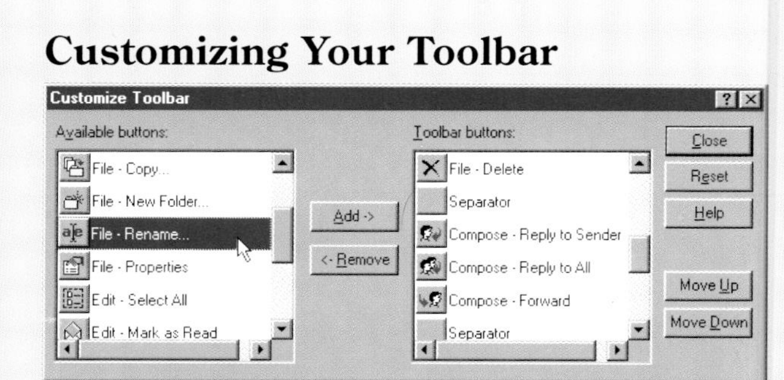

You can customize your toolbar in Microsoft Exchange by adding, removing, or rearranging buttons. Choose *Customize toolbar* from the *Tools* menu of the *Microsoft Exchange* window to display the *Customize Toolbar* dialog box. To add a new button you simply select the relevant icon in the left-hand pane, then click *Add*. The tool appears in the right-hand pane and, after you have clicked *Close*, it appears on the toolbar.

How Windows 95 Handles Electronic Mail

With Microsoft Exchange, you can send electronic mail to another user on your network or to someone on a distant network via a modem.

The Windows 95 network postoffice works in many ways like a "real" post office. For example, when Bill sends a message to Dave, it first goes to the postoffice. Here it is "sorted" (that is, the name and address on the message are checked for accuracy against the postoffice Address List that the postoffice administrator maintains and against Bill's personal Address Book). The message is then sent from the postoffice to the Inbox on Dave's PC.

Microsoft Exchange will talk to the central postoffice every few minutes to check for new mail and to send any messages. You can adjust how often Microsoft Exchange checks for incoming mail by following the instructions in the "Slow Delivery?" box on page 84.

Make Sure They Get the Message!
If you want to know that the receiver has actually read your message, you ask Microsoft Exchange to send you a receipt when the message has been read. To use this feature, click on the Read Receipt button (to the left of the ! button) before you send the message.

Insert File
Click this button to send a text or image file with the current message.

The To Field
Use the To *field to identify who the message is addressed to; you can list several users. Each network user has a unique name that identifies him or her and the PCs at which he or she works.*

Read Receipt
Click this to receive confirmation that the message has been read by the recipient.

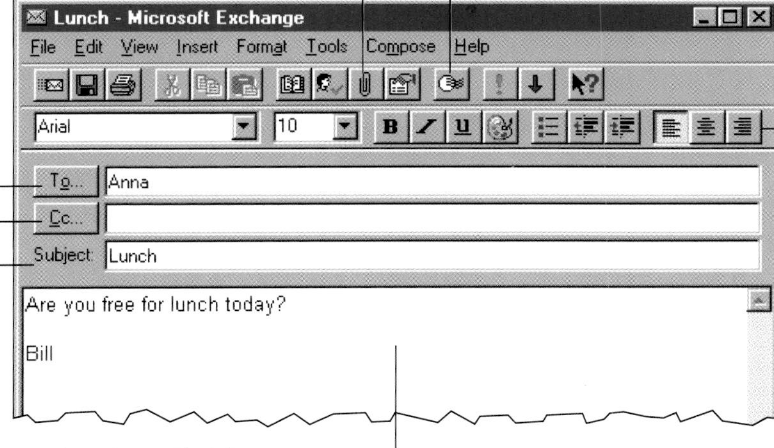

The Formatting Toolbar
Click the icons to access various formatting tools for your message text. If this toolbar does not appear, simply choose it from the View *menu.*

The Cc Field
The Cc *field lets you add the name of any user you wish to send a copy of the message to.*

The Subject Field
In the Subject *field, you can add a short description of the message.*

The Message Area
In the message area you type the message itself. You can include sound files or graphic images and format the message using the tools in the Formatting Toolbar.

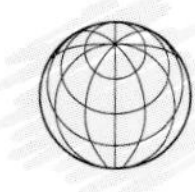

What Is a Workgroup?
A workgroup is a subset of a network: it's a convenient way of naming a group of users in a particular room or with a certain job. A network can have just one workgroup or many small workgroups. Each workgroup might have its own printer and its own electronic mail postoffice. Anyone in a workgroup can access shared files or send mail messages to any other user on the network but, for convenience, each user belongs to a particular workgroup.

Using Network Neighborhood

Using the **Network Neighborhood** folder is the best way to navigate around in your network; it's rather like Windows Explorer, but it shows you all the other PCs and printers connected to the network.

To start Network Neighborhood, double-click on its icon on the Desktop. You'll now see a window with an icon for every PC in your workgroup and an icon labeled *Entire Network*. If you click on the *Entire Network* icon you'll see a list of all the computers on the network, not just those in your workgroup.

To explore what you can share on another PC in the network, double-click on its icon and you'll see a list of shared folders and icons that are available to you.

If you want to see a hierarchical view of the network to help you work out which resource is connected to which PC, click on the *Entire Network* icon and choose the *Explore* menu option from the *File* menu.

HOW TO SHARE A FOLDER

Before you can share a folder, you must first make sure that the "File and Print sharing" option is enabled for your PC. See the first two paragraphs on page 79.

1 Create a new folder called **Freeforall** on Bill's PC. Right-click on the **Freeforall** folder icon and choose *Sharing*.

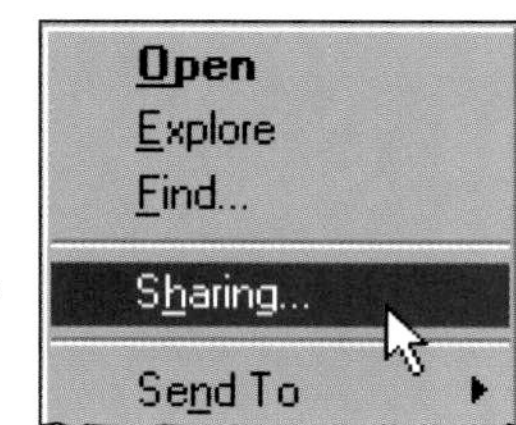

Read-Only
Allows other users to open and copy information but not to modify or remove files.

Full Access
Allows other users to change, add, or remove files.

Depends on Password
Allows users different types of access.

Freeforall Properties
General | Sharing
Not Shared
Shared As:
Share Name: FREEFORALL
Comment:
Access Type:
Read-Only
Full
Depends on Password

2 In the *Freeforall Properties* dialog box, click on the *Shared As* option and FREEFORALL appears in the *Share Name* box. Check the *Full* option under *Access Type*, and click *OK* to save the changes.

3 The folder's icon will now include a hand to show that the folder is shareable.

Make the Most of Sharing
One of the main advantages of installing a network is that you can share the resources of one PC with other users. For example, if your PC has a particularly large hard disk, you could create a shared folder that could be used by any other user who is running short of disk space. Similarly, if you have a color or high-speed printer connected to your PC, you can share it with other users on the network.

The Network Neighborhood Window

In this example, Bill's *Network Neighborhood* window shows all the PCs containing shared folders and printers that he can currently access. By clicking on any icon, Bill will usually be able to open that folder on his desktop and access the files in that folder. He can copy files to and from that folder as if it were a folder on his own PC. If you are wondering what has happened to Dave's PC, it doesn't appear because it hasn't been switched on! Only active PCs appear in the *Network Neighborhood* window. Sometimes it will not be possible for Bill to use a shared folder or printer without taking some additional steps, but Windows 95 will normally give clear instructions on what to do. Sometimes you may need to type in a password, for example, before you can access a shared folder. Also, when you first try to print to a network printer, Windows 95 may prompt you to install the relevant drivers on your own PC by asking you to insert a Windows 95 installation CD or floppy disks.

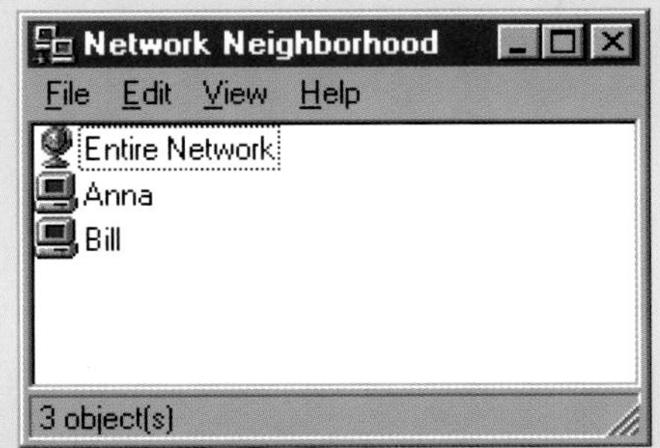

What Can I Share?
Click on any icon in the Network Neighborhood *window to explore shared folders and resources.*

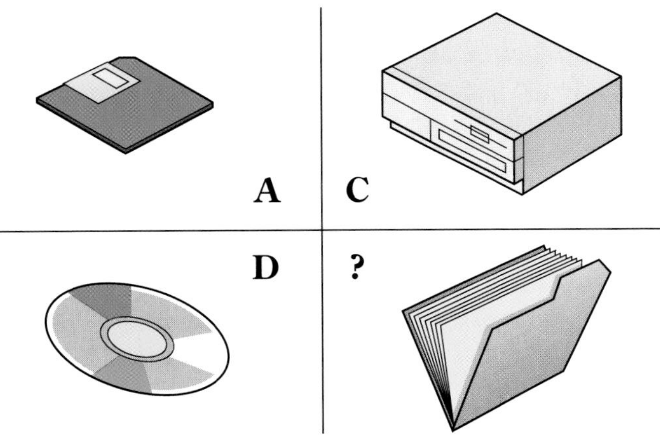

MAPPING TO A SHARED RESOURCE

Now that your network is up and running and you can see the other users who are connected to it, you can start to use some of the special network functions included with Windows 95. For example, you can assign a drive letter to any network resource so that it appears in your **My Computer** folder. Just as drive A usually designates a floppy drive, drive C designates a hard disk, and drive D designates a CD-ROM drive, you can assign any other letter to designate a shared folder on another user's PC. This means that if you want to use a shared folder on a regular basis, you can refer to it as a drive letter from Windows Explorer rather than having to run Network Neighborhood each time.

Assigning a Drive to a Shared Folder

1 From Anna's PC double-click on the *Network Neighborhood* icon.

2 Double-click on *Bill.* Right-click on the icon for the **Freeforall** folder and select *Map Network Drive* from the menu.

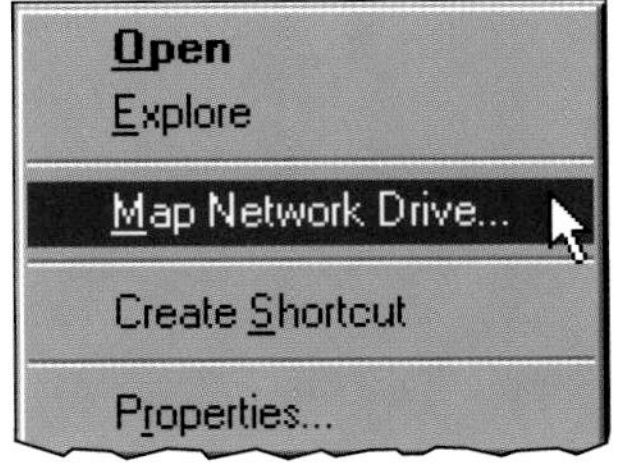

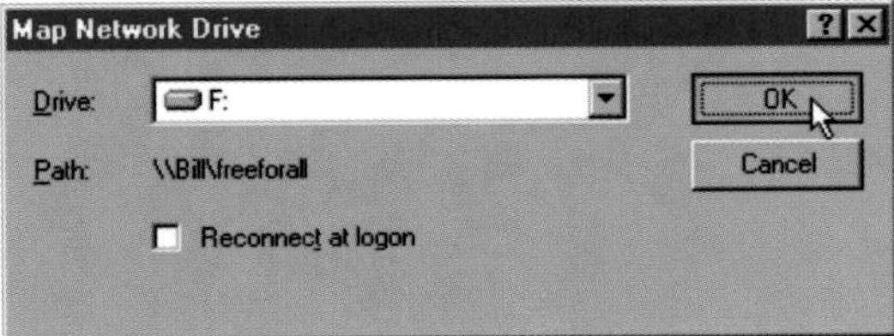

3 Select a drive letter from the list of available drive letters. In this case, choose the F drive. Choose *OK* to save the settings.

4 This drive will now appear in the *My Computer* and *Windows Explorer* windows and can be used from any Windows 95 application.

Working with a Modem

WITH A FAX MODEM ATTACHED TO YOUR PC, you can send e-mail and fax messages and receive similar messages from anyone who has a fax machine or who also uses a fax modem. You can also connect to the Internet and talk to tens of millions of other users around the world. Windows 95 makes it easy to set up and use your fax modem.

What Is a Modem?

Contacting a distant computer by modem is similar in many ways to calling a friend on the telephone. If you wanted to phone a friend you would dial the number and speak into the handset. The "handset" used by your computer is called a modem (which stands for **mo**dulator/**dem**odulator).

The modem converts data into sound signals — a process known as modulation — so that they can then be sent through the telephone line.

Windows 95 provides communications software that controls your modem. It can tell the modem to dial a telephone number, to connect to a remote computer, or to answer a call from another computer. Most modems produced today can send and receive faxes. This means that you can send a letter from your PC to a fax machine or receive faxes that can be displayed on-screen or printed.

Modem
An external fax modem.

INSTALLING YOUR MODEM

An external modem usually plugs into the serial port of your PC and into your phone socket; an internal modem is a card installed inside your PC. An internal fax modem is installed in a similar way to a network adapter card (see pages 76 and 77). Installing an external fax modem is very similar to installing a printer (see the example on page 89).

First connect the modem to your PC. You will usually connect an external modem to the PC's first serial port (labeled "COM1") with a modem cable. If a mouse is plugged into a serial port or if you are connected to a serial printer, plug the modem into the second serial port (labeled "COM2"). The modem cable has a D-shaped connector to prevent it from being plugged in upside down. For an external modem, connect the modem to its power supply and switch it on. Click on the *Start* button and select the *Settings* option, then the *Control Panel* option.

Do I Have the Right Modem?
You don't need a special telephone line to use a modem, but some countries (such as the United Kingdom and Germany) are very strict about the equipment that's plugged into the phone system, and you can only plug in equipment that's been approved. If in doubt, it is usually best to speak to your computer support person for advice.

Buying a Modem?
The speed of a modem will define how quickly you can transfer data or download a file — so it is usually best to buy the fastest modem you can afford. Transfer speeds are measured in bps (bits per second), and most new modems now work at 14,400 bps (a standard called V32) which is equivalent to 1.75KB every second. To prevent errors, make sure your modem has error conversion (a standard called V42). To send more data, modems use data compression technology called V42 bis.

1 From the *Control Panel* window, double-click on the *Modems* icon.

2 In the *Install New Modem* window, click on *Next*. Windows 95 will now try to detect your modem. This can take a minute or so.

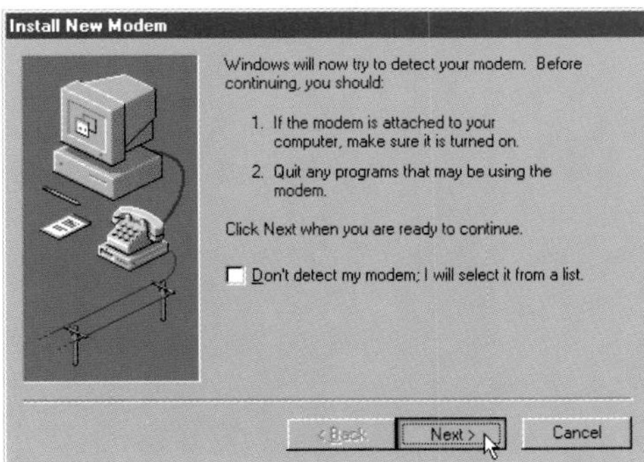

Why Is My Modem Not Recognized?

Make sure that the modem is connected to the PC and switched on before you run the New Hardware wizard. If Windows does not identify your make or model, you might need to get a special driver disk from the modem manufacturer.

3 Once Windows 95 has detected the new modem, the *Verify Modem* dialog box appears. This box displays the type of modem that has been detected. Each modem is slightly different, but Windows 95 can identify hundreds of models. Click on *Next* to accept this selection, or click on *Change* to select your specific make and model from a list.

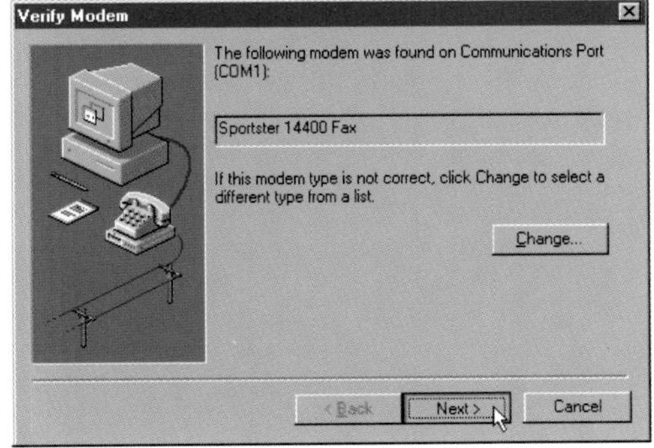

4 In the *Location Information* window that appears, choose the country from which you are using your modem by clicking on the arrow and selecting from the drop-down list. After you have typed any further details in the appropriate boxes, click on *Next*.

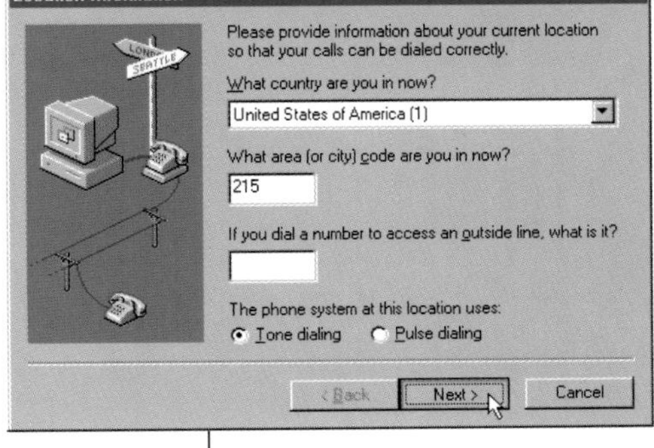

5 In the *Install New Modem* window, click *Finish* to complete the installation.

6 The *Modems Properties* dialog box appears. Here you can change any settings relating to your modem. To return to this box at any time, right-click on the *Modems* icon in the Control Panel and choose *Properties*. For now, click *OK* to return to the Desktop.

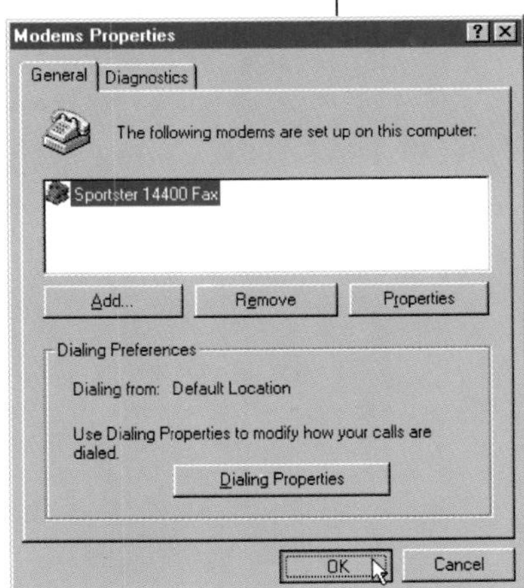

Using Windows 95 to Send and Receive Faxes

Before you can begin to use the fax capabilities of your fax modem with Windows 95, you need to install the Microsoft Fax component by following the instructions on page 123. Then follow the steps below:

1 Double-click on the *Mail and Fax* icon in the Control Panel, click on *Add* in the *Microsoft Exchange Settings Properties* dialog box. In the *Add Service to Profile* dialog box, choose *Microsoft Fax* under *Available information services*, and click *OK*.

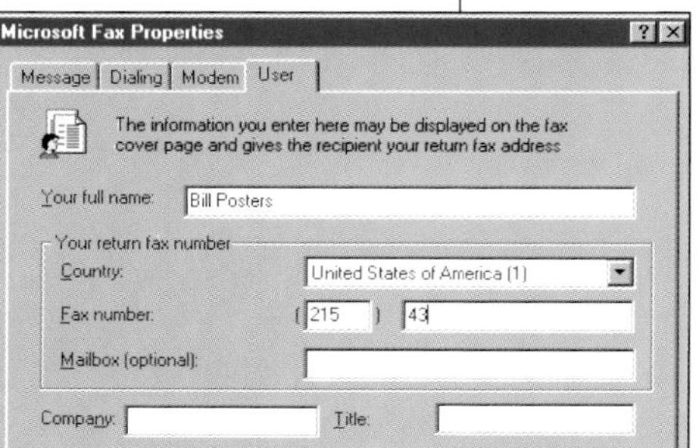

2 Click *Yes* in the warning box that appears and type your details in the *User* page of the *Microsoft Fax Properties* dialog box. Click *OK* when you are ready. Read the message in the warning box that appears and click *Yes*.

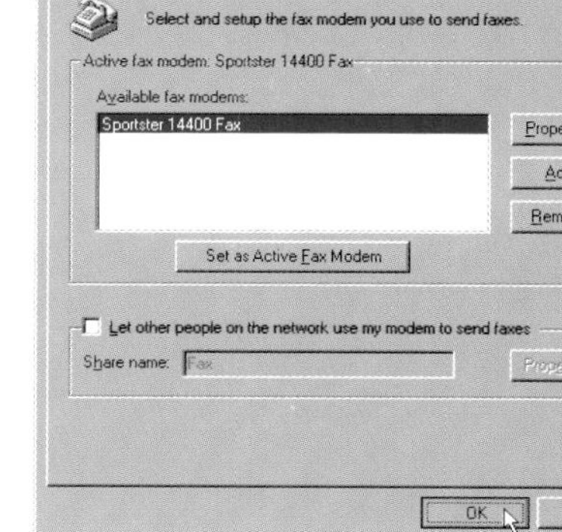

3 In the next box click *OK*. (If you can see more than one modem in your list, you should first select a modem, click on the *Set as Active Fax Modem* button, then click *OK*.) Finally, click OK in the *Microsoft Exchange Settings Properties* dialog box.

Cut-price Communication?
To set up Microsoft Exchange so that it only sends faxes during discount telephone rate periods, click on the *Message* tab in the *Microsoft Fax Properties* dialog box, check the *Discount rates* box, and click on *Set*. You can now specify the start and end of the discounted phone rate period in the *Set Discount Rates* dialog box.

How to Send a Fax from your PC

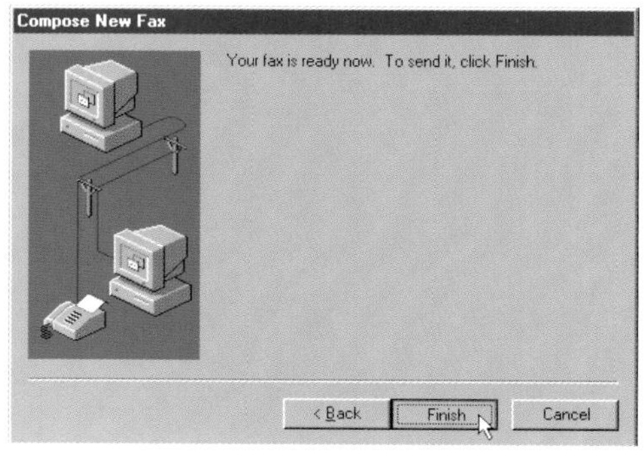

1 Double-click on the Inbox icon. From the *Microsoft Exchange* window, select *New Fax* from the *Compose* menu. Click *Next* in the *Compose New Fax Wizard* box that appears.

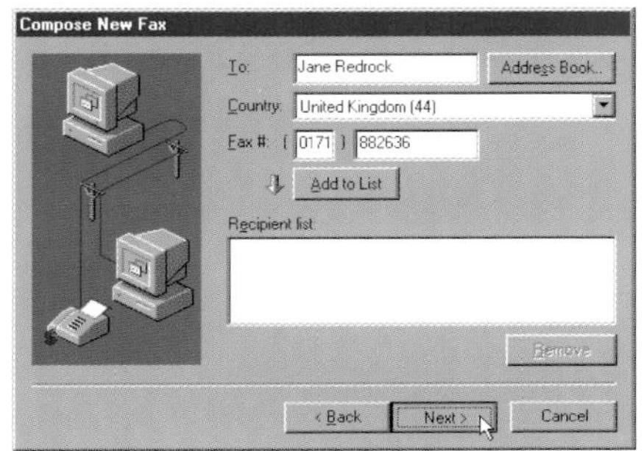

2 Type the name, the fax number and, if appropriate, the country for the person (or organization) you are going to send your message to. (If these details are already included in one of your address books, click the *Address Book* button, select the name from the list in the *Address Book* dialog box that appears, click the *To* button and then click *OK*. The name will then appear in the *Recipients* box in the *Compose New Fax* box.) When you are ready to continue, click *Next*.

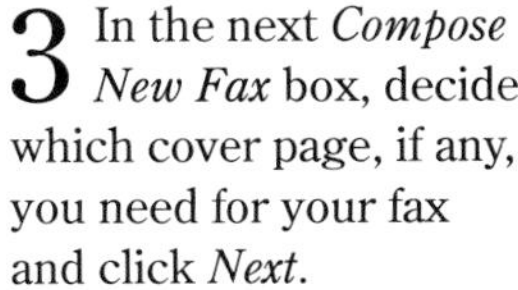

3 In the next *Compose New Fax* box, decide which cover page, if any, you need for your fax and click *Next*.

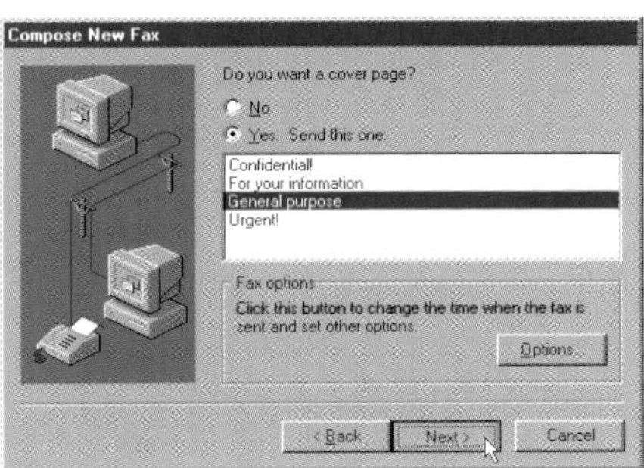

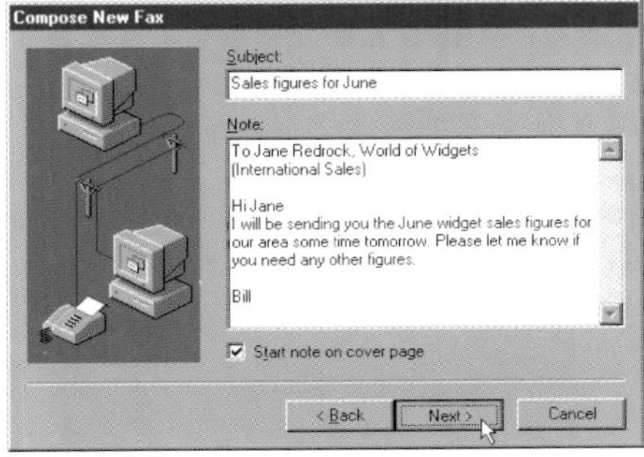

4 In the next box, type your message in the *Note* box and a short description of the message in the *Subject* box. When you have finished composing, click *Next*. To send a simple text message, click *Next* in the next box that appears. (If you click the *Add File* button, you can send additional files with your fax message. See the tip box at right.)

Add Files to Your Fax!

From the *Compose New Fax* box, click on the Add File button if you wish to include files with your fax message. You can then select the relevant files from the Windows Explorer-like dialog box that appears. The names of any files you have selected will then appear in the *Files to Send* box and you can click *Next* to continue.

5 In the next box, click *Finish*. Windows 95 will now send your fax message.

Keep Track of Your Fax

After you have composed and sent a fax using the steps above, you will see a number of windows, dialog boxes, and messages on your Desktop and on your Taskbar.

Windows 95 lets you know when your modem is dialing out, when it is answering an incoming call, and when it is sending or receiving data, so the Desktop and the Taskbar can get pretty busy!

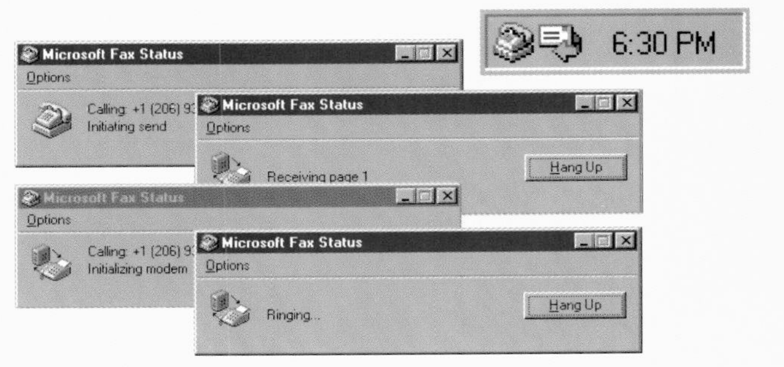

Making the Most of Your Modem

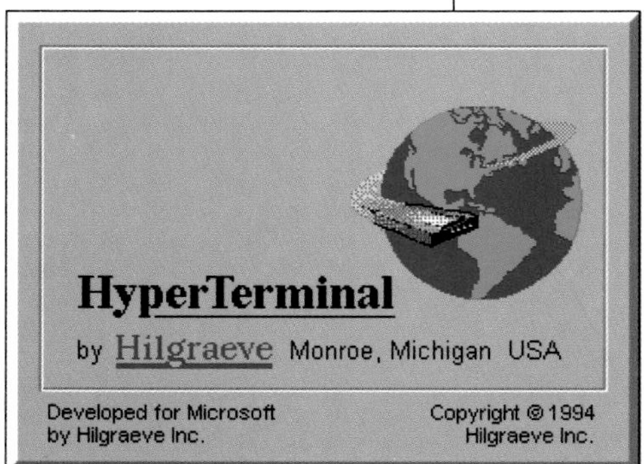

With a modem attached to your PC, you can use another Windows 95 program to make your communications tasks easier and more efficient. With HyperTerminal you can use your modem and the telephone network to connect to other PCs, commercial online services, the Internet, and other electronic bulletin boards — although many information services, like Compuserve, provide their own software for subscribers. (If the HyperTerminal Windows 95 accessory is not already installed on your PC, follow the instructions on page 123.)

USING HYPERTERMINAL

If you need to connect to another computer to send or receive files via a modem or to access an online service or the Internet, you will find that HyperTerminal makes the task easy. When you make a connection to a remote computer or bulletin board for the first time, HyperTerminal prompts you for all the information it needs to begin the connection. Hyperterminal stores this information about dialing properties and modem settings and allows you to assign an icon and a name to each connection. The next time you need to make a particular connection, all you have to do is double-click on the relevant icon in the *HyperTerminal* window.

What Is the Internet?
The Internet is a vast, world-wide network of thousands of computers linked together, to which tens of millions of users are connected. Each central computer can exchange information with all the others, so if you're connected to one, you can send mail or files to any other user who is connected to one of these central computers. You can connect to the Internet using HyperTerminal and an access provider, or you can connect with The Microsoft Network.

How to Connect with HyperTerminal

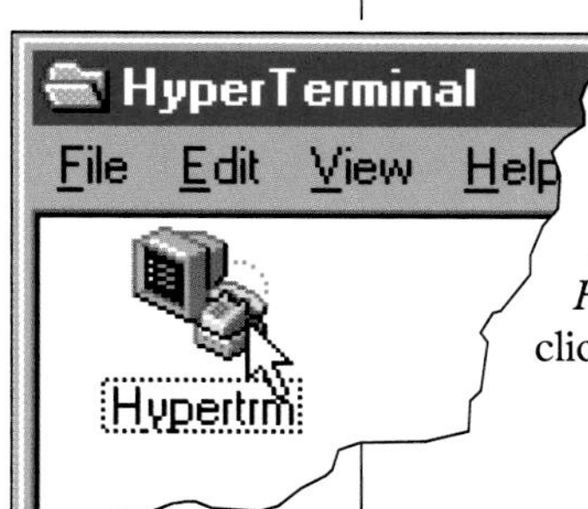

1 Click on the *Start* button and choose the *Programs* menu, then the *Accessories* submenu, and then *HyperTerminal*. In the *HyperTerminal* window, double-click on the icon labeled *Hypertrm*.

2 In the *Connection Description* dialog box, type a name for the connection in the *Name* box (usually the name of the bulletin board or PC you are trying to connect to) and choose an icon by clicking on one of the icons in the *Icon* box. Click *OK*.

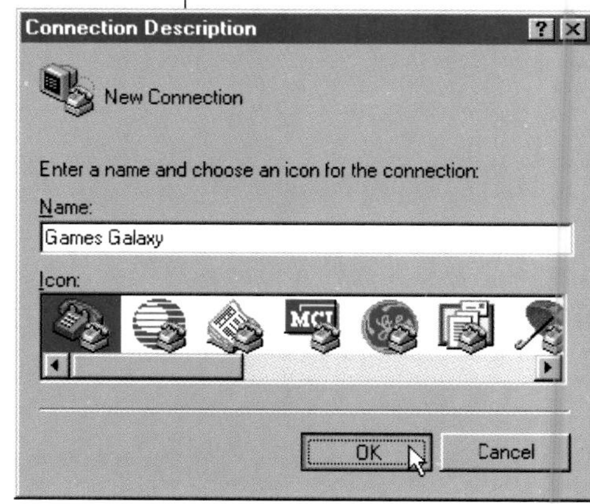

3 In the *Phone Number* dialog box that appears, type in the country and area codes and the phone number for the service you want to connect to and click *OK.*

4 In the *Connect* dialog box, check the details displayed. If they are incorrect, click *Modify* or *Dialing Properties* to make modifications. If you are happy with the settings, click *Dial.*

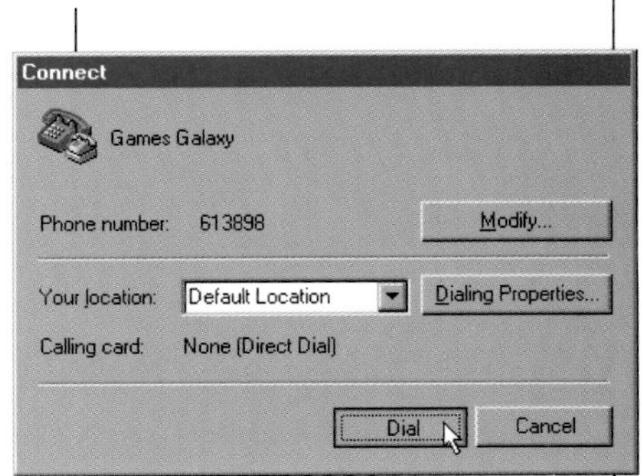

When you have connected to the bulletin board, follow any instructions onscreen. You'll find that most bulletin boards have their own way of doing business, so after connecting with HyperTerminal, you're on your own!

The Microsoft Network

As a Windows 95 user, you will have access to Microsoft's own online service, The Microsoft Network.

The Microsoft Network (MSN) is a global network with which you can access vast amounts of information and communicate with friends or business contacts anywhere in the world from your PC. Here are some of the things you may want to do when you have signed up:

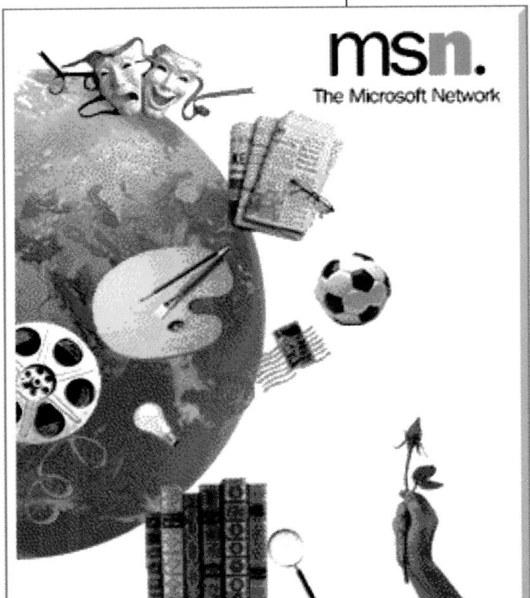

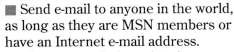

- Send e-mail to anyone in the world, as long as they are MSN members or have an Internet e-mail address.
- Access regularly updated information (news, sports, weather, etc.) at any hour of the day or night.
- Exchange information with others who share your interests via special interest MSN groups, and access many thousands of Internet newsgroups on subjects ranging from gardening to academic research to solutions for computer games.
- Download the latest games, shareware, utilities, graphics, sound files, and more to your PC from the File Download Libraries. On pages 94 and 95 you will find out how to sign up for The Microsoft Network and get a taste of what is available. Because the service is growing daily as more groups and services appear, it is difficult to imagine what will be available in a year's time!

How to Sign Up for The Microsoft Network

Before you can start using The Microsoft Network you need to complete the signup procedure, during which you will need to supply the information necessary for establishing your user account. You have plenty of opportunity to "cancel" the procedure at any time. To begin the signup procedure, simply double-click on the *Set Up The Microsoft Network* icon on your Desktop. If the Windows 95 software for The Microsoft Network is not installed, you will be instructed to insert your installation CD or floppy disks.) When you are ready, follow the steps below:

Global Connections at Local Rates?
When your modem dials the local phone number you choose in step 1 at left, you are connected via a high speed link to the Microsoft Network Data Center. All information is routed back to you via the same link to your local number. This means that you can read news, send mail, or chat with friends online for the cost of a local call — even though you may be connected to a PC on the other side of the world!

1 When the box above appears, click *OK*.

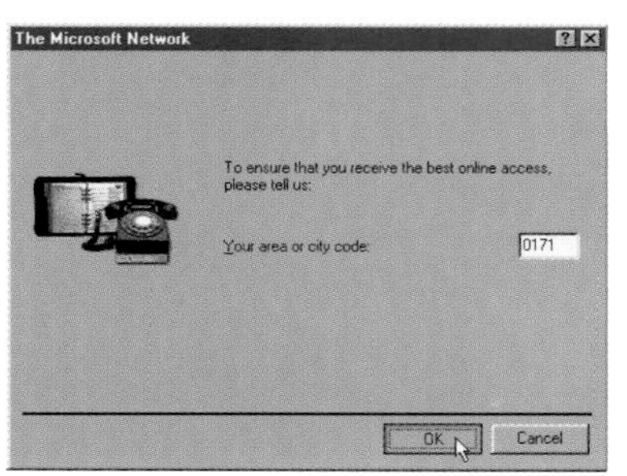

2 In the next dialog box, check that your area or city code is correct (type the correct information if necessary) and then click *OK*. The *Calling* dialog box will appear.

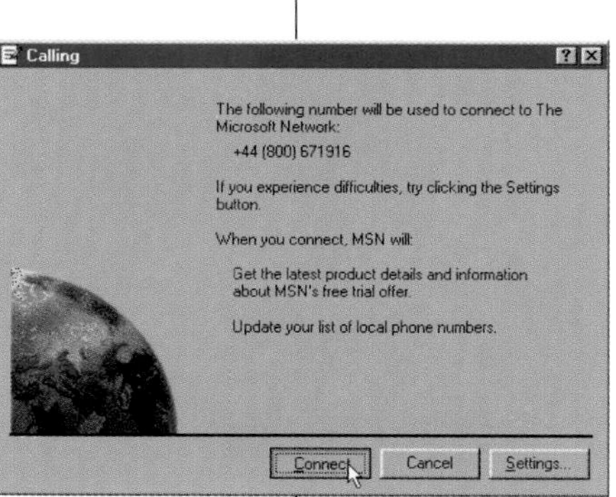
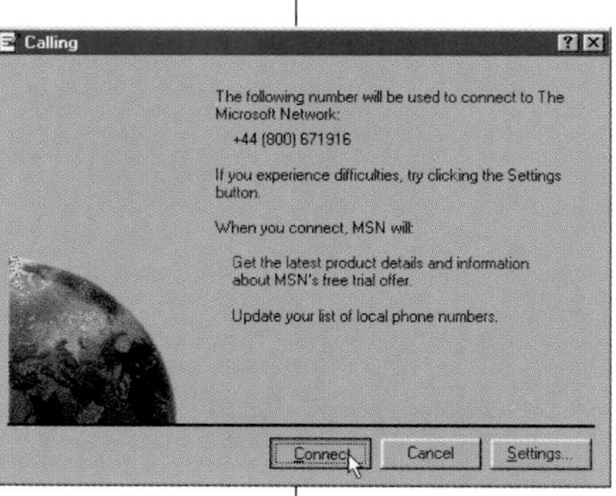

3 Click the *Connect* button. (If you have difficulty connecting, follow the instructions in the *Calling* dialog box).

4 In the next dialog box, click the buttons to find out more about the membership rules for The Microsoft Network and the methods of payment. When you are ready, click on the box labeled *Tell us your name and address,* type the necessary information in the dialog box that appears, and click on *OK*. You are now returned to the previous dialog box. Click on the *Join Now* button and, in the *Calling* dialog box, click the *Connect* button.

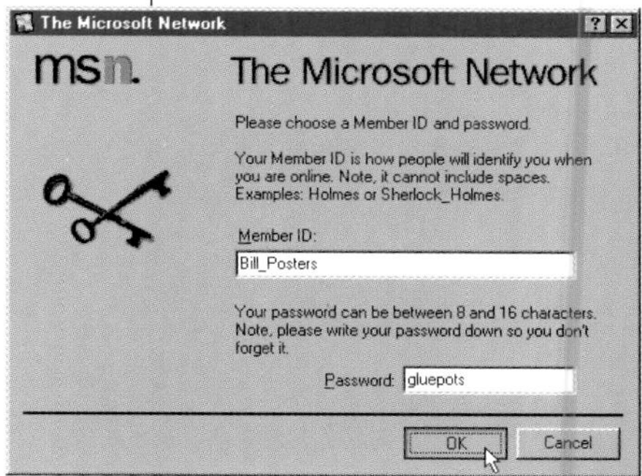

5 In the next dialog box, type a name in the *Member ID* box. This is the name that you will be identified by on The Microsoft Network. Also, type a password that you will easily remember (but that isn't too obvious for someone else to guess) in the *Password* box. Click *OK*.

6 In the *Sign In* dialog box, the name you have supplied should appear in the *Member ID* box and a line of asterisks will appear in the *Password* box. Click on the *Connect* button. In the next dialog box, click on *Yes*. An upgrade to your Microsoft Network software may be downloaded onto your system. When this operation is complete, another dialog box appears. Click on *Yes* to restart your computer and log in to The Microsoft Network.

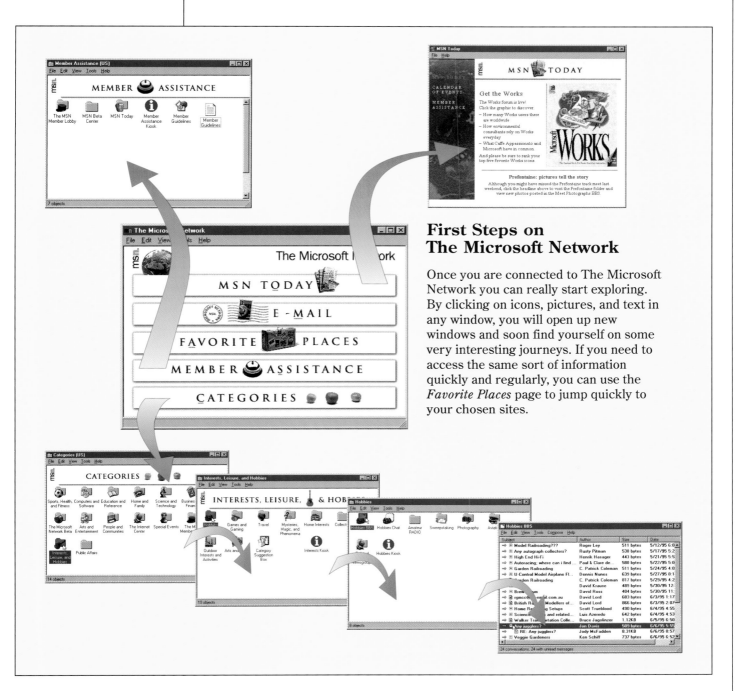

First Steps on The Microsoft Network

Once you are connected to The Microsoft Network you can really start exploring. By clicking on icons, pictures, and text in any window, you will open up new windows and soon find yourself on some very interesting journeys. If you need to access the same sort of information quickly and regularly, you can use the *Favorite Places* page to jump quickly to your chosen sites.

Useful Laptop Tools

IF YOU USE A PC AT WORK OR AT HOME AND A LAPTOP WHEN TRAVELING, you'll know what a chore it can be to keep your documents up-to-date. When you've been working on a spreadsheet for hours, it's very annoying to discover that it's not the most up-to-date version!

The Windows 95 program called Briefcase can help solve this problem. It works just like a briefcase you might carry to work. You can put documents, spreadsheets, or any other file into Briefcase, then carry this around on a floppy disk. If you insert the disk into your laptop you can continue to work on the files; then, once you are back at the office, Windows 95 will automatically update files with any changes you made on the files in Briefcase.

You may need to install the Briefcase accessory by using the *Add/Remove Programs* feature in the Control Panel. (Follow the instructions on page 123.)

Using Briefcase

1 Create a new text document on your Desktop and call it **Week in progress**. Open the document, type **Monday's agenda**, and then close the document. Now drag the text file icon over the *My Briefcase* icon and release the mouse button.

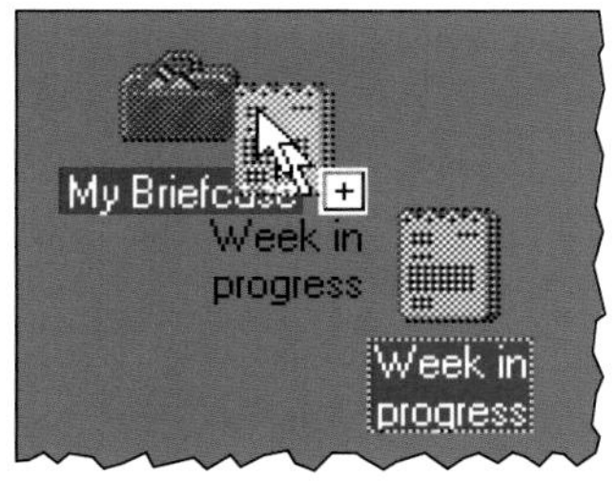

2 Insert a formatted floppy disk into your disk drive. Drag the *My Briefcase* icon over the icon for the floppy disk drive and release the mouse button. Your Briefcase will now be moved to the floppy disk. It will no longer appear on the Desktop. When you want to edit the file on your laptop, drag the *My Briefcase* icon from the floppy drive window onto the Desktop. Open *My Briefcase* by double-clicking on it and then open the **Week in progress** file. Type **Meeting at 9.30 a.m.** under the words **Monday's agenda** and save the changes. Now close *My Briefcase* and drag its icon back to the floppy drive icon.

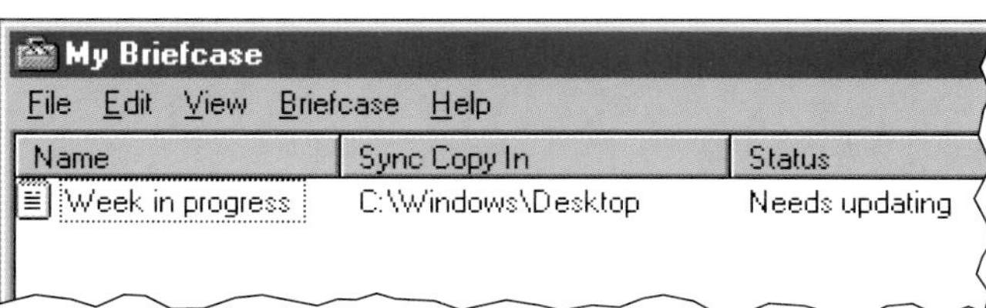

3 Back at work, insert the floppy disk into your PC's floppy disk drive. The icon for the **Week in progress** file should still appear on your Desktop. Double-click on the *My Briefcase* icon and choose *Details* from the *View* menu. Note the "Needs updating" message under *Status*.

4 Click once on *Week in progress* under *Name*, choose *Update selection* from the *Briefcase* menu.

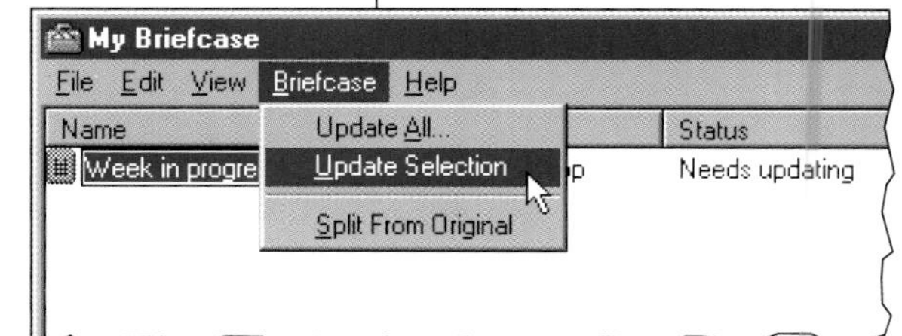

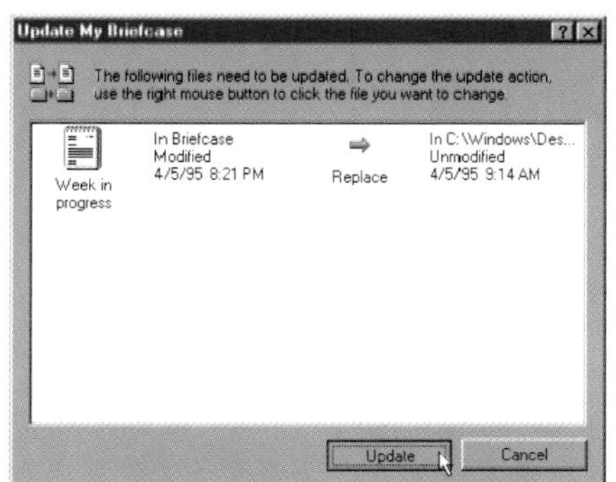

5 The *Update My Briefcase* dialog box appears, telling you that the **Week in Progress** file in your *Briefcase* has been modified and that the **Week in Progress** file on your Desktop needs to be updated. Click on *Update*.

If you open the **Week in Progress** file on your Desktop at this point you will see that you now have the updated version, and if you look in your Briefcase again you will see that the status of this document now reads "Up-to-date."

Not Just for Laptops
The Briefcase and Direct Cable Connection features described on these pages are not just for laptops. You can use them just the same with any PCs running Windows 95.

Direct Cable Connection

Transferring files from one PC to another can be slow if you use floppy disks. If you don't have a network, a direct cable connection will link two PCs together so that you can exchange files. This is very useful if you have a laptop and need to exchange Briefcase files or folders when you get back to base. It's also useful if you are installing a new PC and need to copy a database or a set of files.

Direct Cable Connection (another Windows 95 optional accessory) connects the two PCs, known as the "host" and the "guest," via a cable that plugs into a serial or parallel (printer) port at the back of each PC. You may need to buy a suitable cable from your local computer supplier (see "Get the Right Cable" at right).

Get the Right Cable!
A serial cable is not as fast at transmitting data as a parallel cable, but it is often less expensive. If you buy a serial cable, ask for a null modem cable with the correct size of connector (usually a 9-pin D-connector) for your serial port. If you buy a parallel cable, don't ask for a printer cable, but do make sure that you get a cable that will plug into the parallel printer port on the back panel of each PC.

Power Management Tools

You can set your power management preferences by double-clicking on the *Power* icon in the Control Panel. Double-click on the *Power* icon and the *Power Properties* dialog box will appear. The *Power* status box shows the type of power your laptop uses and information about how much time remains in your power supply if you are using a battery. Check the *Enable battery meter on taskbar* box if you would like the battery meter icon to appear on the Taskbar. You should choose *Advanced* in the *Power management* box to use all the additional power-saving features provided by Windows 95.

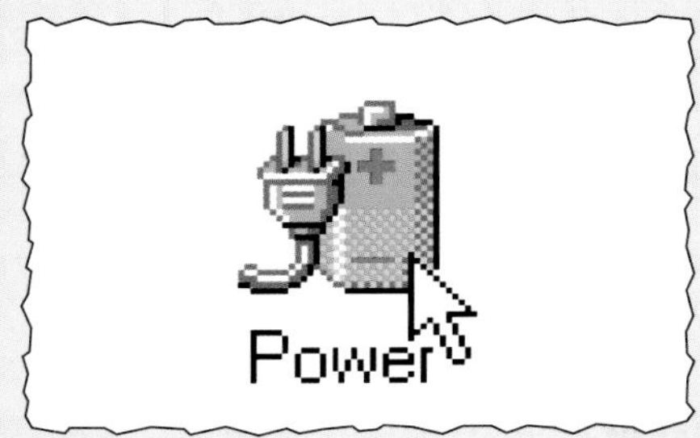

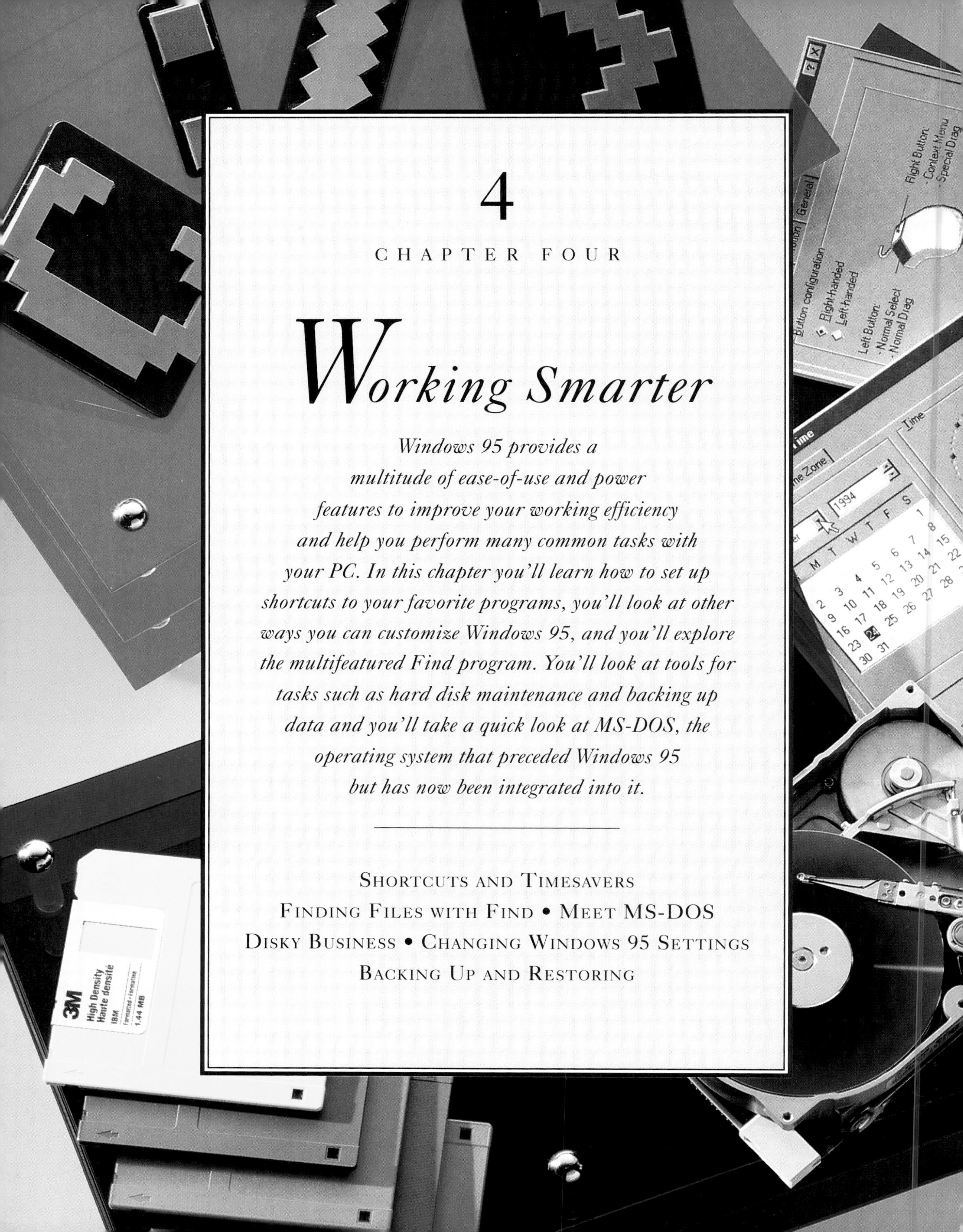

4

CHAPTER FOUR

Working Smarter

Windows 95 provides a multitude of ease-of-use and power features to improve your working efficiency and help you perform many common tasks with your PC. In this chapter you'll learn how to set up shortcuts to your favorite programs, you'll look at other ways you can customize Windows 95, and you'll explore the multifeatured Find program. You'll look at tools for tasks such as hard disk maintenance and backing up data and you'll take a quick look at MS-DOS, the operating system that preceded Windows 95 but has now been integrated into it.

SHORTCUTS AND TIMESAVERS
FINDING FILES WITH FIND • MEET MS-DOS
DISKY BUSINESS • CHANGING WINDOWS 95 SETTINGS
BACKING UP AND RESTORING

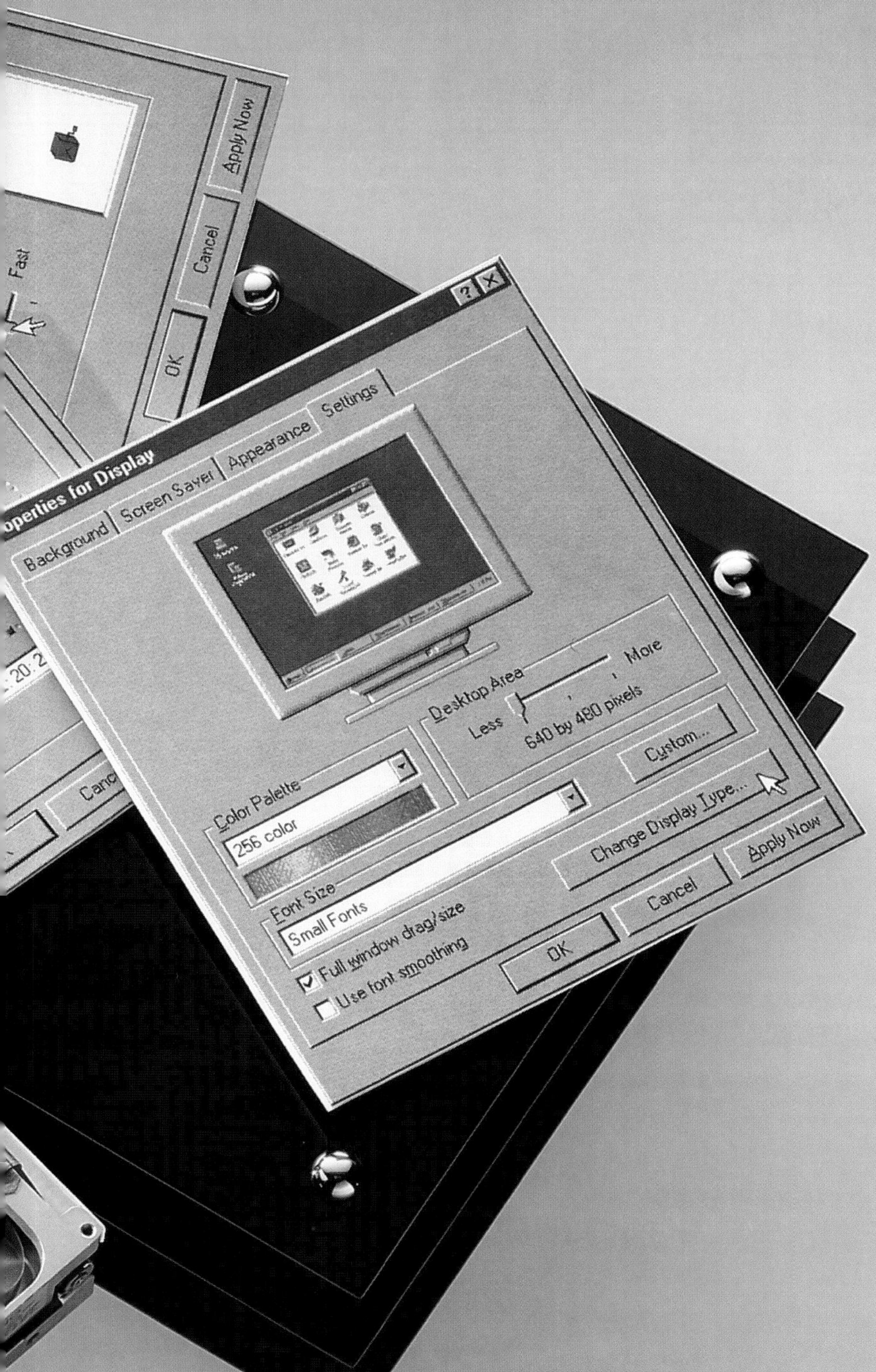

Shortcuts and Timesavers *100*

Learn how to put shortcuts on your Desktop or *Start* menu, so that you can quickly launch the programs or documents you use most often.

Finding Files with Find *104*

Can't find a file or folder? Discover how you can track it down using the Find program, and learn how to perform more sophisticated searches, such as for recently modified files.

Meet MS-DOS *106*

Find out how you can access the MS-DOS command line from within Windows 95. If you've never encountered MS-DOS before, discover what you've been missing!

Disky Business *108*

Take a tour of the Windows 95 tools for formatting or duplicating floppy disks, scanning your hard or floppy disks for errors, optimizing file storage on disks, and compressing disks to increase their storage capacity.

Changing Windows 95 Settings *114*

You'll be amazed at how much you can change the way Windows 95 looks and behaves — for example, find out how to change the color scheme for your desktop.

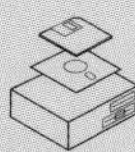

Backing Up and Restoring *118*

If you use your PC to store important files that you update frequently, you should back up the data at regular intervals. Microsoft Backup helps you perform backups quickly and efficiently.

Shortcuts and Timesavers

IN CHAPTER ONE, YOU PRACTICED VARIOUS METHODS for launching programs and opening documents. If you use particular programs or documents every day, you'll find it useful to create "shortcuts" to these items. You can put shortcuts on your Desktop, in any drive or folder window, on the *Start* menu, or on the *Programs* menu. In this section, you'll find out how to create shortcuts so as to optimize access to your everyday programs and documents.

Creating Shortcuts

A shortcut is a file that instructs your computer to look for another file at a particular location and then launch or open that file. For example, a shortcut for Calculator tells your PC to look for the Calculator program file in the **Windows** folder on your hard disk and then run that program.

Shortcut files are represented by icons that are identical to the icons for the files they "point" to, except that they contain a small arrow at the bottom left.

PUTTING A PROGRAM SHORTCUT ONTO THE DESKTOP

Putting a program shortcut onto your Desktop is easy. First you find the program file in your drive and folder structure, and then you drag and drop its icon onto the Desktop. Windows 95 automatically creates the shortcut on the Desktop, while the original program file stays in its original location. Try the following:

1 Open the *Windows* window and find the icon for the Calculator program.

2 Drag the icon onto the Desktop and then release the mouse button.

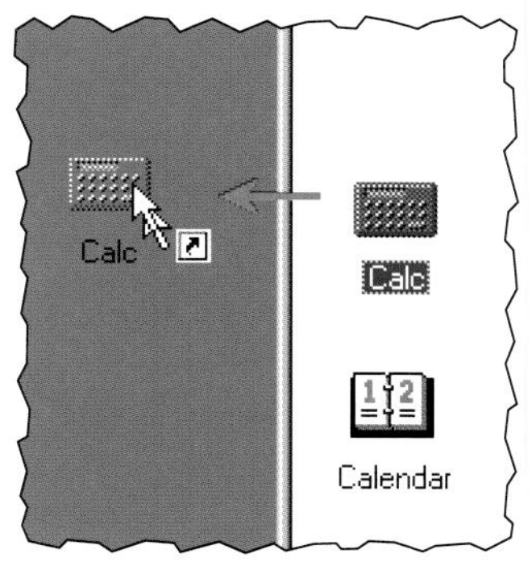

3 You can now launch Calculator anytime directly from the Desktop by double-clicking on its shortcut.

What Else Can I Put on My Desktop?
In addition to program and document short-cuts, you can create shortcuts to folders, to files or locations on a network, or to printers in the **Printers** folder (accessible from the *My Computer* window). The procedures for creating these shortcuts are the same as for creating document shortcuts.

PUTTING A DOCUMENT SHORTCUT ONTO THE DESKTOP

Putting a document shortcut onto the Desktop is a tiny bit more complicated. If you drag and drop a document file icon onto the Desktop in the normal way, Windows 95 will not create a shortcut. Instead, it will move the document file itself onto the Desktop.

To avoid this, you must either create a shortcut icon within the same folder as the original file and then drag the shortcut to the Desktop, or you must perform the drag and drop using the *right* mouse button. Do the following to practice each method in turn.

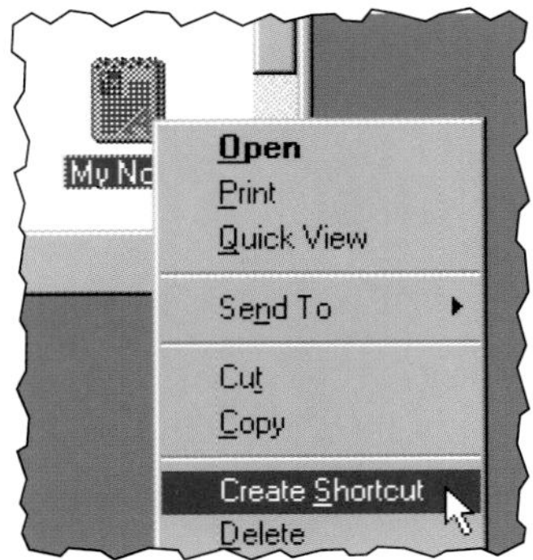

1 Look anywhere on your hard disk for a document that you work on frequently — perhaps that novel you're writing, or a spreadsheet that you use to keep track of your finances. Right-click on the icon and choose *Create Shortcut* from the pop-up menu.

2 A shortcut to the icon appears in the window. Now just drag and drop the shortcut onto your Desktop.

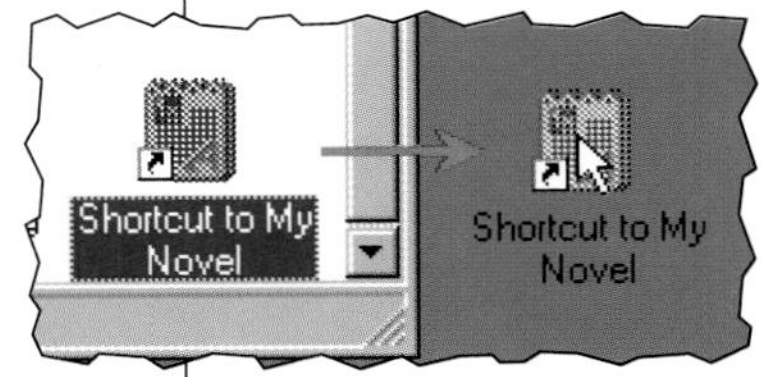

3 Find another file you use often. This time, drag and drop it onto the Desktop using the *right* mouse button. When you release the button, a menu pops up. Click on *Create Shortcut(s) Here*.

Note that with the second method, the pop-up menu also contains the options *Move Here* and *Copy Here*. Choosing one of these options will move or copy the document file itself onto the Desktop. You can choose one of these options if you like — you can then open the document from the Desktop by double-clicking on the file itself. However, moving files to the Desktop is not good practice from the point of view of keeping your files in order, and making unnecessary copies of files wastes space on your PC's hard disk.

Shortcut to Oblivion?
To remove a shortcut from anywhere in Windows 95 just right-click on it and choose *Delete* from the pop-up menu. Because a shortcut is just a pointer, you can delete (or move) it without affecting the original file.

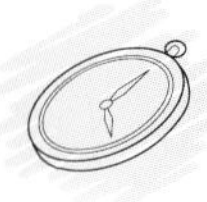

ADDING A SHORTCUT TO THE START MENU

When you create a shortcut, you don't have to put it on the Desktop. You can put a shortcut into any folder on your computer just by dragging and dropping it into that folder's window.

You may also find it useful to put a program or document shortcut onto the *Start* menu. Like most tasks in Windows 95, this is easy — you just drag and drop the file icon straight onto the *Start* button. (You can drag either program or document files — and it doesn't matter whether you use the right or left mouse button.) For example, follow the steps at left to put the Sound Recorder program onto your *Start* menu.

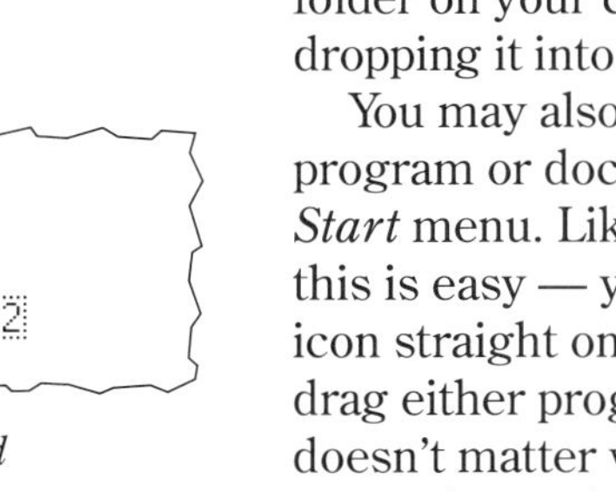

1 Find the *Sound Recorder* icon in the *Windows* window.

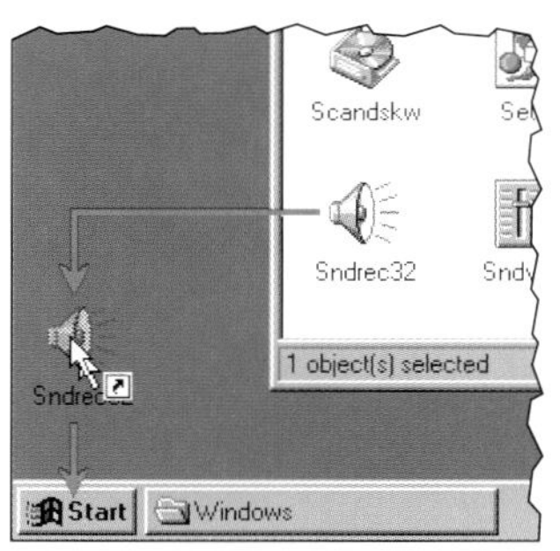

2 Drag and drop the icon onto the *Start* button. (You can use either the left or right mouse button.)

3 Click on the *Start* button and you'll see the shortcut to Sound Recorder as an option at the top of the *Start* menu. You can click on it anytime to start the accessory.

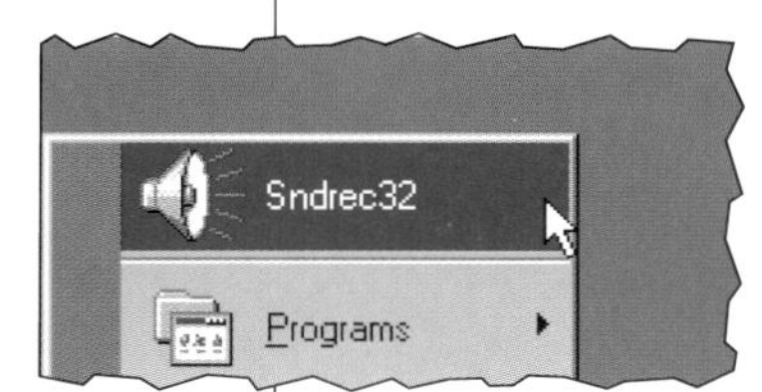

ADDING PROGRAMS TO THE PROGRAMS MENU

If you often use the same program, you might want to add its name to the *Programs* menu, which you can access via the *Start* menu. You can't drag and drop program icons straight onto the *Programs* menu. Instead, you must create a shortcut to the program by following the steps below. Once you've done that, the program will automatically appear as an option on the *Programs* menu.

The steps show how to add a shortcut to CD Player to your *Programs* menu.

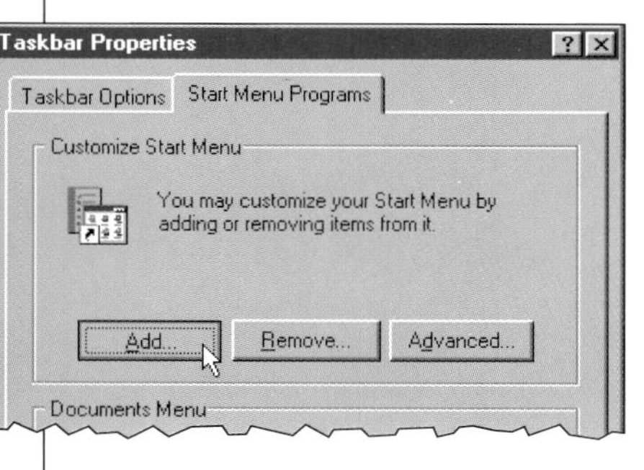

1 Right-click on the Taskbar and choose *Properties* from the submenu. In the *Taskbar Properties* dialog box, click on the *Start Menu Programs* tab and click on *Add*. In the *Create Shortcut* dialog box, click on *Browse*.

2 In the *Browse* dialog box, navigate to the **Windows** folder and double-click on the *Cdplayer* icon. Click on *Next* in the next dialog box.

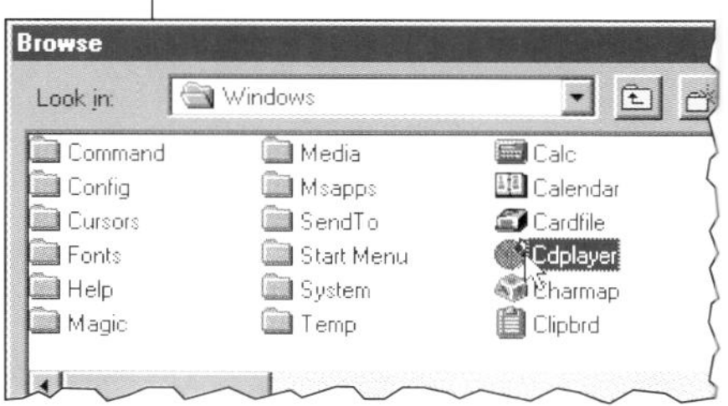

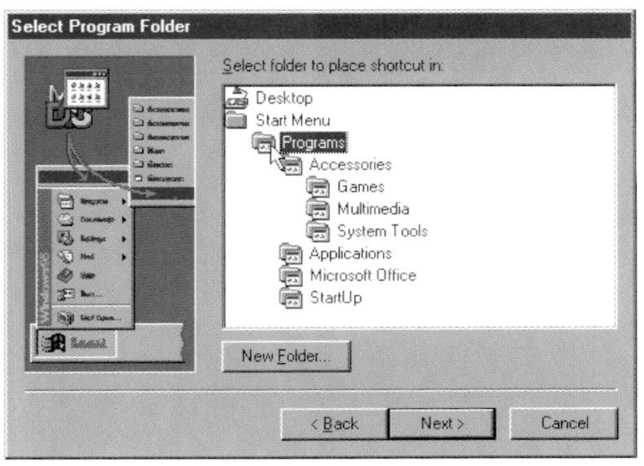

3 In the *Select Program Folder* box, double-click on the *Programs* folder.

4 In the *Select a Title for the Program* dialog box, type **Cdplayer** and then click the *Finish* button. Click *OK* to leave the *Taskbar Properties* dialog box. *Cdplayer* will now appear as an option on your *Programs* menu.

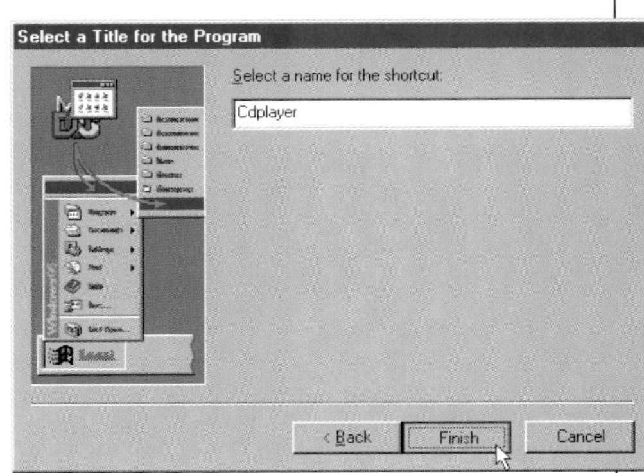

Reorganizing Your Program Groups

As you install new software onto your computer and the number of programs on your PC grows, you may find that your *Programs* menu becomes a little disorganized. You may decide you'd like to create new program groups, redistribute programs between groups, delete any empty or unused program groups, and so on. To perform such operations, you must customize the **Programs** folder within the **Start Menu** folder within your **Windows** folder.

As an example, practice creating a new program group that will contain shortcuts to the programs Paint and WordPad.

1 In the *Windows* window, double-click on the **Start Menu** folder, and then double-click on the icon for the **Programs** folder. When the *Programs* window opens, choose *New* from the *File* menu and *Folder* from the submenu.

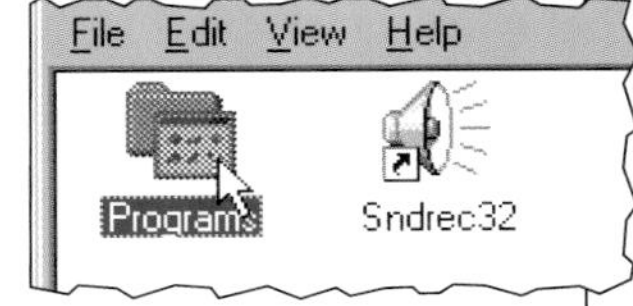

2 A new program group folder icon appears in the window. Type **Creative** to name this folder and press Enter.

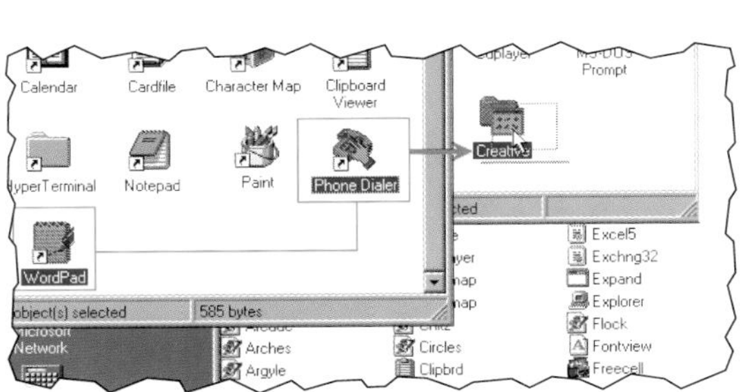

3 Double-click on the *Accessories* program group icon to open the *Accessories* window.

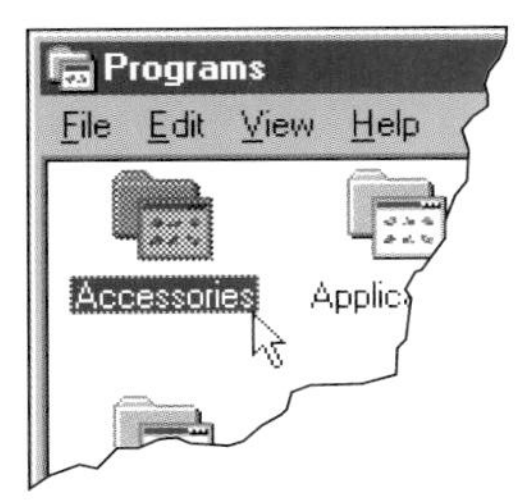

4 Select the shortcuts in the *Accessories* window for Paint and WordPad. Now drag and drop these shortcuts onto the *Creative* program group icon in the *Programs* window.

5 Open the *Start* menu and point to *Programs*. You'll see that there's now a program group labeled *Creative* on this menu. Point to it and you'll see that it contains shortcuts to the Paint and WordPad programs. If you point to *Accessories*, you'll find the shortcuts for Paint and WordPad are no longer there.

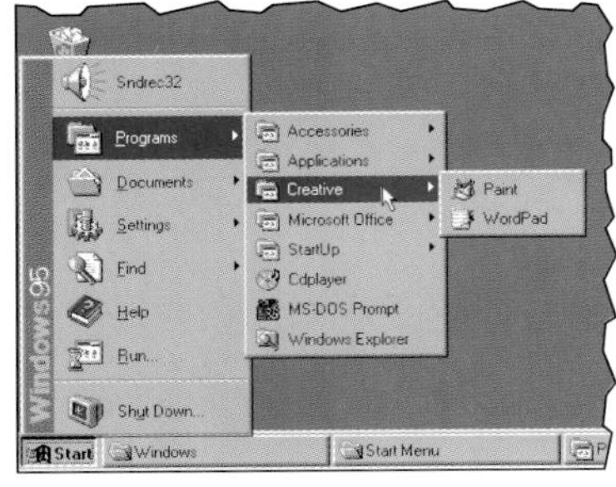

Finding Files with Find

WINDOWS 95 MAKES FINDING ANY TYPE of file or folder very simple. You can employ the *Find* command to quickly locate a lost or "mislaid" document that you know you've stored somewhere in your drive and folder structure. You can use this facility even if you can't remember the name of the file or folder but do know some other information about it, such as what type of file it is, some of the text it contains, its size, or the date it was last worked on. Locating files and folders has never been easier.

What's a Pathname?
When search results are displayed in the *Find* dialog box, folders are identified by their "pathnames." These identify the route that must be followed through your computer drive and folder hierarchy to reach a file or folder. For example, the pathname C:\Windows\Media refers to the **Media** folder within the **Windows** folder on your C drive.

A Simple Name Search

Rather than browsing through your folders on your computer to look for a document, you can instruct Windows 95 to do the searching for you. It's much faster. You can search for a document even if you don't know its full name. Follow the steps below to search for the document called **Practice File** that you originally saved on page 16. Let's assume you can't remember whether you spelled **Practice** with a "c" or an "s."

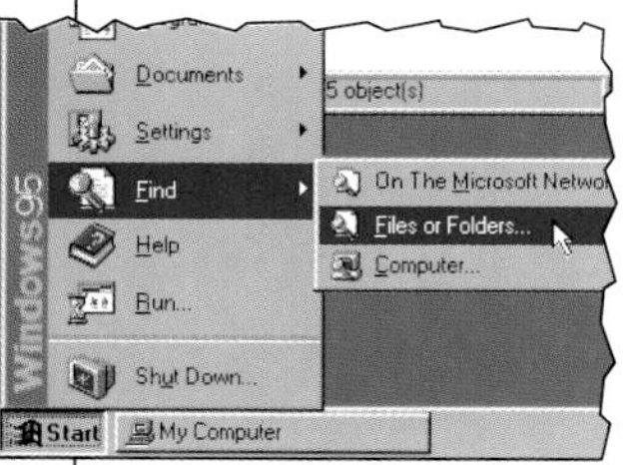

1 Choose *Find* from the *Start* menu and *Files or Folders* from the submenu.

2 The *Find* dialog box opens. The title bar displays the search attributes currently selected. As no modifications have been made to narrow the search, the title bar displays *Find: All Files*. Now type **practi** in the *Named* box. Any filename that starts with these six letters will then be located by the search.

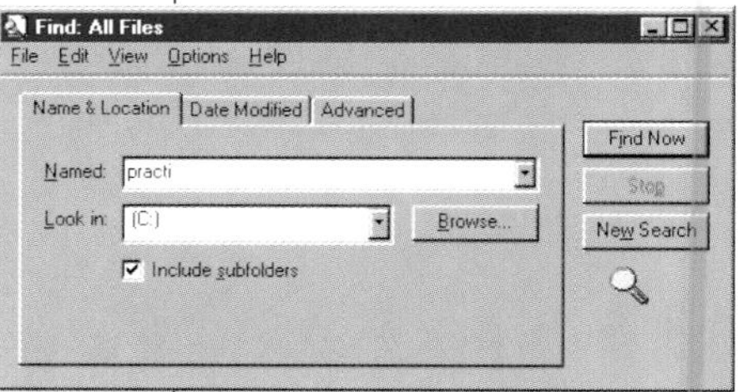

3 In the *Look in* box, leave *[C:]* selected to instruct Windows to look for the document on your hard disk. If you want to look in a different location, you can click on the down arrow to see a list or you can click on the *Browse* button. Make sure that *Include subfolders* is checked. Then click on *Find Now*.

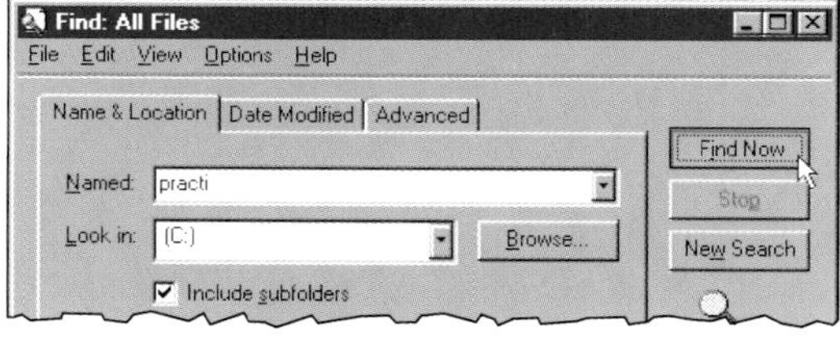

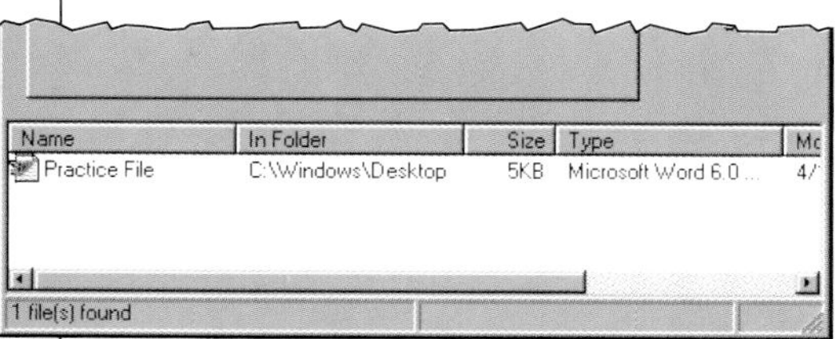

4 You'll see an animation representing the search operation. The dialog box extends to reveal the search results. The name of the file you are looking for is listed, together with the folder it is stored in (see "What's a Pathname?" above right), its size, its type, and when it was last modified.

5 If you wanted to open **Practice File**, you would click on its icon and choose *Open* from the *File* menu. You can also perform other operations from the search window, such as previewing, deleting, and printing files.

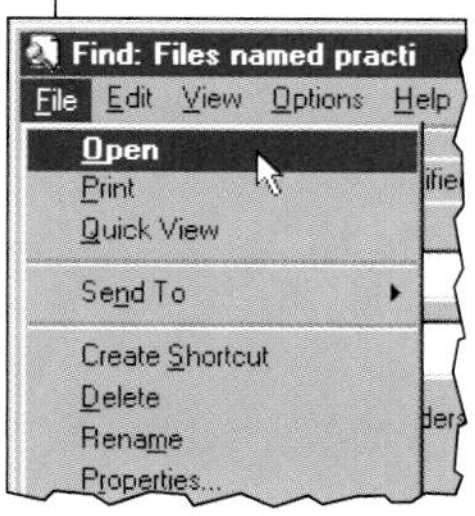

Doing a Complex Search and Saving the Results

Windows 95 offers more than just a simple name search. Additional information may help you find a file or folder, even if its name has escaped you. For example, earlier in this book, you opened a text file called **Country** in the **Dos** folder and saved a copy of it in another folder somewhere on your hard disk. You now want to open the copy of the **Country** file but cannot remember what you called it or where you saved it. Nevertheless, you can recall something about the file. Here is what to do to find it:

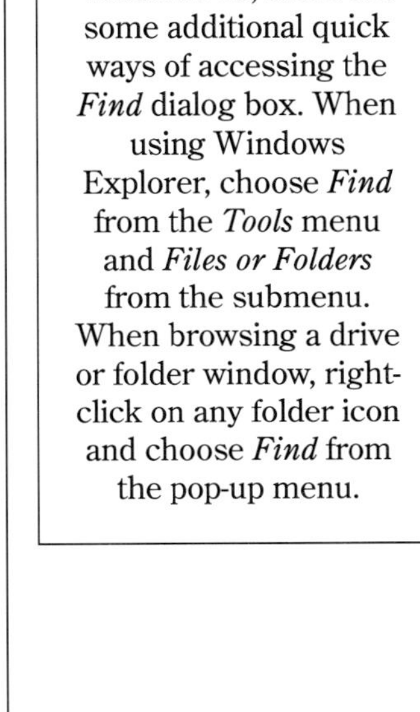

1 With the *Find* dialog box still open from the previous search, click on *New Search*. Click on *OK* when you see the message at left.

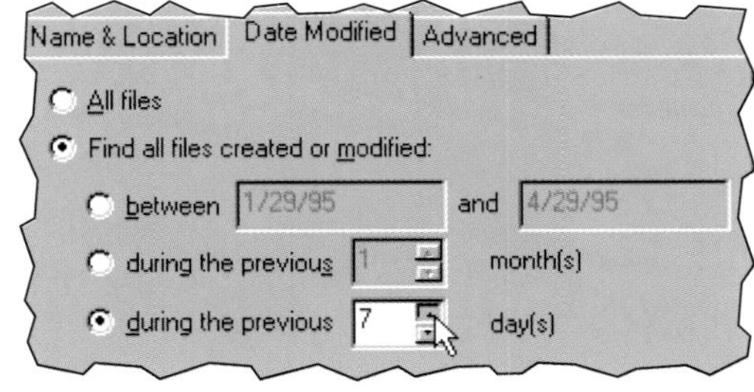

2 Click on the *Date Modified* tab. Let's suppose you are certain you created the missing file within the last 7 days. Click on the option button next to *during the previous day(s)*. Then click on the up arrow until you reach *7*.

3 Click the *Advanced* tab. In the *Of type* box, leave *All Files and Folders* selected. You know that you inserted the word "wizard" in the file before saving it, so type **wizard** in the *Containing text* box. Then click on *Find Now*.

4 The missing file called *Wysiwyg* soon appears in the extended dialog box — along with any other files that have been created or modified in the last 7 days and contain the word "wizard." Choose *Save Search* from the *File* menu.

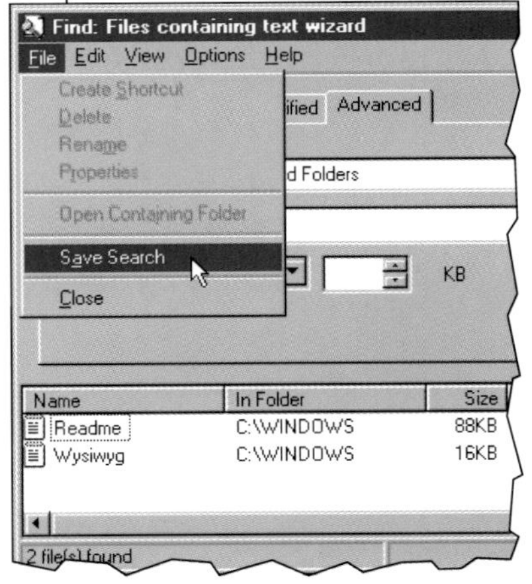

5 An icon labeled *Files containing text wizard #1* appears on your Desktop. You can double-click on this icon any time and the *Find* dialog box will appear with the results of the search. When you want to delete the icon, just drag and drop it into the Recycle Bin.

More Ways to Find
Depending on your current activity in Windows 95, there are some additional quick ways of accessing the *Find* dialog box. When using Windows Explorer, choose *Find* from the *Tools* menu and *Files or Folders* from the submenu. When browsing a drive or folder window, right-click on any folder icon and choose *Find* from the pop-up menu.

Meet MS-DOS

UNTIL THE ARRIVAL OF WINDOWS 95, MS-DOS (Microsoft Disk Operating System) was the operating system used by most PCs. Earlier Windows versions ran "on top of" MS-DOS, leaving the basic jobs, such as the control of hardware resources, to MS-DOS and providing a new, graphical interface that you could control with a mouse. Windows 95 goes one better: it includes all the functions of MS-DOS within its own programs.

MS-DOS vs. Windows

Before Windows 95, many applications would not run while Windows was running and had to be launched by typing at the MS-DOS command prompt — a rather bleak-looking string of symbols set on a black background, considerably less friendly than the mouse-operated Windows interface.

Now you can launch nearly all MS-DOS based programs from Windows 95 simply by double-clicking on the file for that program in its folder window (although you may still need to run some programs in *MS-DOS mode* — see next page). Therefore you are likely to want to access an MS-DOS command prompt only if you are an "old hand" with MS-DOS and would prefer to carry out certain tasks from a command prompt — or are just curious about how things used to be.

OPENING AN MS-DOS WINDOW
To access an MS-DOS command prompt while running Windows 95, you must open an MS-DOS window. Just do the following:

MS-DOS Alone!
To access an MS-DOS prompt without starting Windows 95, restart your PC. When you see the message "Starting Windows 95...", press Shift-F5 or, for more options, F8. You are likely to want to do this only if you are an experienced MS-DOS user and want to drastically reconfigure your PC, for example, by removing Windows 95 from your system.

1 Choose *Programs* from the *Start* menu and *MS-DOS Prompt* from the submenu.

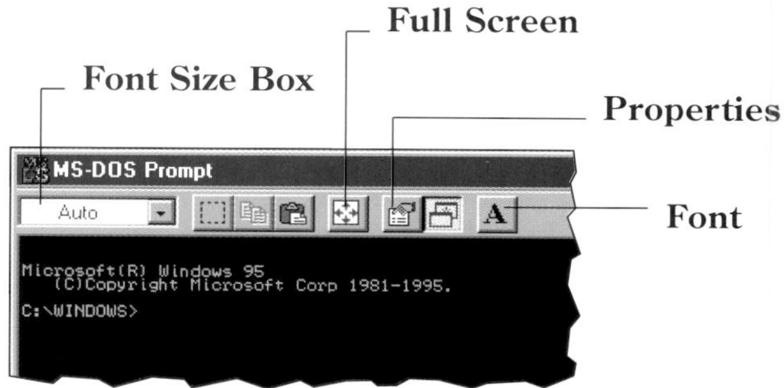

2 In a new window, titled *MS-DOS Prompt*, you will see an MS-DOS command prompt (normally the characters C:\ followed by the name of the current folder and the > character) and a flashing cursor. The functions of some of the buttons on the window's toolbar are labeled above.

Hot Properties!
The *MS-DOS Prompt Properties* dialog box, which can be accessed by clicking on either the Properties or Font buttons on the MS-DOS window's toolbar, allows you to change various MS-DOS settings, for example, whether or not a screen saver can start while the MS-DOS window is active. However, options such as memory settings are best left to experts.

USING AND CUSTOMIZING THE MS-DOS PROMPT WINDOW

If you've used MS-DOS before, you'll find that most of the familiar MS-DOS commands, like DIR, CLS, and MEM still work perfectly well when used at a command prompt in a window. You can move and resize the *MS-DOS Prompt* window, and you'll also notice a number of other new features. For example, from the *MS-DOS Prompt* window's toolbar you can paste text from the clipboard into the window or you can change the font size of the displayed text as follows:

1 Click once on the Font button on the toolbar. The *Font* flipcard of the *MS-DOS Prompt Properties* dialog box appears.

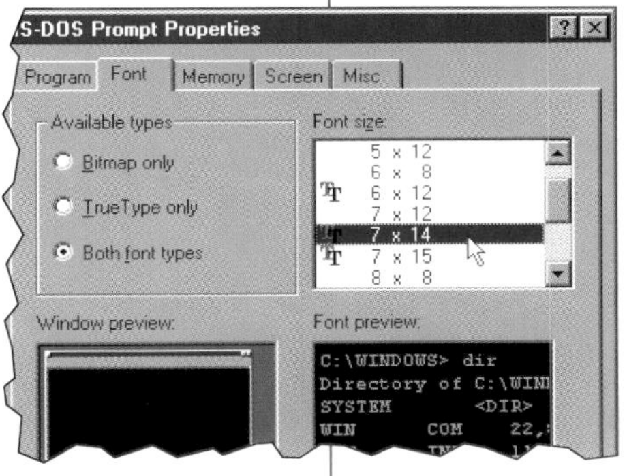

2 Select your preferred font size by clicking in the *Font size* box. The *Font preview* box will show you what the font will look like on your screen, and the *Window preview* box will show you the size of the MS-DOS window relative to your desktop. Click *OK* when you have finished.

To close the MS-DOS window, type **exit** and press Enter or simply click the window's close button.

RUNNING PROGRAMS IN MS-DOS MODE

Some MS-DOS based programs, such as Microsoft Flight Simulator, may only run properly when launched from Windows 95 in MS-DOS mode. When a program is run in this mode, the system must first close all other active programs, so that the MS-DOS based program can control the entire system. When you exit the program, your system will automatically take you back to the Windows 95 Desktop.

Flight Simulator 5.0

This program is set to run in MS-DOS mode and cannot run while other programs are running. All other programs will close if you choose to continue.

Do you want to continue?

Yes No

Windows 95 will usually warn you automatically if a program needs to run in MS-DOS mode. For example, the dialog box at left appears if you double-click on the *Microsoft Flight Simulator* icon (if the program is installed on your system).

Want the Big Picture?
You can convert an MS-DOS window to a full screen display by clicking on the *Full Screen* button or by pressing Alt-Enter. Press Alt-Enter again to switch back to a window. A few MS-DOS based programs, although they can be launched from Windows 95, will not run in a window but must be run in full screen mode.

Disky Business

TO PROTECT THE DATA ON YOUR HARD AND FLOPPY DISKS, and to improve your PC's performance, it is very worthwhile to practice some basic disk maintenance. Windows 95 provides a variety of tools, such as ScanDisk, and Windows Disk Defragmenter, that make disk maintenance simple and easy to learn. You'll also learn in this section how to format floppy disks, how to duplicate the contents of a floppy disk, and how to create extra storage space on your hard disk.

Is Your Hard Disk Healthy?

You can quickly find useful information about the size and condition of a hard or floppy disk, and the amount of used and free space on it, by looking at the *Properties* dialog box for the disk. Try the following:

1 Right-click on the *[C:]* icon in the *My Computer* window and choose *Properties*. The dialog box that appears shows you how much space is available on your hard disk.

2 Click on the *Tools* tab. The *Tools* flipcard shows you when you last carried out disk maintenance operations such as error-checking (using ScanDisk) and disk defragmentation (using Windows Disk Defragmenter). These Windows 95 accessories are explained over the next few pages.

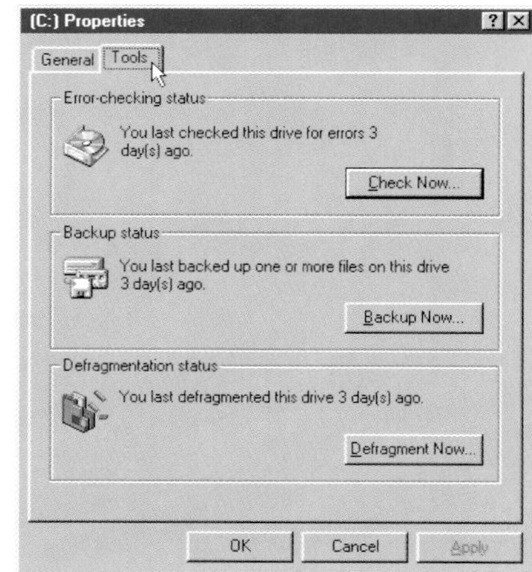

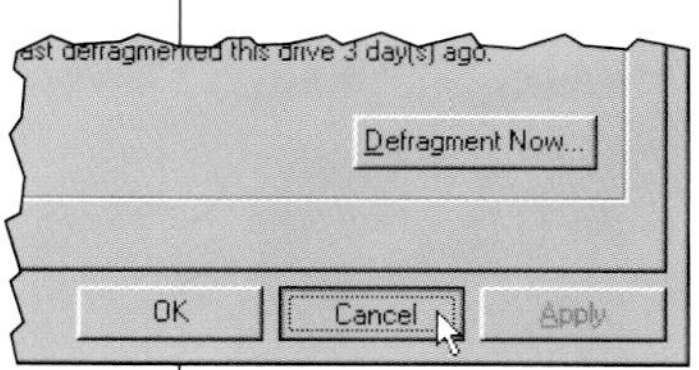

3 Click *Cancel* to return to the Desktop.

Running ScanDisk and Windows Disk Defragmenter regularly will help your disks last longer and perform better, and you may also find that your computer treats your data more kindly! You don't need to be an expert to use these tools. If you find any serious problems, these programs will allow you to give valuable information to your technical support person.

Recycle Your Disks!
You can format a floppy disk that already contains some files, but be warned that the files will be erased during the formatting. Just follow the same procedure as you would to format a new floppy disk. If you are not sure whether the floppy disk contains files, double-click on the icon for the floppy disk drive in the *My Computer* window to display the disk's contents.

Format that Floppy!

You can't do anything with a disk until it is formatted. Your hard disk will already be formatted when you buy your computer and you should never attempt to reformat it unless you are an experienced user and have good reason to do so. New floppy disks are sometimes unformatted when you buy them, so you need to use Windows 95 to format them before you can use them.

USING FULL FORMAT AND QUICK FORMAT

Windows 95 can format floppy disks in two ways. With a *full format*, Windows checks a disk for bad sectors and tries to repair any it finds before formatting the disk. Bad sectors are small areas of a disk that are faulty and unreadable. With a *quick format*, Windows does not scan a disk for bad sectors before formatting. Use this option if you know the disk you wish to format is undamaged.

Formatting Floppy Disks

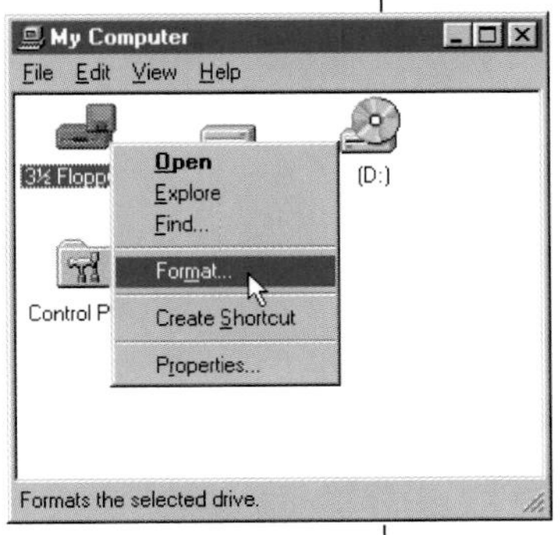

1 Insert a disk into the floppy disk drive. Right-click on the icon for the floppy disk drive in the *My Computer* window and choose *Format*.

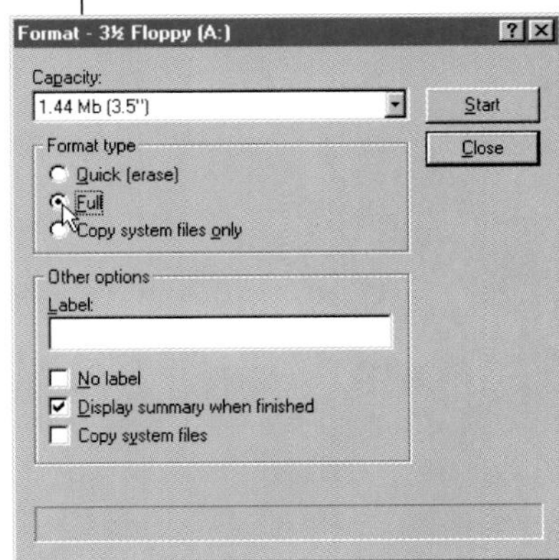

2 In the *Format* dialog box, click on the *Full* option box under *Format type*. Make sure the *Display summary when finished* box is checked under *Other options*.

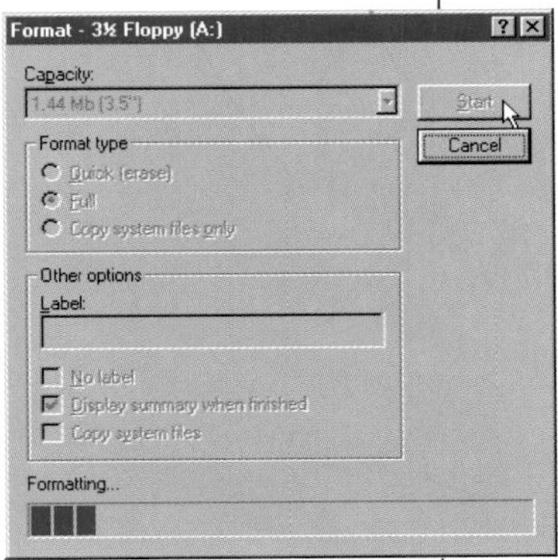

3 Click *Start* to begin formatting the disk. The formatting process may take a few minutes. The box at the bottom of the dialog box shows how the process is progressing.

4 A *Format Results* box appears once formatting is complete, providing information about the disk. Click on *Close* and then on *Close* again to exit the *Format* dialog box.

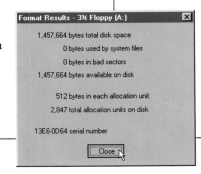

Format Results - 3½ Floppy (A:)
1,457,664 bytes total disk space
0 bytes used by system files
0 bytes in bad sectors
1,457,664 bytes available on disk
512 bytes in each allocation unit
2,847 total allocation units on disk
13E6-0D64 serial number
Close

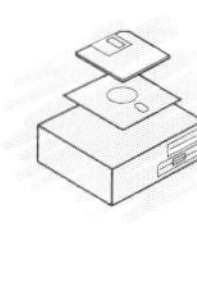

Copying Entire Disks

It is always a good idea to make a backup copy of your software in case you damage or lose the original disks. The MS-DOS DISKCOPY command is the best way to duplicate entire disks. It makes an exact copy of the "source" disk, holds it temporarily in your computer's memory, and then transfers it to a blank "target" disk that you provide. This means you can copy disks even if you have only one floppy disk drive. Just follow the steps below. First make sure you label your source and target disks clearly.

First Write-Protect!
Usually, disk copying requires just one swap of the source and target disks, but sometimes you may be asked to swap them several times. Before copying a set of disks, it's a good idea to write-protect them. By doing this, you prevent any chance of the data on a source disk being overwritten if you make a mistake during the duplicating procedure.

1 Open an *MS-DOS Prompt* window (see page 106), type **diskcopy a: a:** at the command prompt, and then press Enter. Insert the source disk (the one you want to copy from) into floppy disk drive A and press any key.

2 When your PC tells you it is ready, insert the target disk (the one you want to copy to) and press any key.

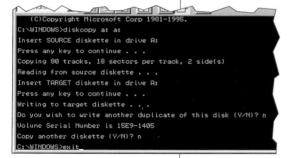

```
(C)Copyright Microsoft Corp 1981-1995.
C:\WINDOWS>diskcopy a: a:
Insert SOURCE diskette in drive A:
Press any key to continue . . .
Copying 80 tracks, 18 sectors per track, 2 side(s)
Reading from source diskette . . .
Insert TARGET diskette in drive A:
Press any key to continue . . .
Writing to target diskette . . .
Do you wish to write another duplicate of this disk (Y/N)? n
Volume Serial Number is 15E9-1405
Copy another diskette (Y/N)? n
C:\WINDOWS>exit_
```

3 When copying is completed, which may take a little while, type **n** (for no) to any further questions to return to the command prompt. Type **exit** and press Enter to leave the MS-DOS window.

Scanning for Errors with ScanDisk

ScanDisk is a utility you can use to run a sort of "health check" on the condition of a disk. ScanDisk detects and repairs errors in the way that files and folders are stored on a disk and will clean up any useless file fragments that have accumulated on a disk, possibly as a result of your PC halting unexpectedly. You can also use ScanDisk to check the surface of a disk for errors. If it finds any areas of a disk affected by surface errors, ScanDisk will tell Windows 95 to avoid writing to them. Since all disks wear out eventually (and usually some parts of the disk give out before others), this feature can prove useful for protecting your data.

Running ScanDisk

1 Right-click on the *[C:]* icon in the *My Computer* window, and choose *Properties* from the pop-up menu. In the *Tools* flipcard of the *[C:] Properties* dialog box, click on *Check Now* under *Error-checking status*. The *ScanDisk* window appears.

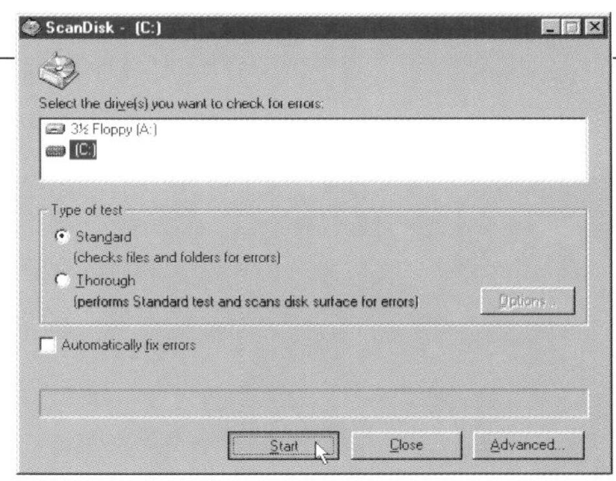

2 Make sure *[C:]* is highlighted under *Select the drive(s) you want to check for errors*. Choose between the *Standard* and *Thorough* option boxes and click *Start*. Follow any instructions that appear on your screen. When the *ScanDisk Results* dialog box appears, click on *Close*, and then click on *Close* in the *ScanDisk* window.

Creating Order

The jumbled mosaic of colors suggests the way files become fragmented on your disk. The neater pattern of colors shows how Windows Disk Defragmenter condenses the files into better order.

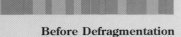

Before Defragmentation

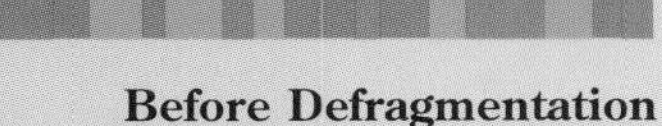

After Defragmentation

Disk Defragmenter

When Windows saves a file to your hard disk, it places it wherever there is a convenient slot. If it can't find a large enough slot for the whole file, Windows splits the file and places the parts in different areas of the disk. Eventually, your disk can become full of fragmented files. This can make your programs run more slowly and can cause some extra wear on your hard disk drive since the read/write heads of your disk drive have to do a lot more work to access the data.

Windows Disk Defragmenter looks at the way programs and files are stored on your hard disk and then rearranges the "filing system" by placing all the parts of a file in consecutive areas of the disk.

Pause for Breath!
Windows Disk Defragmenter works "in the background" so you can carry on with other tasks while it is running. If you find your computer is running too slowly to carry out other tasks, you can temporarily stop the Defragmenter by clicking *Pause* in the *Defragmenting* window.

Running Disk Defragmenter

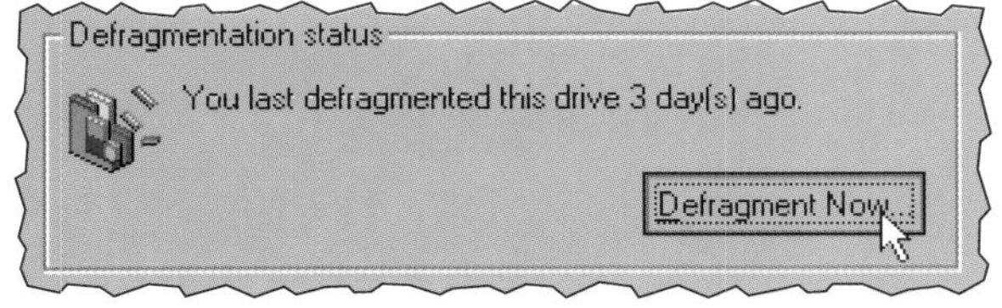

1 In the *Tools* flipcard of the *[C:] Properties* dialog box, read the text under *Defragmentation status*. This tells you the last time you ran Windows Disk Defragmenter. Click on *Defragment Now*.

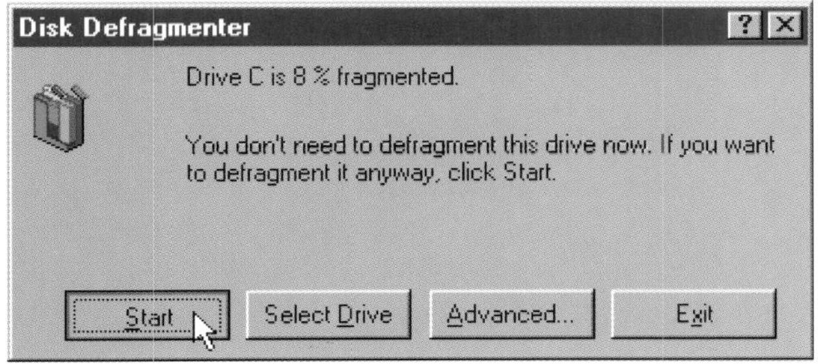

2 Follow the advice in the *Disk Defragmenter* dialog box. In this case, click on *Start*. Once the defragmentation is complete, click on *No* in the *Disk Defragmenter* dialog box.

Freeing Disk Space

Some Methods For Freeing Space

- Run ScanDisk to remove any unwanted data from your hard disk.
- Reduce the size of your Recycle Bin (see page 54) — although, of course, this also reduces the safeguards provided by the Bin.
- Delete documents and folders that you no longer need — or transfer files you rarely use to floppy disks.
- Remove any Windows 95 components you never use.

All hard disks fill up quickly — no matter how large they seemed when you bought them. Eventually, you'll have to find some space to install a new program. You should never allow your hard disk to get too full, even if you are not installing any new programs, because some programs use part of your hard disk to write temporary files.

A number of options are available to you for freeing up space on your hard disk. To create large amounts of extra space, you could run the DriveSpace utility (see next page), although this is not recommended for absolute beginners. Remember, whenever you perform any such operation on a hard disk, you should always back up your data first!

REMOVING AN UNWANTED COMPONENT
Here is an example of how you could free disk space by removing all of Windows 95's multimedia-related programs and media clips from your hard disk:

1 Double-click on *Add/ Remove Programs* in the Control Panel.

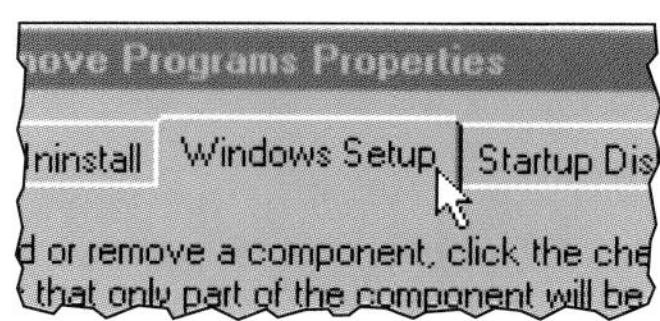

2 Click on the *Windows Setup* tab.

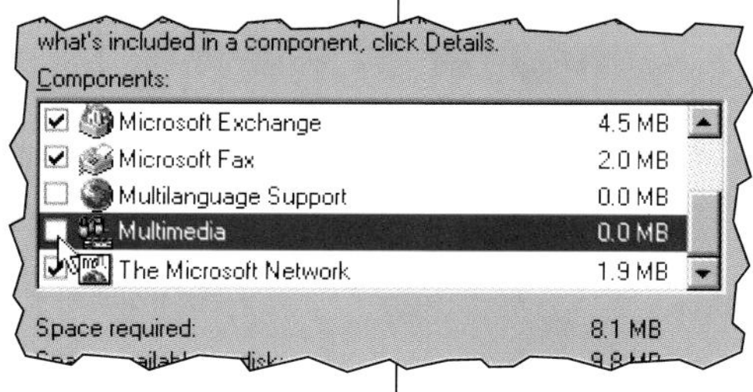

3 Click on the down arrow until *Multimedia* appears in the *Components* box. Clear the *Multimedia* check box. Click on *OK*. You can reinstall this component at any time by clicking on the check box, clicking *OK*, and inserting the appropriate Windows 95 installation disk when prompted.

How Full is Your Hard Disk?
You can see at a glance how much free space is available on your hard disk by right-clicking on the *[C:]* icon and accessing the *Tools* flipcard of the *Properties* dialog box. A pie chart shows you the amount of used space on your hard disk in blue and the amount of free space in pink.

Don't Forget To Back Up!

Before compressing the files on your hard disk, back up your important data files (and any programs if you have lost the program installation disks) by copying them to floppy disks or by using the Microsoft Backup program (see page 118).

COMPRESSING FILES WITH DRIVESPACE

DriveSpace frees space on a disk by compressing most of the files on the disk. These files are stored as a single file, called a compressed volume file (CVF), on the disk. To you, the user, however, the CVF does not look like a file at all but appears in Windows as though it were a disk drive and retains its original name (i.e., drive C) when you compress the files on your hard disk. You can think of it as a "virtual" disk drive within your hard disk. After the compression, this virtual disk drive contains far more space than it did originally.

The following steps show how you would begin the process of compressing your hard drive.

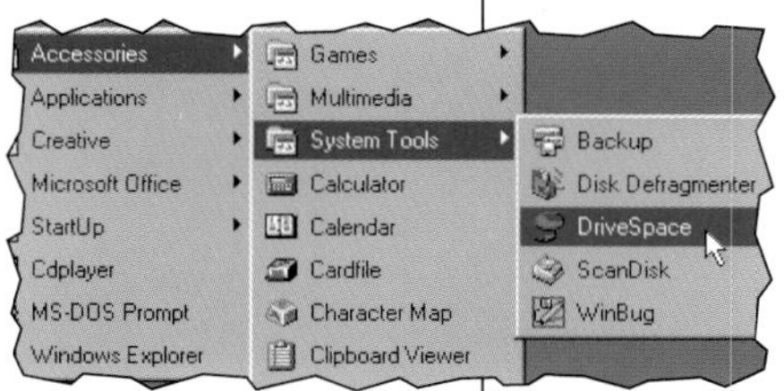

1 Make sure there is no floppy disk in your floppy disk drive. Then, via the *Start* button, choose *DriveSpace* from the *System Tools* program group within the *Accessories* program group.

2 The *DriveSpace* window opens. To find out more about DriveSpace before proceeding, choose *Help Topics* from the *Help* menu and, in the *Contents* flipcard of the *Help Topics* box that appears, double-click on *Overview* and then on *Understanding disk compression*. Read the help topic and then close the window.

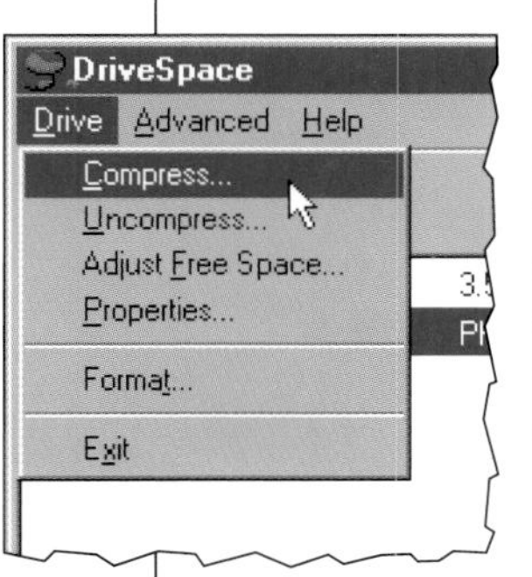

3 Click on the *[C:]* drive icon in the *DriveSpace* window if it is not already highlighted and choose *Compress* from the *Drive* menu.

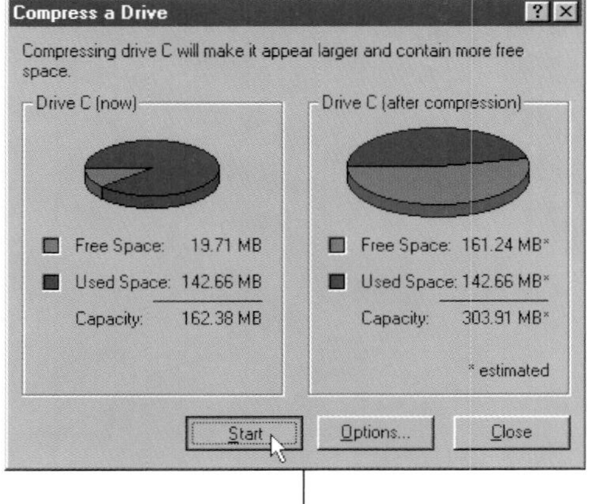

4 The *Compress a Drive* window opens, showing the estimated effects of the compression on the amount of free and used space on the disk drive. Click on *Start*.

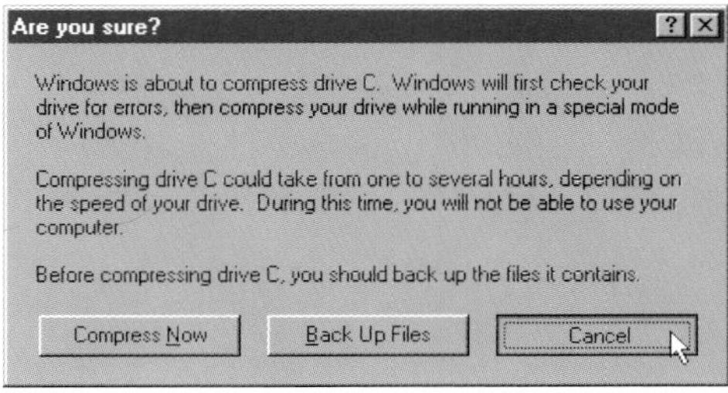

5 Read the message in the *Are You Sure?* dialog box. Since we do not intend to use Drivespace in this example, click *Cancel*.

Changing Windows 95 Settings

If you're not happy with the way Windows 95 looks or behaves, why not change it? You can change just about every part of the Windows 95 interface, from the color scheme used for your windows to the way your mouse behaves. You'll see over the next four pages how to carry out many useful changes to your system settings. If you decide to experiment, make sure that you know what you're doing, since some changes can have unexpected results.

Setting the Time and Date

You can easily check the current time and date in Windows 95 because it is displayed on the Taskbar. Move your mouse pointer over the time box on the right end of the Taskbar. After a pause, the date will appear in a pop-up box. If you need to change the time and date, you can run the Date/Time utility directly from the Taskbar. Just follow these steps.

1 Right-click on the time box on the Taskbar and choose *Adjust Date/Time*. The *Date/Time Properties* dialog box appears.

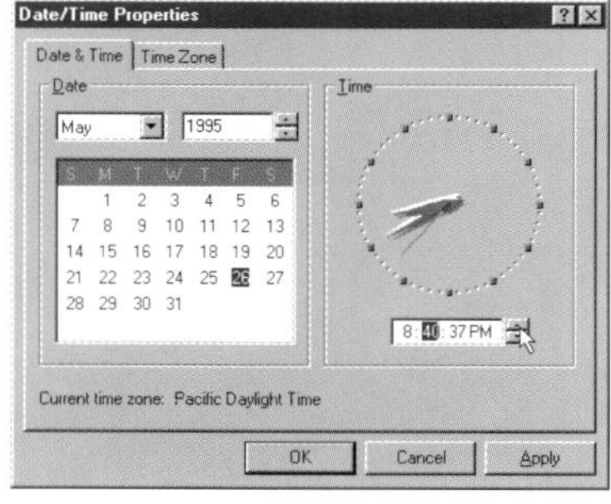

2 Move the mouse pointer over the digital time readout below the clock. Click on the hours, minutes, or seconds and then click on the up or down arrows to make changes.

3 Choose the correct day, month, and year from the *Date* panel to the left. Click on the *Apply* button to save your changes and click on *OK* to close the window.

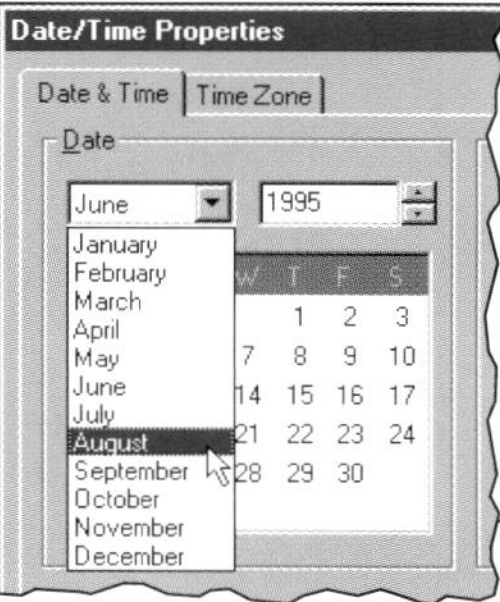

Clockwatching?
Are you an 18:30 or a 6:30 PM kind of person? To change the way Windows 95 displays times, dates, numbers, and currencies, double-click on the *Regional Settings* icon in the Control Panel. In the *Regional Settings* flip-card, click on a part of the world, and standard settings for that country will be used.

Display Settings

If you right-click on the Desktop and choose *Properties* from the pop-up menu, a dialog box titled *Display Properties* appears. This dialog box allows you to change how your Windows 95 screen display looks. You've already seen how to put a wallpaper on your Desktop (see page 35), but many other aspects of your screen display can also be customized.

CHANGING THE COLOR SCHEME

You can easily change the color of all the windows, menus, and message boxes, as well as the background by choosing from one of the color schemes provided.

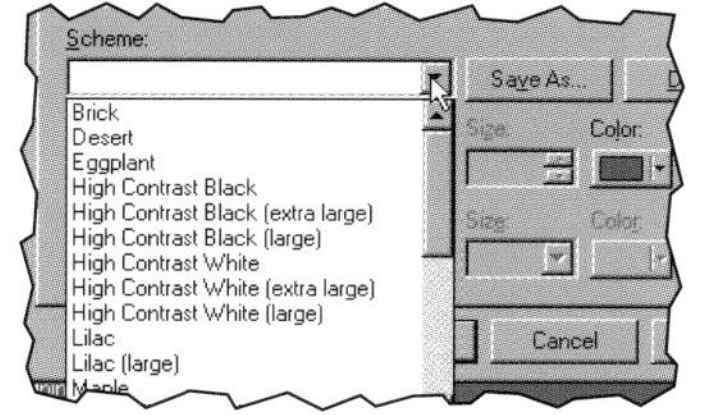

1 In the *Display Properties* dialog box, click on the *Appearance* tab, and then click on the down arrow next to the *Scheme* box.

2 Choose a color scheme from the list. You'll see a preview in the window above. Click on the *Apply* button.

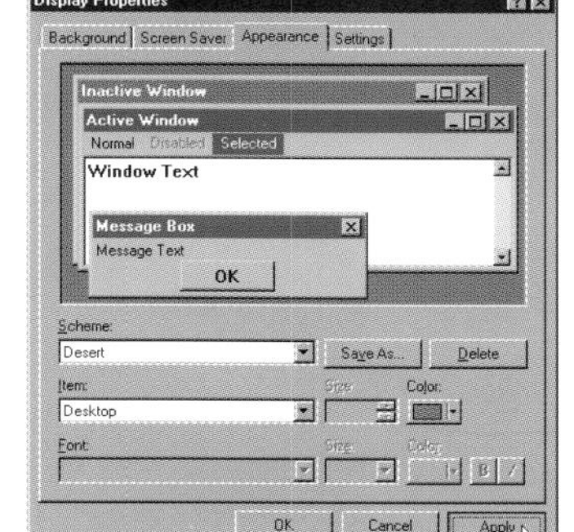

CHANGING RESOLUTION AND COLOR PALETTE

The *Settings* flipcard in the *Display Properties* dialog box allows you to change the resolution and color depth used for your screen display. The options vary according to the make and model of your monitor and display adapter (hardware inside your PC).

The resolution, or sharpness, of the screen display depends on the number of pixels (picture elements) used for the display. With a high resolution, items like icons and windows take up less space on the screen, leading to an apparent increase in the Desktop area. The color depth defines the number of different colors that can be used for displaying images.

To change the resolution and/or color depth, click on the *Settings* tab of the *Display Properties* dialog box, and follow these steps:

1 Choose the number of colors you want for your display from the *Color palette* box and choose the resolution by dragging the slider in the *Desktop area* box. Then click on *Apply*.

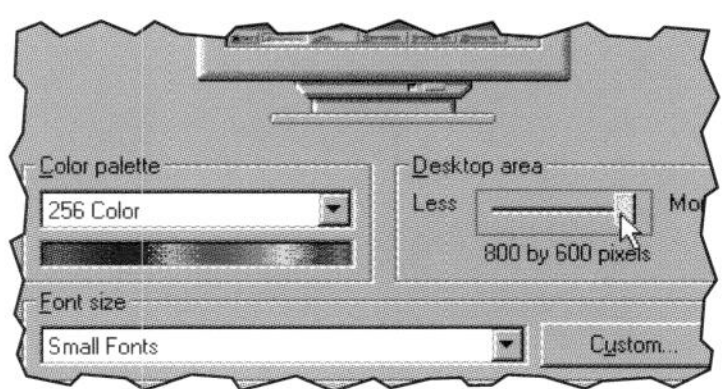

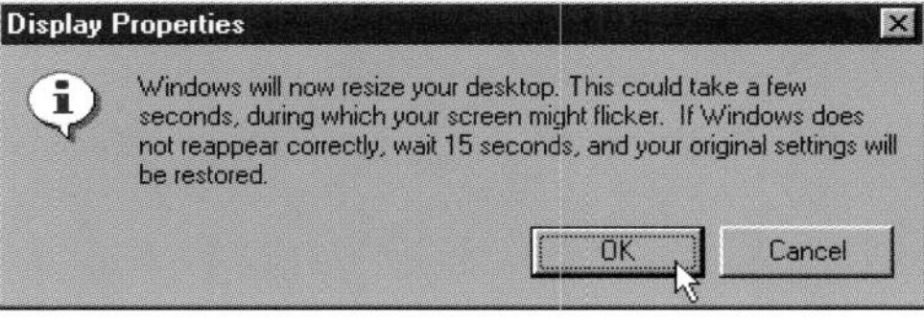

Display Properties
Windows will now resize your desktop. This could take a few seconds, during which your screen might flicker. If Windows does not reappear correctly, wait 15 seconds, and your original settings will be restored.
OK
Cancel

2 You may see the message shown at left or one asking you to restart Windows 95 for the changes to take effect. Click on *OK*.

Save Your Screen!
If you use your PC intermittently throughout the day, it's a good idea to set up a screen saver to reduce wear on your monitor. Open the *Screen Saver* flipcard in the *Display Properties* dialog box, click the down arrow next to the *Screen Saver* box, choose a screen saver (you will see a preview in the miniscreen), set the number of minutes of inactivity you want to have elapse before the screen saver appears, and click on *OK*.

Why Change the Display?

You might want to change the resolution or color depth of your monitor display for the following reasons:

- A high resolution allows you to fit more onto the screen, although everything — windows, their contents, and icons — appears smaller.
- A high color depth enhances the display of images and allows you to use image-editing programs to their full potential.
- Some software, such as some games and CD-ROM titles, will operate only at specific resolutions or color depths.

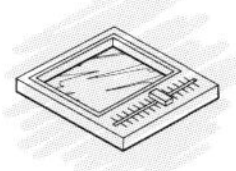

Taming Your Mouse

There are many ways in which you can change how your mouse behaves. You can change the speed of the mouse pointer or add a trail that follows the pointer around. You can choose from a variety of mouse pointer shapes to change the shape of the pointer associated with a particular function. You can swap the functions of the left and right mouse buttons, and if you are having a problem double-clicking fast enough to operate Windows 95, you can adjust the double-click speed setting.

Swapping the Mouse Buttons and Adjusting the Double-Click Speed

1 Choose *Settings* from the *Start* menu and then choose *Control Panel*. Double-click on the icon labeled *Mouse*.

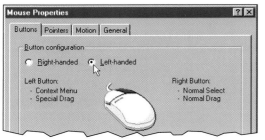

2 The *Mouse Properties* dialog box appears. Under *Button Configuration*, click on the *Left-handed* option button if you want the right mouse button to take over the functions normally associated with the left mouse button and vice-versa.

3 To test whether your personal double-clicking action is fast enough to meet the requirements of the current double-click speed settings, move the mouse pointer into the *Test area* panel and double-click.

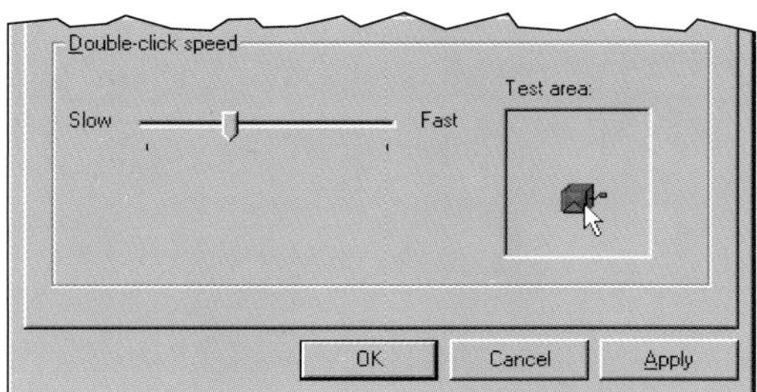

4 If nothing happens, you need to decrease the current double-click speed setting. Drag the slider toward *Slow*. Then double-click in the *Test area* again. If the test works, click the *OK* button to save the settings and close the dialog box.

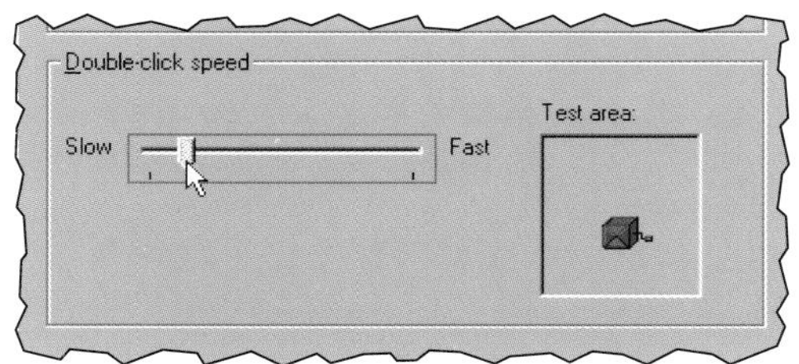

I've Lost My Pointer!
If you are running Windows 95 on a laptop, you will find it easier to see the mouse pointer if you add a trail and slow down its movement. These can be controlled from the *Motion* flipcard of the *Mouse Properties* dialog box.

Swap Pointers?
If you want to change the shape of the pointer associated with a particular mouse function, access the *Pointers* flipcard in the *Mouse Properties* dialog box. You can change any of the pointers used by Windows 95 by clicking on the pointer icon you want to change and then using the *Browse* option to choose a replacement.

Accessibility

If you have poor eyesight or hearing or problems using the keyboard or mouse, you can tailor Windows 95 to work with you. Via the *Accessibility Options* icon in the Control Panel, you can adapt many sound, keyboard, display, and mouse features to suit your needs. For example, try activating the SoundSentry feature by following the steps starting at left. (If you see no *Accessibility Options* icon in your Control Panel, you may need to install it; see page 123).

Activating the SoundSentry

1 Double-click on *Accessibility Options* in the Control Panel.

2 In the *Accessibility Properties* dialog box, access the *Sound* flipcard and check *Use SoundSentry*. Click on *OK*.

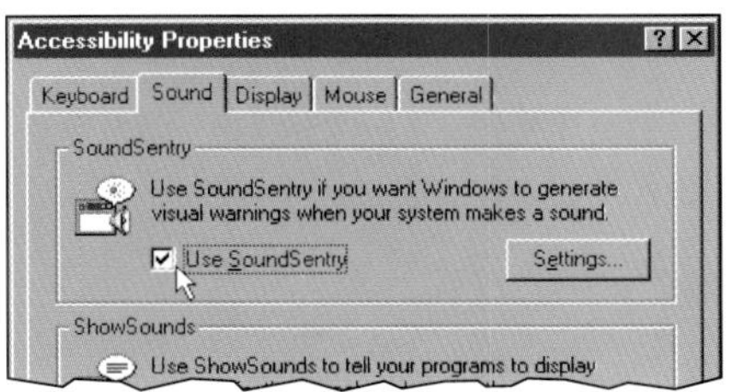

When SoundSentry is active, Windows 95 will generate visual warnings by causing the Desktop display to flash when your system makes a sound.

Sticky Keys

If you have difficulty pressing two keys simultaneously, you may want to use the StickyKeys feature. This allows you to press any of the modifier keys (Ctrl, Alt, and Shift) and have that key remain active until you press any key other than Ctrl, Alt, or Shift. Turn the StickyKeys feature on or off from the *Keyboard* flipcard of the *Accessibility Properties* dialog box.

Customizing the Taskbar

You might have thought that the Taskbar was stationary —well, it isn't. You can position it along the top of the screen or vertically along either the right or left edge. To do this, just drag the Taskbar to the new position.

The *Taskbar Properties* dialog box allows you to customize the Taskbar in a number of other ways — for example, to have the Taskbar hidden except when you choose to see it, or to specify whether or not the Taskbar stays "on top" of other items on the screen.

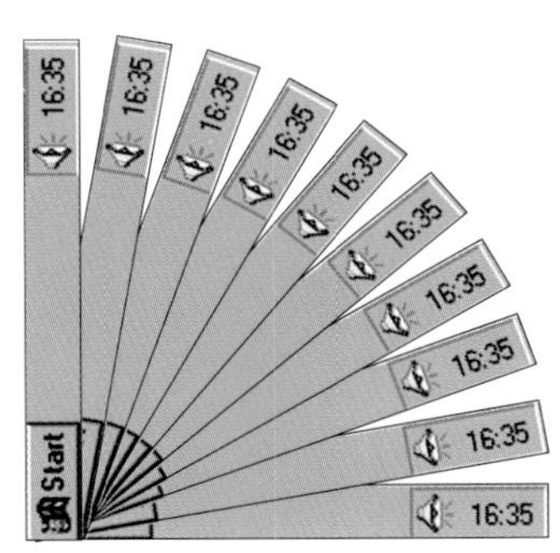

Auto Hiding Your Taskbar

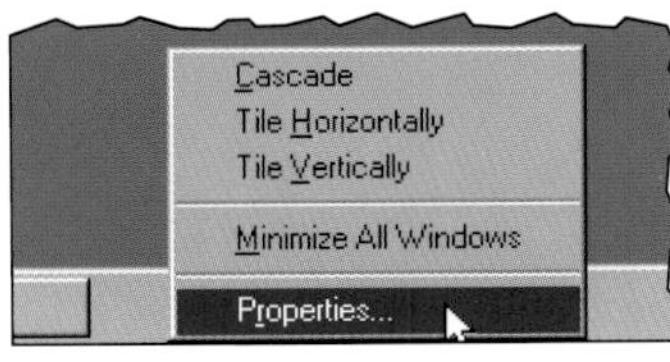

1 Right-click on a blank area of the Taskbar and choose *Properties* from the pop-up menu. The *Taskbar Properties* dialog box appears.

2 In the *Taskbar Options* flipcard, click on the *Auto hide* check box. If you wish, clear or check any of the other Taskbar customization options. Then click on *OK*. The Taskbar will now be hidden by default but will reappear whenever you move the pointer so that it hits the edge of the screen where the Taskbar was displayed.

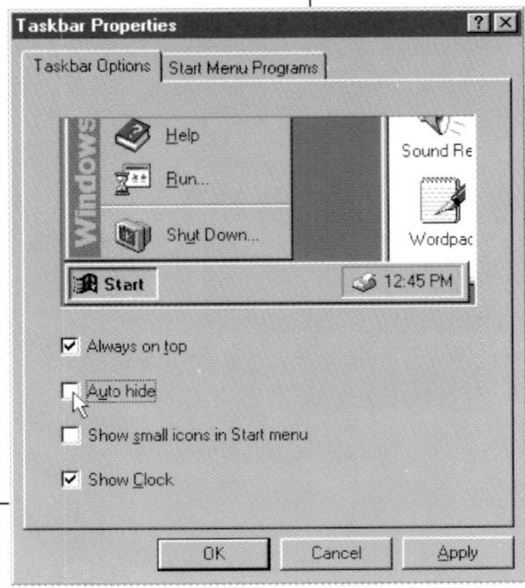

Backing Up and Restoring

BACKING UP YOUR IMPORTANT DATA FILES REGULARLY is a good idea. If you've ever lost some important files — maybe through hard disk failure — you won't need to be reminded of this simple fact. You can back up your files on a number of different storage media, such as tape, removable hard disk, or floppy disks. It's quickest and easiest to use a tape backup unit or a removable hard disk if you are backing up a lot of data, but there is nothing wrong with using floppy disks — it just takes longer and you may need a lot of them. If you are backing up an entire hard disk containing a fairly modest 65 MB of data, for example, you might need as many as 46 floppy disks.

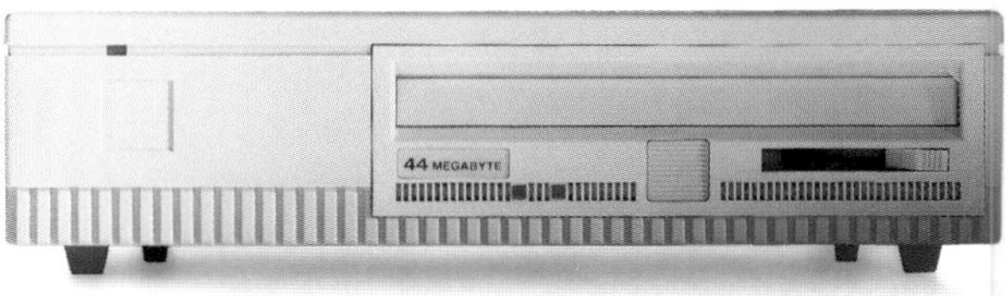

Removable Hard Drive

Floppy Disks and Removable Cartridge

Backup Methods

You can back up any file by dragging the file you want to copy onto the floppy drive icon. This method is fine on a small scale, but what if you need to back up larger files? Some files may be bigger than the 1.44 MB storage capacity of a high-density 3½-inch floppy disk. If you try to copy such a file directly to a floppy disk, Windows 95 tells you that "The file being copied is too large for the destination drive" and suggests that you insert a higher capacity disk. This is not possible when you are using a 1.44 MB floppy disk.

MICROSOFT BACKUP

Backing up is generally a lot easier if you use Microsoft Backup. This Windows 95 system tool can help you organize how, when, and where you back up your data.

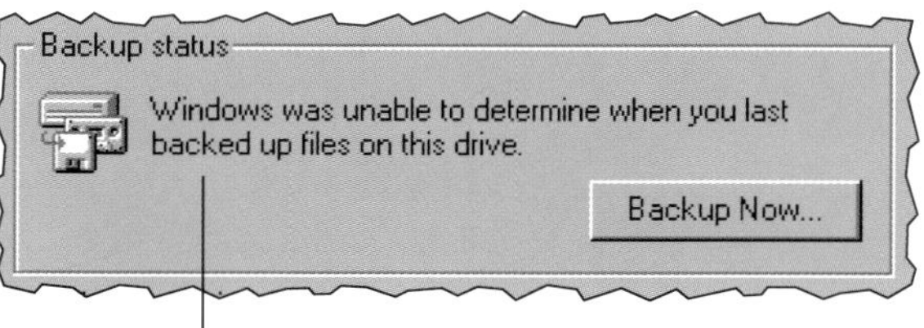

Checking Backup Status
You can run Backup from the Tools *flipcard of the* [C:] Properties *dialog box. After you run Backup for the first time, the* Backup status *box will tell you when you last backed up your files.*

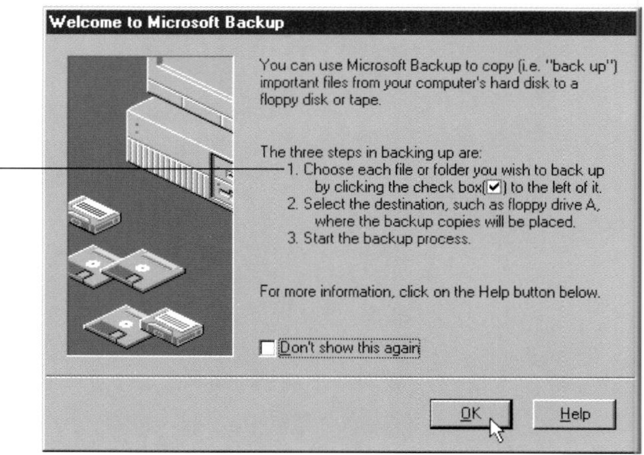

Using Microsoft Backup for the First Time
The first time you click the Backup Now *button you will see the* Welcome to Microsoft Backup *window. (In fact, you will see this window every time you run the program unless you check the* Don't show this again *box). The window provides a three-point summary of how to use Microsoft Backup, as shown at right.*

No Need to Copy!
You do not usually need to make a copy of the folder you intend to back up. In the example on this page and on page 120, you make a copy of a folder so that, after you have backed up the copy, you can delete the copy from the hard disk and subsequently practice restoring it from your backup storage medium.

A SIMPLE BACKUP

Let's try backing up the **Dos** folder using floppy disks. Make a copy of the **Dos** folder. (Right-click on its folder, choose *Copy* from the menu, then right-click on a free area of the *[C:]* window and choose *Paste* from the menu.) You will now back up the **Copy of DOS** folder to make a "backup set" called **Wysiwyg Backup**. You will need to have one or more blank formatted floppy disks ready for this backup. (Make sure the disks are clearly labeled.) The first time you use Microsoft Backup, read the information both in the "Welcome" window and in the "Warning" window that subsequently appears. Read the information in these boxes and, if you don't want to see the boxes the next time you run Backup, check the *Don't show this again* box. You may also see a dialog box relating to tape drives. If your PC does not have a tape drive, click *OK*. If it does, follow the instructions in this box.

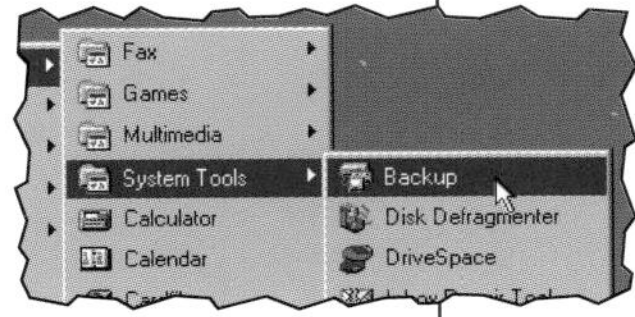

1 Start Backup either from the *Tools* flipcard of the *[C:] Properties* dialog box or by choosing *Backup* from the *System Tools* group via the *Start* menu. A window called *Untitled - Microsoft Backup* appears.

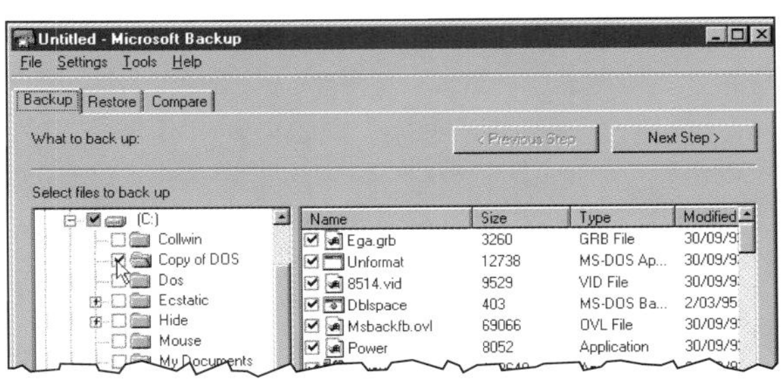

2 Under *Select files to back up*, click on the box containing a plus sign next to *[C:]*, then check the box next to the icon for the **Copy of DOS** folder. A check mark will appear in this box, and the files in the folder will appear in the right-hand pane (also with check marks in the boxes next to them). A check mark also appears in a grayed out box next to *[C:]* at the top of the left-hand pane. Click *Next Step* to continue.

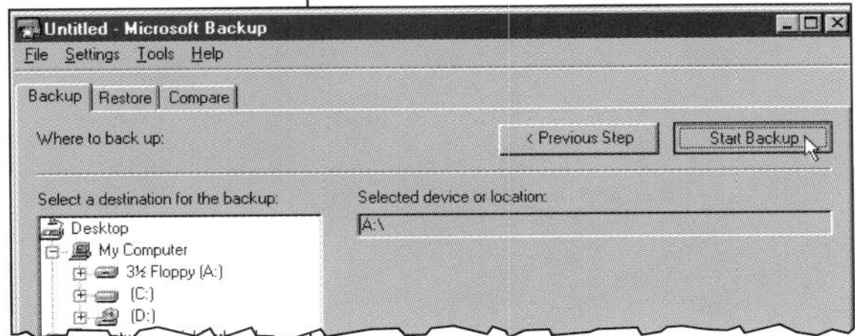

3 Insert a blank formatted floppy disk in the disk drive. Then, under *Select a destination for the backup*, click on the *3½ Floppy (A:)* icon. The grayed-out *Selected device or location* box will now show *A:*. Click the *Start Backup* button. In the *Backup Set Label* dialog box that appears, type **Wysiwyg Backup**.

4 The *Backup* window appears and reports on progress. Click *OK* to continue. Insert the next blank floppy disk when prompted and click *OK*.

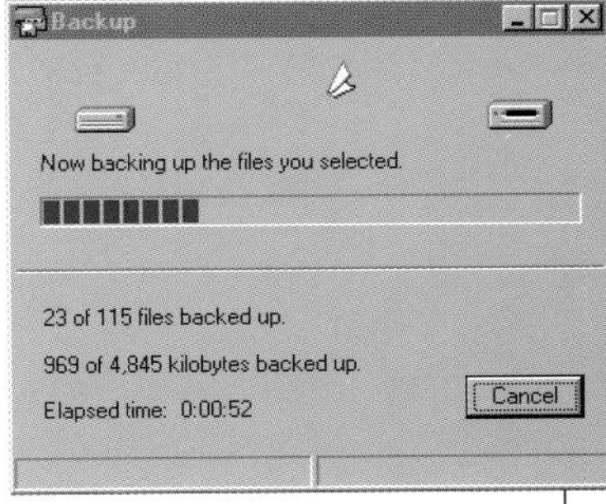

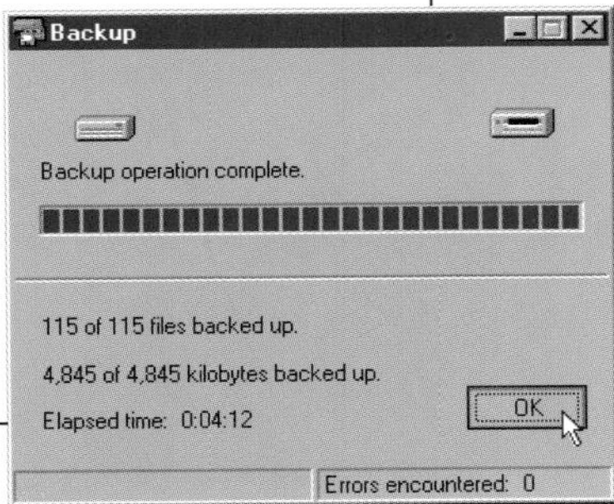

5 When the "operation complete" message appears, click on *OK*, and then on *OK* again in the *Backup* window to return to the *Microsoft Backup* window. Close this window in the usual way. You should now delete the **Copy of DOS** folder.

FULL SYSTEM BACKUP

In the example on the previous page you backed up a single folder, but you can select any combination of files and folders for backup by checking the appropriate boxes in the *Microsoft Backup* window before starting the backup. If you want to back up your entire hard disk you must choose the "Full System Backup" backup set provided with Windows 95. This is intended only for "disaster recovery," so you should not use the file for differential or partial backups. The Full System Backup backup file set includes a number of special files that are not selected when you simply select the entire hard disk for backup. You can access this full backup set by choosing *Open File Set* from the *File* menu in the *Backup* window, clicking *Open* in the *Open* dialog box, and following the instructions onscreen.

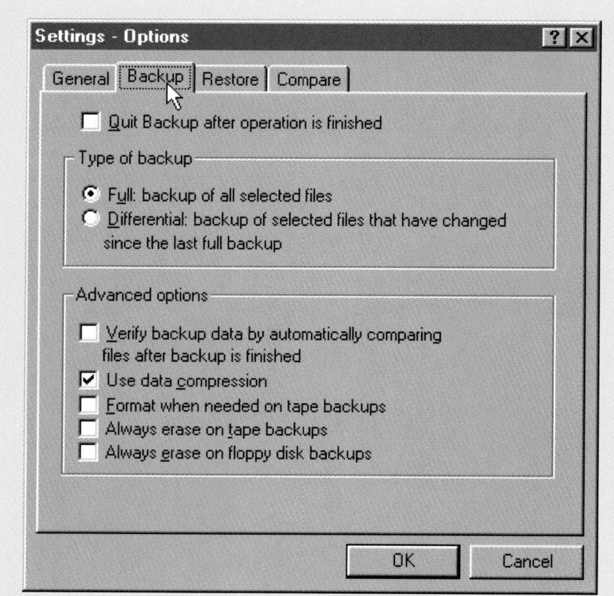

Full vs. Differential Backups

From the *Settings - Options* dialog box (which can be accessed by choosing *Options* from the *Settings* menu of the *Microsoft Backup* window) you can customize many of the ways in which Backup works. For example, in the *Backup* flipcard, you can choose either a *full* or a *differential* backup. Every time you run a full backup, all your selected files are backed up from scratch. A differential backup, on the other hand, backs up only the files that have changed since you last ran a full backup. If you regularly back up the same folders and files, it is probably best to make a full backup once a week and a differential backup every day.

Restoring Backups

You make backups to protect yourself from losing data that could be accidentally erased from your hard disk; therefore, you should not need to restore backup sets often. To restore a backup set, you reverse the backup procedure, as set out in the steps below. By default your files are written back to their original locations, overwriting any files currently located there. To change the location to which your backup files are restored, you need to choose *Options* from the *Settings* menu. In the *Restore* flipcard of the *Settings - Options* dialog box you have various options; for example, you can restore files to an alternate location or overwrite only older files.

Restoring the Wysiwyg Backup Set

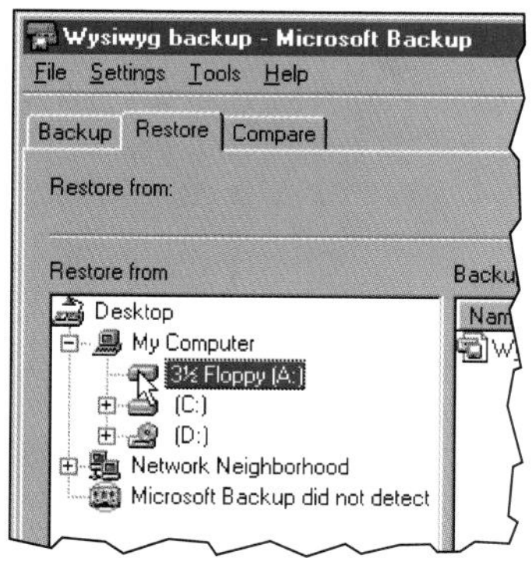

1 Access the *Microsoft Backup* window. Insert the last disk containing the backup set in your floppy disk drive. Click the *Restore* tab. Click on the floppy disk drive icon in the *Restore from* box.

2 Click on *Wysiwyg Backup* in the right-hand pane and then click on *Next Step*. Now check the box next to **Copy of DOS** in the left-hand pane and click *Start Restore*. Follow the onscreen instructions, inserting each floppy disk when prompted. Now follow step 5 on page 119 (only the dialog box names may be different). You will now find the **Copy of DOS** folder restored to its original location on your hard disk.

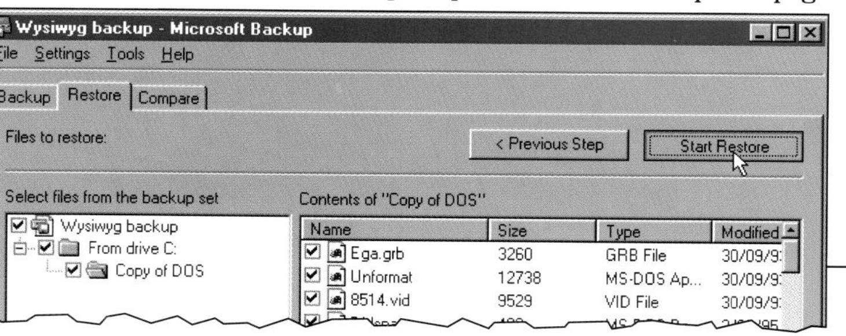

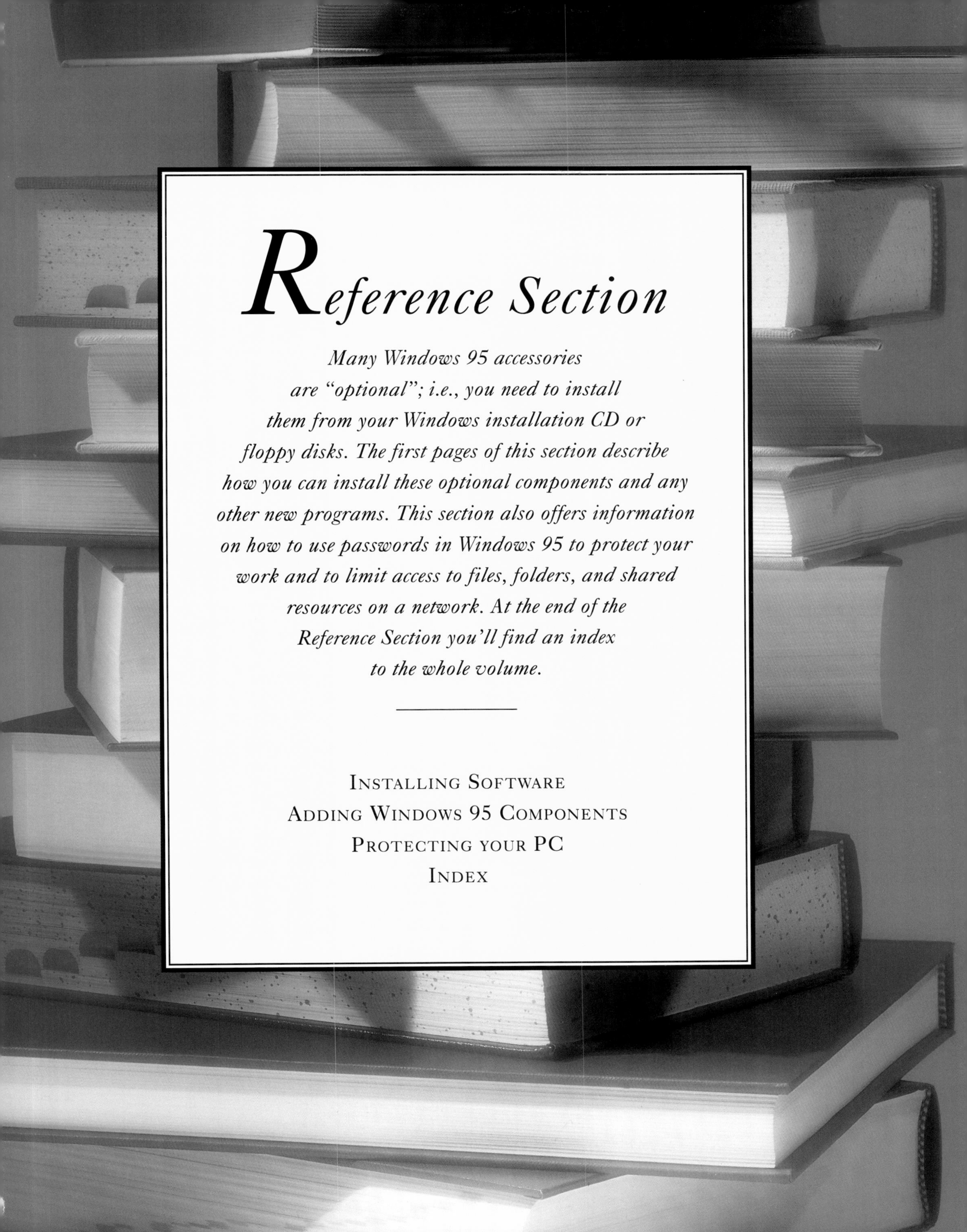

Reference Section

Many Windows 95 accessories are "optional"; i.e., you need to install them from your Windows installation CD or floppy disks. The first pages of this section describe how you can install these optional components and any other new programs. This section also offers information on how to use passwords in Windows 95 to protect your work and to limit access to files, folders, and shared resources on a network. At the end of the Reference Section you'll find an index to the whole volume.

Installing Software

INSTALLING NEW SOFTWARE HAS NEVER BEEN SO EASY. You no longer have to remember any of the old MS-DOS commands such as SETUP or INSTALL to integrate a new application into your Windows 95 environment.

Software

Various types of applications can run with the Windows 95 operating system. Some applications are especially designed for Windows, which means that they are generally highly graphical, and their menus, commands, and dialog boxes are similar to those in Windows. Others are designed to run with MS-DOS rather than Windows and their interface, commands, and overall look and feel may differ considerably from the Windows look. However, the procedure for installing new software remains basically the same. Here is what you have to do:

1 In the Control Panel, double-click on the icon labeled *Add/Remove Programs.*

2 The *Add/Remove Programs Properties* dialog box opens. In the *Install/Uninstall* flipcard, click on the *Install* button.

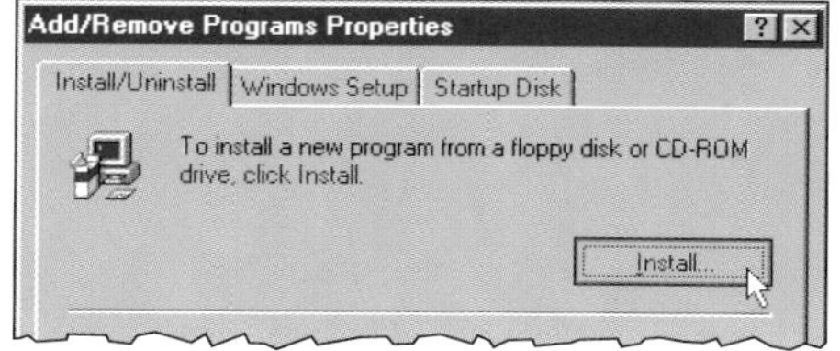

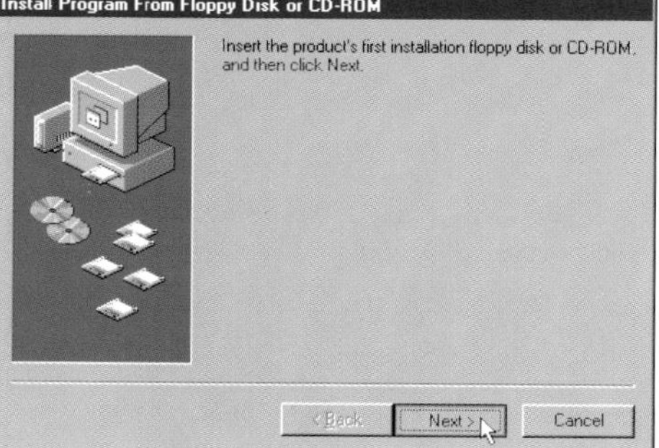

3 A box titled *Install Program From Floppy Disk or CD-ROM* opens. Insert the correct setup floppy disk, which (if there is more than one disk) is often marked "Disk 1" or "Installation," in the floppy disk drive or insert the relevant CD-ROM in the CD-ROM drive. Click on *Next.*

4 Windows 95 now starts looking for the setup program on the floppy disk or CD-ROM. Setup program files are traditionally called **Setup** or **Install**. Once a program with such a name is found on the disk, you are asked to verify that this is the correct program by clicking on the *Finish* button.

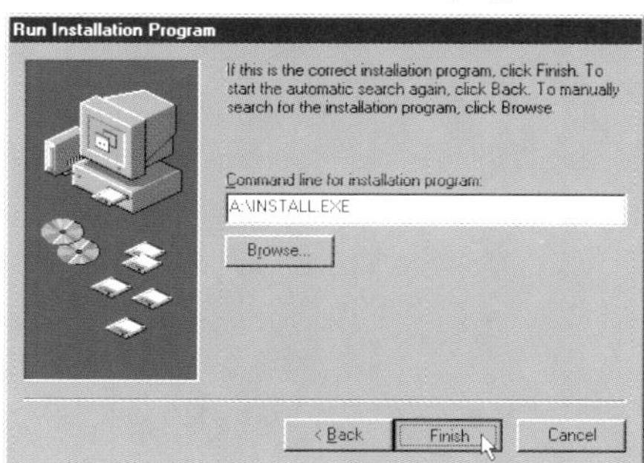

5 Individual setup or installation windows will appear, asking you to confirm or specify certain settings relevant to the software you are installing. These suggestions and queries, such as the message below, are usually clearly written instructions that you can easily follow on the screen. In the window shown, you would click on the *Continue* button to continue installation.

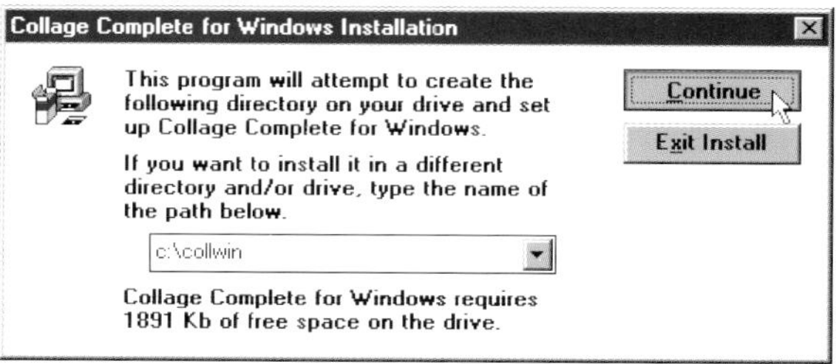

6 Eventually the setup program reports that the installation has been successfully completed. You can usually use the new software immediately, although you may sometimes be asked to restart Windows 95 in order to launch the newly installed software.

TROUBLESHOOTING
If you have trouble installing new software, carefully read the instructions that come with the software. If there aren't any, print out the **Readme** file, which is usually stored on the first installation disk. To get to the **Readme** file, double-click on the relevant floppy disk drive or CD-ROM drive icon in the *My Computer* window. You will see the **Readme** file among other files on the installation disk.

Adding Windows 95 Components

UNLESS WINDOWS 95 WAS INSTALLED on your PC with a "complete" installation, you may find that some Windows 95 components, such as Microsoft Exchange, appear to be unavailable. However, it's easy to install any "missing" components, as long as you have the Windows 95 installation disks or CD-ROM at hand.

Types of Setup

When Windows 95 was installed on your PC, any of several setup options may have been chosen, and the setup option chosen will determine which components may be missing on your system. If a "Compact" installation was chosen, most Windows 95 accessories will not be installed by default. If a "Typical" installation was chosen, most accessories, such as WordPad, will be available, but other components, such as Microsoft Exchange, will not. If a "Custom" installation was chosen, the range of components available will vary.

INSTALLING MISSING COMPONENTS

To install any Windows 95 component that has not yet been installed, just follow these steps:

1 In the Control Panel, double-click on the icon labeled *Add/Remove Programs.*

2 In the *Add/Remove Programs Properties* dialog box, click on the *Windows Setup* tab.

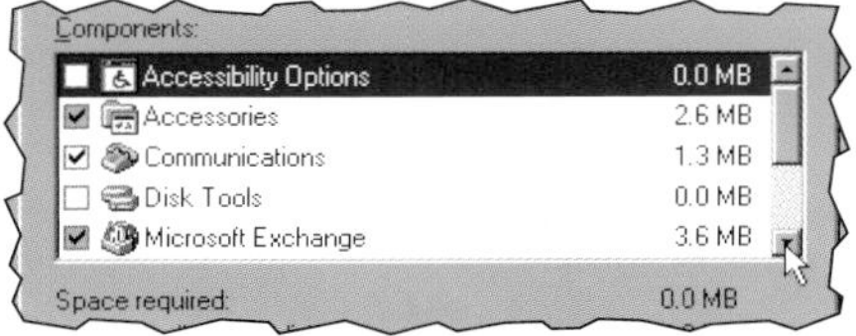

3 In the *Windows Setup* flipcard, use the scroll bar arrows to the right of the *Components* box to browse the list of optionally installed groups of components. A check mark next to the name of a group indicates that at least some of the components in that group are already installed.

4 To specify which of the components in a group to install (or remove) from your system, click on the group's name (for example, *Accessories* or *Multimedia*) and then click on the *Details* button.

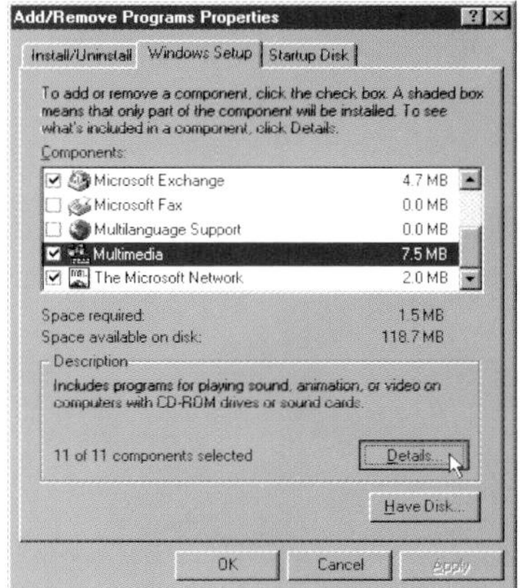

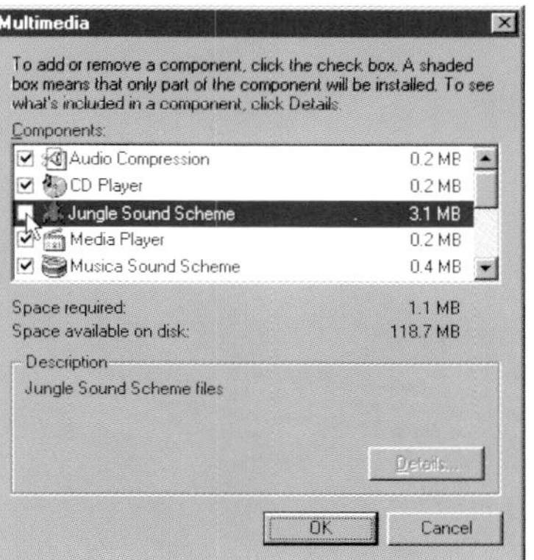

5 A dialog box appears, giving a list of specific components. Check the box next to those components you wish to install, and clear the box next to any components already checked that you wish to remove. Then click on *OK*.

6 Repeat steps 4 and 5 for any other groups for which you wish to add or remove individual components. Check the information shown in the dialog box to see whether there is enough space available on your hard disk to install the extra components. If there isn't, you may have to remove some components that are already installed, or change your options.

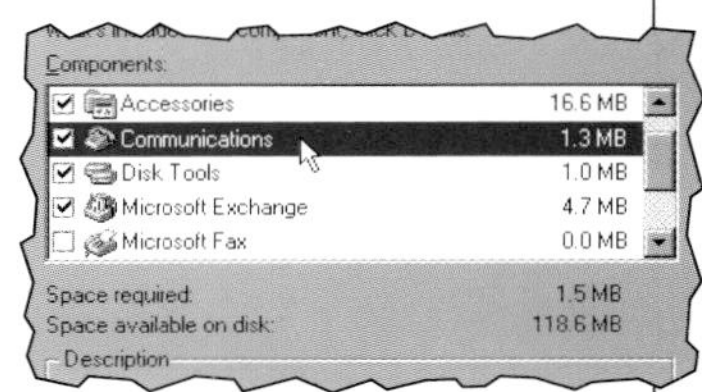

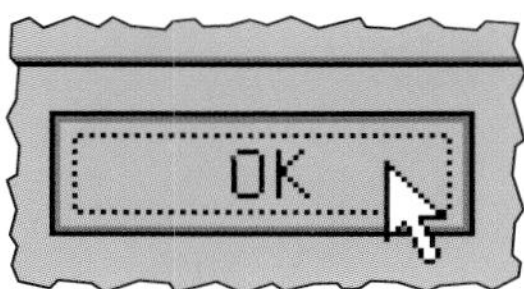

7 Once you've finalized your choice, click on OK in the *Add/Remove Programs Properties* dialog box.

8 One or a series of message boxes will appear asking you to insert the appropriate installation disk(s) or CD-ROM. Follow these instructions carefully. When you've finished, you should find that the new components are available on your system.

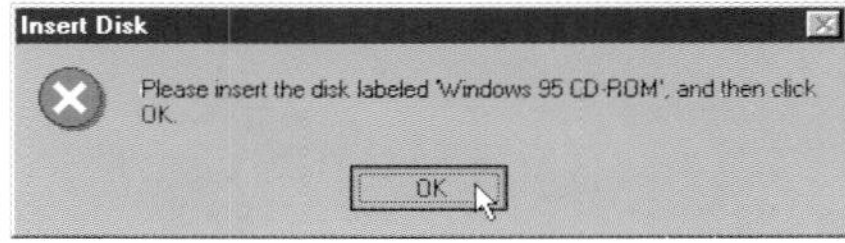

Protecting Your PC

WINDOWS 95 MAKES IT EASY TO LINK YOUR PC to different online services, check your personal electronic mail, and manage all your files. With this amount of access, the last thing you want is for someone to be able to read your private mail messages or copy files.

Windows provides many different security systems that can help make your PC more secure; you can assign a password to a network drive so that only authorized users can share your resources over a network, or you can protect your PC using passwords.

Passwords

The files on your computer are at their most vulnerable when you leave your PC — for example, when you go for a coffee break. If you are worried about someone snooping through the files on your system or copying or printing your files while you are away from your PC, you need to consider password protection. If you are logged on to a network, a snooper would have access to the same files that you have access to across the network unless the files are password protected. If you are connected to a large network, your network administrator will usually have made sure that some sort of security is in place. That's why you need a password to log on and why there are probably some resources you can access and others you can't.

One simple way of using a password to protect your files is to assign a password to a Windows 95 screen saver. (See the tip box on page 115 for instructions on how to set up a screen saver.) With a screen saver, if you don't touch the mouse or keyboard for a few minutes, the screen will clear and display a pattern. You can get back to your programs from a screen saver to which a password has been assigned only by typing the password. Anyone who doesn't know the password would need to restart your PC. The password can be different from your usual network password, for added security. This won't cause any problems for someone who seriously wants to tamper with your files, but if you are only away from your PC for a short time, it may deter the casual snooper or prankster!

PERSISTENT PASSWORDS

Some users can find it tedious to have to type a password frequently, so they delete the password or use a very short password; this is not advisable if you want your PC to be very secure. One way to avoid getting bored is to use the "persistent passwords" feature of Windows. When you first log on to your network with a new password, Windows asks you to confirm whether you want to remember this password. If you do, in the future when you are accessing network resources Windows will automatically enter your password for you. It avoids the tedium of re-entering the same password many times during the day. Of course, you will still need to enter the password to log on each morning.

ONE PC, SEVERAL USERS

Most people like to customize the way Windows 95 looks and sounds (see pages 114 through 117). If you share your PC with others, you can use Windows 95 to assign passwords for each user. This allows each user to customize his or her Desktop (by setting up a favorite screen saver or sound scheme, for example) and these settings will be activated every time that user logs on with the relevant password.

1 From the Control Panel window, double-click on the *Passwords* icon.

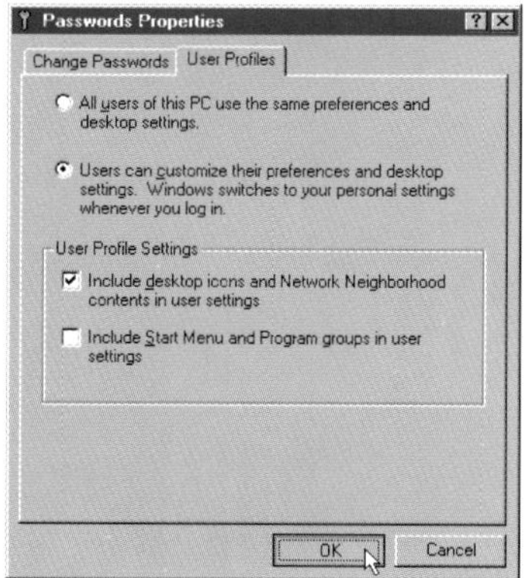

2 In the *Passwords Properties* dialog box, click the *User Profiles* tab and check the button next to *Users can customize their preferences and desktop settings.* Also check either or both boxes in the *User Profile Settings* box. Click *OK* to save your settings.

3 In the *System Settings Change* dialog box, click on *Yes* to restart your system If you are working on files that need to be saved, click on *No.* The new settings will be in effect the next time you switch on or restart your computer.

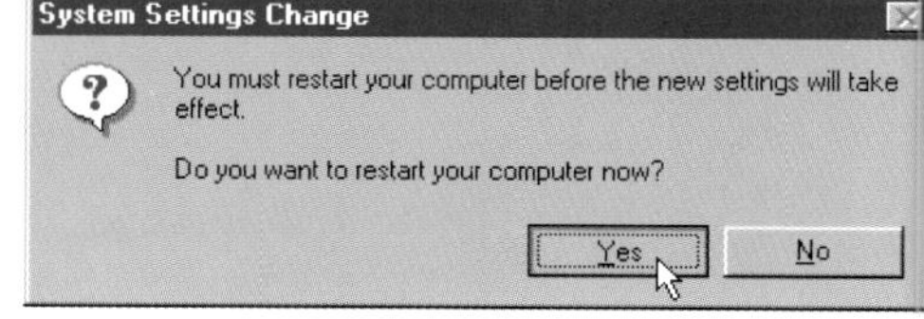

The next time you start your PC, a dialog box will appear asking you to confirm that you want your personal Windows 95 settings to be saved and reloaded every time you log on to your PC. Any other users who share your PC will see the same dialog box when they next log on.

CHANGING YOUR PASSWORD

You can change your password at any time by using the Password utility.

1 In the Control Panel, double-click on the *Password* icon. In the *Passwords Properties* dialog box, click on the *Change Passwords* tab and click on the *Change Windows Password* button. (You will also see a *Change Other Passwords* button. Use this to change your password for other password-protected services.)

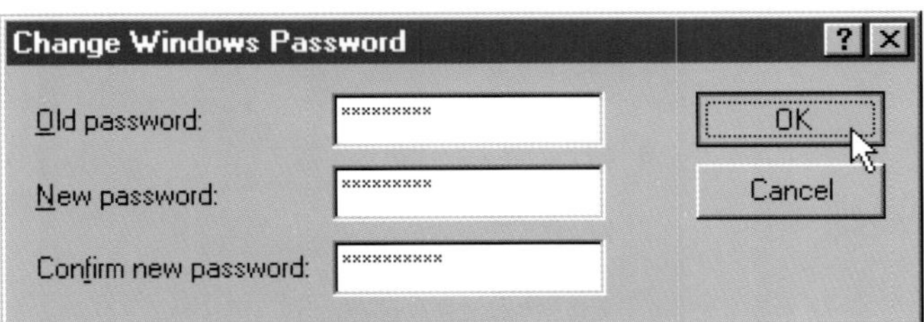

2 In the appropriate boxes, type your current password and your new password. You will have to type your new password once more to confirm.

3 A dialog box appears confirming that you have successfully changed your password. Click *OK* and then, in the *Passwords Properties* dialog box, click on the *Close* button.

Make Sure You Choose a Sensible Password!

To be effective, passwords need to be easy to use but difficult for a snooper to crack! It's no good setting up a complicated password system and then using your name as the password — anyone can guess that! You need to set up passwords that are changed regularly but that are not too easy to guess.

Network Security

If you are using Windows 95 on a network, you will have already had to enter a password. Windows asks for a password before you log on to a network or, as the administrator, before you make any changes to the network setup. Because anyone else on the network can gain access to your files, it's important that you set up network security correctly.

When you decide to share a resource, like a folder on your PC, you need to declare that it can be shared. At this stage you can also define the security associated with the resource: the password and the type of sharing. In this way you can control who can access the folder, and the level of access permitted to individual users or groups of users.

USER-LEVEL AND SHARE-LEVEL

Two types of sharing are possible under Windows: "user-level" and "share-level" sharing. Both are useful and offer different advantages. With user-level sharing, each resource (such as a printer or folder) is assigned a share name and a list of authorized users; it is also given an access password. Users can only share this resource if they know the password and are on the list. Share-level security is less secure but easier to set up: just declare that a resource is sharable and, if you want, assign a password. (The same password is used for all users.) Unless you're very worried about users being able to read your private files, share-level security will be fine for most cases.

You can set up the security settings for the shared object from the same *Properties* window that you used to share the object. You can require any user to have to enter a password before he or she can use the resource or limit the user's rights to "read only" (which means the user can look at files but cannot make any changes to them).

INDEX

a

b

c

d

e-f

Equipment Suppliers: Computer on page 10 supplied by Apricot Computers. The items on pages 37, 59, and 104 supplied by Clark Davis Ltd. Toolcase on page 42 supplied by Argos Distributors Ltd. Satellite image on page 70 supplied by Earth Satellite Corporation/ Science Photo Library. Facsimile machine on page 90 supplied by Panasonic UK. Globe image on page 93 supplied by NASA.